Another Way the River Has

Another Way the River Has

TAUT TRUE TALES FROM THE NORTHWEST

Robin Cody

Oregon State University Press

Corvallis

A Northwest Reader
Robert J. Frank, Series Editor
The Northwest Readers Series presents collections of writings by notable
Northwest authors and anthologies on provocative regional themes.

Drawing on page i by Heidi Cody

The paper in this book meets the guidelines for permanence and durability of
the Committee on Production Guidelines for Book Longevity of the Council
on Library Resources and the minimum requirements of the American
National Standard for Permanence of Paper for Printed Library Materials
Z39.48-1984.

Library of Congress Cataloging-in-Publication Data
Cody, Robin, 1943-
  Another way the river has : taut true tales of the Northwest / Robin Cody.
    p. cm.
  ISBN 978-0-87071-583-9 (alk. paper)
  1. Northwest, Pacific--History--Anecdotes. 2. Northwest, Pacific--
Biography--Anecdotes. 3. Northwest, Pacific--Social life and customs--
Anecdotes. 4. Cody, Robin, 1943- I. Title.
  F852.3.C63 2010
  979.5--dc22

                                    2009053061

Oregon State University Press
121 The Valley Library
Corvallis OR 97331-4501
541-737-3166 • fax 541-737-3170
www.osupress.oregonstate.edu

With large thanks to Jack Hart,
coach, critic and outdoorsman,

and a nod to Jo Alexander's sharp pencil.

Contents

A Note

My devious nefarious giggling plan with this introductory note was originally to tell a howling pack of lies about Robin Cody for sheer entertainment, such as the whole Maori tattoo inguinal area misadventure, or the thing with the buffalo calf and the laundromat, or the time he was going to ask out Miss Refrigeration 1966 but got distracted, or the time he actually did hit a badger with his boat, or maybe tell some stories about his colorful baseball career at Yale University, where he may or may not have deliberately hit George Walker Bush in the throat with a throw from shortstop, or how he tried to surf a sturgeon once, or how he can curse like a sailor in French, or how he courted his lovely bride by actually no kidding begging and pleading on his knees, or how he used to ride his bicycle while balancing not one but two excellent bottles of wine on the handlebars, but then I read through all the essays in this book in one day, and it seemed to me that only a roaring idiot would get between the reader and one of the finest writers Oregon ever hatched, and while I am indeed a roaring idiot, as my friends would be more than happy to tell you if I gave you their phone numbers at the county jail, I am not *that* much of an idiot.

Robin writes the leanest cleanest sinewiest most honest most unadorned most egoless true tales I think I have ever read, and he has a really remarkable ear for stories and the glories who tell them, and no one loves Oregon as much as Robin, who was spawned on the banks of the Mighty Columbia and raised pretty much *in* the Clackamas River, as far as I can tell. The guy is a total river junkie, and as soon as you have read this book you ought to read his *Voyage of a Summer Sun*, about canoeing the entire Columbia, and then read *Ricochet River*, a great novel made into the worst movie in the history of the world, trust me on this.

I've known Robin almost twenty years, and much as I like to razz him, and make bets that lead to beer for me, the fact is that he has a heart as big as a river, a really cool wife, and a silver-plated storyteller's engine in his head. He listens for grace and guts and laughter and courage, and he mills and planes what he hears into stories that will echo and shiver in you for a really long time. Trust me (again). Ladies and gentlemen, one of the great storycatchers and storytellers who ever hatched in the Great North Wet: Robin Cody.

—*Brian Doyle*

Another Way the River Has

The Clackamas River

Nobody ever called the Clackamas "old man river. " This young rascal is full of mischief and rebellion, brash and impatient, rising from the south slopes of Mt. Hood to catch up with the mature Willamette in the city.

Lucky for me, I grew up swimming across and drifting down and poking around and puzzling over the Clackamas. We lived on an unpaved dead-end road called Lakeshore Drive, almost in Estacada. A flat deep green beautiful part of the river lay right out our door. The wild laughing lyrical part struck up again below the dam.

My ninth-grade English teacher, Miss Davis, insisted that Henry David Thoreau's *Walden* was a good book. Can you believe that? I read about Walden Pond and said we'd do better to take Miss Davis for a float down the Clackamas.

She thought I was kidding.

I didn't have the brass or the words at the time to defend my position with Miss Davis. But it's a known fact that rivers can be as good as books for getting outside yourself. Other kids, maybe, had an imaginary friend. In the Clackamas River I had a substitute teacher, a supplementary instructor, not imaginary at all.

~~~~

The river was a physics lab.

A rock, you know, will sink like a stone in water. But a *flat* rock, slung spinningly near the water surface and at an angle parallel to it, will go *skipping across* the water in defiance of gravity and common sense. How cool is that?! The first time a boy pulls this off ranks just short of first-time sex on the scale of things he'll want to do over and over whenever he can and as long as he lives.

~~~~

The river taught anthropology.

From riverside one day I brought home a curious bowl-shaped stone, large enough to hold half a cantaloupe. Mom recognized this as an archeological find. It was a mortar, for pulverizing food with a pestle. Clackamas Indians liked their roots mashed. Is this widely known? Mom and I knew that these Indians had been fishers from down by Willamette Falls. Each August, we supposed, they must have come right up the river here on their way to high huckleberry fields.

Broken obsidian from a cliff-side shallow cave was evidence of an arrowhead factory. And so. Outside our front door, where others put decorative pots, sat the stone mortar and a block of obsidian. A band of Indians might drop by any day and find us hospitable.

〜〜〜

There is a mathematics to history.

If Estacada in 1956 was fifty years old, and this vanished people had passed through for ten millennia, how much longer than we had they loved and cried and joked and suffered the rain and known the play of sunlight on water and told stories?

〜〜〜

Stories. So many stories. I could go on and on, and I have, writing fiction. But here is a very short true story:

The preacher, attempting a baptism at Eagle Fern Park, lost his footing and fumbled Mary Ethel Harbert into an eddy while God evidently had His back turned. We kids splashed in and hauled out Mary Ethel sputtering and eternally thankful. She was saved.

〜〜〜

The river demonstrates biology. Natural history. That is to say, it teaches humility.

The banks of the lower Clackamas are watched over by Douglas fir trees that witnessed the first wagons crossing the very last stream on the Oregon Trail. The trees are descendants of vast conifer forests that for millions of years covered these western Oregon slopes. The poet Gary Snyder called them "Doctors of Perennial Habitat, experts at staying put, and we are the little grazers and grifters who are shouldering them aside."

I wouldn't go that far, but it's something to think about is what the Clackamas River says.

Cutting It Close

Lydell Reed is among the first to arrive at Cruz Inn, a tiny coffee shop and hamburger joint just a short piece up the Clackamas River Road from Estacada. It's 4:30 a.m., still dark. One by one the loggers stumble in, gathering before their day's work, grateful that there is any work at all this summer of 1983. Three years of cutthroat competition have meant trouble for Reed Logging Co., a small, family-owned operation. Although it counts itself among the survivors in the Northwest woods, the company's future is by no means secure. And at Cruz Inn this morning, everyone has his own idea about what the trouble is. Opinions flow as freely as the steam off morning coffee mugs.

The trouble is transportation costs.

The trouble is high interest rates and the finance company with little imagination or tolerance for risk.

The trouble is Reaganomics. Fewer housing starts.

The trouble is the Forest Service. Now there's the trouble. The Forest Service and the environmentalists. It's got so a man can't pee in the woods anymore without filing an Environmental Impact Statement.

The trouble is aluminum siding, composition roofing, and plastic toys.

The trouble is big timber corporations that have the political clout to finagle government while they squeeze the little guy dry.

The trouble is the trees. The trees left to log are smaller and harder to get to.

Listening to this babble—with the air of a man who thinks the trouble may be loggers who would rather sit and talk than go to work—is Lydell Reed, patriarch of Reed Logging Co. He keeps his opinions to himself. Except for his gray-striped cotton logger shirt and red suspenders, Reed could be mistaken for a mildly prosperous banker on his mid-morning break. Reed, now in his sixties, has the physique of a strong but not oversized man who has benefited from good home cooking. His blue white hair is carefully parted with a wide-toothed comb. His blue eyes are alert and cautious.

Among his crew, Reed is referred to as The Old Man, That Old Bugger, The Head Nuts, or One Shrewd Son-of-a Bitch.

To his face he is called Lydell. The name is uttered reverentially, as high praise for the one who finds them jobs. To a man, they would walk across a skyline cable for him if he said that would be a smart way to cross the canyon.

Lydell Reed rises to lead his crew up the river road. Time to hit it.

~~~

In the hour before dawn, traffic on the Clackamas River Road is a one-way surge of red tail lights into the dark woods. The trucks show little regard for speed limits, and none at all for no-passing zones. Past North Fork Reservoir the road winds alongside the Clackamas and past place names that spark the imagination and quicken the blood: Memaloose Bridge. Big Eddy. Roaring River. Three Lynx. Reed Logging Co. is headed for a spot way, way out there in the Mt. Hood National Forest. Beyond Austin Hot Springs, the upper reaches of the Clackamas turn visible, silvery, under the first hints of breaking day.

Reed swings his pickup off the river road, climbs another three miles up the steep one-lane blacktop, and then turns onto a rock road that twists another mile into the mountains. He slows and comes around a corner, his truck trailing a roostertail of gray dust into the eerie morning light. Visible ahead is a horseshoe-shaped bend of logging road that wraps around a canyon of felled trees. More vertical than horizontal, this clearcut has been officially named—by someone with a touch of homesickness or a fine sense of irony—Kansas.

On the far side of the canyon stands the yarding tower, its floodlights illuminating the landing and the loader. An advance guard of Reed's crew has already loaded one truck. It is 5:30.

~~~

The term "gyppo logger" binds those who are free to use it into a fraternal order of the oppressed. "Gyppo" comes from the old railroad-building days when laborers might form a little cooperative on their own, gypping their employer out of a job. In the woods today gyppo connotes small size, maverick personalities, and agile moves from one job to the next. It's about independent logging. Anyone with a pair of caulked boots can be a gyppo logger for a little while. Only those who've been in it for a long time are free to refer to theirs and others' as gyppo shows. A gyppo logging outfit will make it—if it makes it—on its own hard work and wits.

The past three years had been a struggle, but Reed stayed busy enough to survive the worst of it. A successful logger knows his costs, is not overextended on credit, and can figure his bids low enough to get jobs and high enough to turn a profit. Lydell Reed has earned a reputation as "a man with a sharp pencil."

Using a dull pencil here—rounded numbers—Reed explains how the skyline show at Kansas costs him roughly $4,000 a day. His personnel and equipment costs are $300 an hour, $2,400 for every day the operation is running. He subcontracts the cutting, bucking, and hauling for the other $1,600.

On the other side of the ledger, the mill pays him $100 a thousand board feet of logs delivered. A log truck carries about five TBF, or $500 worth of product, to the mill. If Reed delivers eight loads today, he earns $4,000 and breaks even. The ninth load of the day is profit. The eighteenth load of the day, which is possible but unlikely, puts enough money in the bank to cover equipment breakdowns like last Tuesday, when only two loads left Kansas.

Vastly oversimplified—every job is different—this is how a gyppo logger puts turkey on the table, or fails to. The sharp pencil comes into play predicting costs down to the last detail, anticipating setbacks, and submitting a bid of $93 per TBF to the mill when the other guys bid $94 and up. A crew member says, "That Old Bugger once lost a $90,000 job by bidding 25 cents too high. He never forgot it. One lousy quarter."

Reed employs a crew of twenty-three men, working two sites at once. He has two full-time mechanics and watchmen to guard against vandalism and fire during off hours. Highly skilled people are paid year-around, whether there is work or not. Others wait for the phone to ring.

Equipment costs are led by the new yarding tower, an $800,000 mobile spar pole by Skagit. The rest of his equipment is nothing to draw a film crew to the site. Its beauty is that it's paid for. The company owns three loaders, six skidders, a lowboy truck, two Caterpillar tractors, two fire trucks, three crummies (crew carriers), and four pickup trucks. Replacing a skyline cable (2,400 feet at $2.86 per foot) will cost $6,864, so Reed has to know how long it will last. He wonders why in the world it costs $1.98 for one of these little bitty spray cans of yellow paint to mark the ends of logs, and why he can't get them in bulk.

Competition is keen, but Reed is not at all comfortable with this "sharp pencil" business. What good is a sharp pencil in predicting the weather? Every winter comes with down time, and an east wind in summer can turn a logging site into dry tinder, shutting him down in prime time. You never know. Soon after he bought the yarding tower, it got snowed in for six months on a high site above Fish Creek. With payments due at $12,000 each month, the tower sat idle.

~~~~~

By 8 a.m., the operation at Kansas is in full swing. The fifth log truck has backed onto the landing. The loader picks logs from a growing pile and lifts them onto the truck. Overhead, the skyline cable stretches between the yarding tower and the far ridge of the canyon. The skyline is a monorail track for the carriage and butt rigging, from which three choker cables swing loose on their quick trip out over the canyon.

A sharp bleep—the signal from choker setters to the tower—splits the drone of diesel engines at the landing. The skyline slackens, dropping its rigging to the canyon floor. Three choker setters, like toy soldiers in the distance below, scurry to hook up another batch of logs. Setting choker is dangerous, more dangerous on the steepest slopes. Imagine a game of giant Pic-up Stix, hooking cables under and around the right sticks when they lie crisscrossed on a forty-degree incline. Poison oak, nettles, and wasps are minor irritants to the choker setter. The big bad dream is a cable snapping or one of these logs moving the wrong way.

With chokers set, the men scramble to a safe distance and radio a piercing two bleeps back to the tower. The skyline comes taut, lifting its load with the crack of dry branches and logs spinning off dust and bark as the haul-back cable pulls them to the landing.

Log trucks move in and out. The loader lurches steadily from log pile to truck. The overhead cables continue their busy dance against the gray morning sky. The smell of fresh timber, pungent fir and raw hemlock, mixes with the exhaust of straining engines. From below rise the syncopated bleeps of the choker setters, and from over the next ridge comes the whine of a cutter's chainsaw.

The operation has hit its stride, has found its rhythm.

Lydell's son Dick maneuvers his blue-and-chrome truck, a White Western Star, onto the landing at Kansas. The loader plucks the trailer off the truck's back, and Dick hooks trailer to truck. From out of the cab springs nine-year-old Benjamin Reed, blond, bright-eyed, wearing a green-and-gold football jersey. Ben, Lydell's grandson, has strict limits on where he can and cannot wander in the vicinity of the landing. Crew members call him Soop, as in Supervisor.

A burly logger says, "Whaddaya think, Soop? Shut down early today?" The kid beams.

On another site, just ten minutes from Kansas, are Colleen Reed, seventeen, and David Reed, thirteen, working with their dad, Don, this morning. Don, Lydell's brother, piles slash with a Cat, and the teenagers help clear a three-foot-wide fire line around the clearcut.

Reed Logging Co. goes one generation deeper than Lydell, who joined his dad when he got out of the service, in 1946. Horse logging at first, with a crosscut saw for felling and bucking, they worked the hills around Estacada. The decision to buy a pair of Caterpillar tractors in 1948 was an agonizing, mind-boggling investment. Next came a portable sawmill and an Army surplus GMC truck. Reed Logging Co. was on its way. Brother Don joined the family enterprise in 1962. Nobody got rich, but the Reeds' sense of purpose goes beyond the family members to influence members of the crew. The pay is as good or better elsewhere, but exceptional people choose to work for Lydell.

Mike Perry, the foreman here at Kansas, can work anywhere. His logging skills are such that he'd been busy all winter—no slump for him—and he took a mind to have a little summer vacation.

"Then I got a call from Old Lydell," Perry says. "Said he needed a little help on a job. What can you do?" he wonders.

Perry is a forty-year-old Estacada native who trails behind him a reputation of near-legendary proportions, not all of it productive. By his early twenties, Perry had established himself as one of the hard-drinkingest, mean-fightingest, bar-wreckingest hombres in the western woods. He also was one fine logger. Not that Perry's off hours these days are all lemonade and PTA meetings, but the years have made him sane. Built thick, with dusty yellow hair and a square jaw, Perry mutters and grins a lot while overseeing this site.

When it's time to move the skyline cable five degrees to the right, Perry heads to the opposite ridge and fires up the D-7 Cat. With the help of choker setters, he repositions a quarter-mile length of cable, thick as his wrist—thick as my forearm—as if it were a rubber band. The Cat climbs the steep slope and crushes wicked obstructions to drag the end of the skyline to, and then wrap it around, a stump that will anchor it for the next couple of hours of logging. Then he rearranges tail blocks and rigging to get the proper angles of declension over the canyon.

Back at the landing, Lydell Reed quietly observes the operation of a twenty-one-year-old loading machine under the deft direction of Ted Copher, a disheveled and stubble-bearded veteran of the woods. The tongs on his battered and doorless loader are suspended by cable, like huge pincers swinging freely from the stub of an upper arm, the manipulation of which can sling the tongs fifty feet or so to clamp a log lying on the ground.

Copher is a virtuoso on this machine. He also knows he is being watched. In one continuous move he snags the end of a twenty-four-foot log and lifts it so that the log is momentarily standing vertical to the ground. The tongs release. And before the log can fall back to the ground, the heavy tongs slide down the length, snapping off unwanted limbs, to clamp the lower end. Now clean enough for loading, the log is lifted onto the truck and nudged into place.

Lydell enjoys the show. He is attending Van Cliburn. He is watching Ozzie Smith at shortstop. More than just loading here, Copher is also grading and sorting these logs. He separates the fir from the hemlock, setting aside the culls for a later truck. If Copher judges a log saleable and the mill at Boring says no, Reed has lost the $150 he could have earned by sending it to Stevenson, Washington, as core stock for plywood. The man on the loader can make or break this operation.

Lydell wonders aloud what keeps Copher coming to work on this antique of a loading machine. Copher owns eight log trucks of his own, some of the most awful-looking machines on the road, but they all run. He has his own airplane to help keep track of them. Copher is . . . well, irreplaceable. Sure, someone else can operate the loader. But not like *that*.

~~~~~

Like any independent producer—the farmer, the primary manufacturer—a logger thinks of government as a Never Never Land of know-nothing authorities filling out forms in triplicate and waiting for retirement pensions. U.S. Forest Service regulations and supervision are anathema to the logger, who thinks of himself as one of the last great Americans. Where would this country be without people who go out and work? To a logger, the Forest Service is visible and immediate. Government drives right up to him, once or twice a week, in a pale green pickup. At the wheel is a real live bureaucrat. Behind every other bush lurks someone plotting new ways to complicate a logger's life.

When the Reed crew sits down to snap open lunch pails and to unscrew the tops of steel thermos jugs, the Forest Service serves as a mother lode of complaints. But not for Lydell. He won't say anything critical of the Forest Service. And he won't say anything complimentary about Lydell Reed. As a result, Lydell says very little at all. He squirms and fidgets as the crew's lunchtime conversation veers off course toward self-pity and excuses.

The Forest Service forbids logging within an eagle's view from its nest, which can shut down an enormous area. The Forest Service will come out with a tape recording of the mating call of the spotted owl. This is called "hooting 'em up." If an owl answers the tape three times, it counts as a "sighting." There will be no logging activity, year-around, over an area of a thousand acres. The elk mating and calving seasons kept Reed Logging Co. off its current sites until July 1. Loggers have to tip-toe around any trickle of water that could be called a creek. Slash piles must be covered with Visqueen to await burning. Raise a berm of mud six inches high next to a tire rut or a skid road, and the Forest Service will shut things down until conditions get dry enough to continue.

Lydell tries to change the subject. Isn't it remarkable, he says, how Don's daughter—sitting nearby and soaking all this in—has grown to look like her big sisters?

This fails to distract anyone except Colleen.

Lydell takes off his hardhat. His white hair is miraculously still parted though he's been wearing the hardhat all morning and working a shovel to clear a second landing. The horizontal mark from the hardhat's sweatband looks permanently embossed across his forehead. It probably is. Reed has been at this a long time, but he's assembled here a bunch of rugged individualists who will talk about whatever the hell they want.

Unmentioned, here at lunchtime, is that great botches such as the French Pete timber sale in the 1960s raised the public consciousness about the social and environmental impact of logging. The profit motive, left unchecked, *does* result in compacted ground on delicate terrain, streams running brown, and the whole resultant mess for salmon and other Northwest inhabitants.

The Forest Service is the great flak-catcher, taking criticism from all sides. The environmentalists cry that its *modus operandi* is to extract maximum profit from the resource, while thrashing the woods and trashing streams. At Mt. Hood National Forest Headquarters, in Gresham, the dilemma is visible in officials' eyes. *Oh, Lord have mercy, not another magazine article.* These people are tense, harangued, defensive. Whatever they do, they cannot win.

~~~

The tenth loaded truck to leave the landing is Dick Reed's, again. Five trucks are hauling from Kansas today, and there will be thirteen loads—a good day for Reed Logging. Dick was fifth in rotation, so this will be his second trip to the mill, and his last. Paid by the load ($150, on this job), Dick needs over $300 a day to make a living and to replace his truck components when things fall apart, as they will. Tomorrow he will be first in the rotation. He should get three loads.

As talkative as his dad is taciturn, Dick is lean, trim-bearded, and brash. He's proud of the family operation and satisfied with his own financial independence from it. He owns this four-year-old truck.

The cab vibrates to the low-range shifting of gears—thirteen speeds forward—as Dick maneuvers slowly down the one-lane road off the mountain. He radios a CB warning that he's on his way out. He fears city folks might wander up here on a weekday. If the driver of an oncoming car panics and does not hit the ditch, it will be left for Dick, sitting in front of forty tons of truck and logs, to find a way through.

This load of hemlock is headed for Vanport Mill, in Boring, and from there to Japan. Dick Reed joins a growing convoy of loaded trucks, like tributaries merging into rivers gaining volume. At two and a half truckloads to a housing start, the potential for a good-sized suburban development will roll out of the Mt. Hood National Forest today.

While stopped at the scaling station, Dick looks up to see Lydell barreling down the Clackamas River Road at the wheel of the lowboy with a Cat on the back. For a boss, Lydell is having himself quite a workingman's day.

~~~

Later, at 6 p.m. and nearly fourteen hours after Lydell's morning coffee at Cruz Inn, his wife, Nona, answers the phone at his house. "Lydell isn't here yet," she apologizes. "You can probably reach him at the shop."

~~~~

"One of these days I'm going to wash the moss off this old airplane," says Ted Copher, Reed's virtuoso loader. He rubs a thin green growth along the underbelly of the fuselage.

On this clear Sunday in August, the plane sits at an obscure airport in the woods south of Sandy. Too busy to fly it recently, Copher regards its tires—one flat, another limp—and searches in the cockpit for the gas key. Like most of the log trucks he keeps on the road, this Cessna 175 is the product of a salvage operation. It was wrecked, and Copher rebuilt it. Still on the instrument panel are radio call numbers for the San Jose, California, area. Missing is the radio itself.

But Copher is at one with machines. "It might not be pretty, but it flies," says the mechanical wizard who draws grease and oil to his person as if it were part of the innate human condition. And sure enough, after he patches the tire and spends another half hour readying the plane for flight, the engine roars to life.

Up over Sandy and north toward the Columbia River Gorge, the plane flies low over private timberland, large tracts of it owned by Publishers Paper Co. After a breathtaking loop past Bridal Veil Falls, with the wide blue Columbia curving suddenly far below, Copher heads back over Bull Run and east toward Mt. Hood. The big rock looms high and white. Copher turns south toward the terrain Reed Logging Co. has been working. Below lies a patchwork quilt of green forest and clearcuts.

The overriding impression is one of limits. From this vantage point, the forest is not infinite, not even vast. To the east rise the brown hills of the dry country. To the west lies a civilized haze over the Willamette Valley. About half the timber under intensive management remains to be cut. Signs of logging are varied, from fresh clearcuts like Kansas, to patches of short seedlings forcing their green upon the brown, to units already mature enough for commercial thinning. Like a trip backstage, however, the overhead view contrasts starkly with the view from Timberline Lodge, say, where outlying hills seem untouched and the forest rolls on and on. It does not. Almost all is being harvested. Regeneration is not just the best option. It is the only option.

The plane flies back toward Estacada, crossing the drainage area of Roaring River Canyon. This is virgin forest. Trees up to eight feet in diameter rise here, creating a solid canopy of branches and a damp forest floor of ferns, free of brush. A hiker can spend a summer day and never be touched by a ray of direct sunlight. This area is off-limits to logging.

Copher is unhesitating in his opinion that prime forest areas like this must remain protected. "We've got enough trees to cut," he says. "That's not the trouble."

What *is* the trouble, Ted?

"The trouble is too many loggers. Too many loggers, bidding each other out of business. The market gets hot and every idiot who can sign a mortgage statement is out to make a quick buck. And then he'll go broke undercutting a solid outfit like Reed's. Nobody but the mill or the finance company comes out ahead."

~~~

After thirty-seven years, after co-founding a company and supporting a crew of over twenty men, Lydell Reed lives in a modest hillside home in Boring. He hasn't taken a vacation in two years. His yacht is a twelve-foot aluminum fishing boat with an outboard. He has a travel trailer that he might pull down to Arizona this winter. One car, a Buick Regal, sits in the driveway. No swimming pool. No hot tub. No extravagant dinner parties for Lydell and Nona, who have been married for forty years.

Eligible now for Social Security, Lydell would be embarrassed to slow down and take those easy checks. What he likes best about his home in Boring is the view toward Mt. Hood and the hills where he works. This summer has been a good one for the company. It had to be good. And he likes the contracts lined up for this fall. Always careful with words, Lydell Reed takes a deep breath and offers a lengthy—for him—commentary, one whole sentence, about his prospects for the immediate future.

"It looks promising."

The Turtle

Sam McKinney's book, *Reach of Tide, Ring of History*, is an account of his poking around in a self-made boat on the lower Columbia River, from its mouth at the Pacific Ocean to Portland. Sam wrote about the river and he wrote about how people—the natives, and then early Euro-Americans—had used the river. Illustrations show a sassy sixteen-foot cabin cruiser that the water clearly loved. The book, too, is of clean design and spare language and large mind. Anybody—not just riverpeople—would like this book.

When I mentioned it to my sister Betsy, she said, "Sam McKinney! He lives right next door to me."

Betsy told Sam I was working on my own Columbia River book. She arranged for my wife, Donna, and me to meet Sam and Gail for drinks at their house in Johns Landing, southwest Portland, before Betsy's Halloween party. Sam was not in costume, but he cut a fine figure of the scholarly navigator at rest. He wore a tweed jacket with leather elbow patches over a bulk-knit sweater, all in river colors, rumpled, as if somebody else had dressed him in a hurry and forgotten to rake his eyebrows. After a vice-grip handshake I guessed he was in his early sixties, a decade older than I, with Viking cheekbones and crow's feet at the eyes. A boyish shock of hair swept sideways across his brow. Sam's best feature was his eyes, mischievous brown-green lasers that might be sizing me up already for partnership in truancy.

No sooner had we downed a drink than Sam led me to the garage and fired up his pipe and showed me the next boat he was building.

All it was, this boat, was a flat-bottom, bottom-side-up hull made of plywood, coated with a hardened goo to waterproof and toughen it. There wasn't much to admire yet about the boat except its size. Fitted to the dimensions of the garage, the hull left only enough room for a Sam-sized person to walk its perimeter. It was twenty feet by five-and-a-half, or slightly longer and wider than his Volvo station wagon, now parked on the street. The hull was rectangular. Viewed from above, I couldn't tell bow from stern. From the side, I saw one end taper like the business end of a paint-scraper. That end was the bow.

"Come back Saturday," Sam said, "for the boat-turning."

Boat-turning, come to find out, is a social event to which Sam invites every able-bodied man and woman he can think of, hoping enough will show up to lift and rotate the hull. A dozen of us lifted the hull and carried it out of the garage. We turned it right side up (water side down). Then we carried it back into the garage. Gail served coffee and buttermilk coffee cake. We stood around at the nautical equivalent of kicking tires, trying to imagine what Sam might build *upwards* from this freshly painted hull.

I lingered longer than the others. I asked him what he would do next. Maybe that's why Sam again invited me back—"Saturdays, or whenever you can"—to help him build this boat.

"I'm no carpenter," I warned him. I didn't yet know that Sam wouldn't have wanted anybody with boat-building skills. What he needed was somebody to sand and to paint and to listen. He, Sam, had all the skills and most of the ideas. We talked, as we worked on successive Saturdays, about rivers and what they are. We talked about how people shaped the Columbia River, and how a river shapes its people. We talked about my sister Betsy, a smart cookie. We agreed that Meriwether Lewis and William Clark and A. B. Guthrie were great men. But Sam didn't include among his heroes, as I did, Charles Darwin and Ken Kesey. And Sam had a gloomier regard for humanity than I did. That's where we found fresh currents for talk. Sam was stunned—he dropped a C-clamp and reached for his pipe—when I said I thought human activities had not yet ruined the Columbia River for salmon and steelhead. With human help, the fish could rally, could make it through.

We talked as we worked.

The only "plan" for this boat had sprung directly from Sam's head onto a single sheet of graph paper with only the rough penciled outlines of length, width, and height. Sam had built several such boats, beginning with *The Gander*, the sixteen-footer in his book. I came to understand that Sam's boats were disposable, as boats go, to him. He would invest a single winter building a boat and then test it for a summer before moving on to another.

"Trial and improvement," he said, distilling into three words the adaptation and selection that lies behind all of humanity's tools for accelerating movement, from the dugout canoe to the Honda Civic. Make it and try it. If it works, keep it. If it could work better, change it. Sam's approach to boat building parallels natural selection. There is heritable variation from one model to the next, and some variants are more likely than others to survive. Sam's way is different from natural selection in that the product arises from a designing intelligence, from Sam's brain. A McKinney-made boat is designed to work on the Columbia River, after the least possible investment of money and time.

"My first boat?" he said, pausing to light his pipe. "I was reading a British architect whose name . . . (puff) . . . escapes me. A British naval architect asked himself, *How big does a boat have to be?* This is the question. Kunnart was his name. Kunnart answered himself, *Big enough to lie down in*. And that," Sam said, "got me started. A boat any bigger invites two kinds of trouble. Expense and guests."

Here in the garage Sam had laid himself out on two slabs of plywood and marked his body length. For width he waved his arms and marked that, too, with a pencil on the wood. He marked places to stand, fore and aft, in this nascent boat. On materials, he spent a total of $650.35. *The Gander* was the first in a series of boats, followed by *Gander II, Gander III*, in which, over a period of four years, Sam completed a 5,200-mile voyage across North America, as much as possible by water. He went up the Columbia and Snake rivers, down the Missouri, through the Great Lakes, and out the St. Lawrence Seaway to the Atlantic.

Sam built several other boats of similar design. Not all of them worked. But in the cosmos of boat design, Sam fashioned a new species. Here in the garage were his most recent design improvements, including an arched roof (the better to shed Northwest rain) and a more gradual flare at the bow (the better to plane the boat across rough waters)..

We talked as we worked. I puttied those little holes in the wood the sunken screws make. I tirelessly sanded and painted. Nothing about building a boat required me to think about building a boat. I looked forward to these Saturdays, waking early and fending off responsibilities at home with the words—technically true—"Sam and I are building a boat."

On successive Saturdays and an occasional Sunday that winter of 1994-95 the boat took shape in Sam's garage. It found its name, *The Turtle*, not for its shape or for the lack of hurry its shape suggested but for its color. Before the boat turning, Sam had painted the hull Atlantic Green, a yacht enamel. I don't recall the first time Sam called *The Turtle* "our" boat. Anyway, I took this to be a figure of speech. He welcomed my dumb labor. No doubt he also liked as much as I did the river talk that filled his garage like pipe smoke. But Sam wouldn't let me pay for materials, not even for paint.

In March, maybe early April, we waterproofed the roof. I shellacked the mahogany trim and painted with a small brush the sills of the Plexiglas windows, applying final touches to a boat I was in love with. *The Turtle* was a triumph of simplicity. Of its twenty feet in length, the middle ten were cabin, with two benches long enough to sleep on. Four separate cubbyholes at each cabin corner could be devoted to cooking or to storage. The cabin, not quite tall enough to stand up in, was rescued from stark boxiness by sloping lines from the roof to each corner of the hull. Forward lay a five-foot-square deck, for standing or sitting in the open. Aft was another open deck with benches port and starboard. *The Turtle* was symmetrical except for the upward flare of the hull at the bow.

~~~

By the time we launched her, on April 19, 1995, I had adopted Sam's habit of calling *The Turtle* our boat. My family members—amazed, snapping photos— dominated the launch party. We jiggered a set of fulcrums and rollers and ramped *The Turtle* from the floor of Sam's garage onto a flatbed trailer. We trucked it a quarter of a mile down Nebraska Street and across Macadam Boulevard to the river at Willamette Park. After the first splash, there was a hold-your-breath moment to see how she would come to rest in the water.

The Turtle bobbed at dockside just fine. I crawled inside and probed the nether spaces with a flashlight, looking for leaks. I found none.

And so on that blustery spring day a clumsy immobile object became a slippery and water-friendly vessel. She's no ballerina, but *The Turtle* showed from the get-go that a fifteen-horse Honda four-stroke, short shaft, was enough to plane her. She slid, instead of plowing, downstream on the Willamette River. Sam took her the first hour, through Portland, while I stood forward on the deck feeling like a hood ornament. I'd been on the river plenty, but I poke around by canoe. Here on *The Turtle*, clipping along water, rushing through air, I had this manic impression of sensational, and unearned, speed. We were moving along at . . . what? . . . maybe seven knots. We passed the ramparts of downtown Portland and on past ocean-going ships at their wharves.

Downstream from the industrial area, the Willamette River splits. Its narrower and more wind-protected branch, on the left, is Multnomah Channel. The right branch, the ship channel, merges with the wide Columbia River just a mile or two farther on. Between Multnomah Channel and the Columbia lies Sauvie Island, a big one, a twenty-mile stretch of lush farmland and wildlife refuge. On this day, the wind was up. The Columbia River would be a washboard of whitecaps. So Sam aimed *The Turtle* into Multnomah Channel.

And then I ran the boat. Its outboard motor has a telescoping extension to the handle. The extension lets the operator stand up, facing forward, to see over the cabin where the boat is going. We slid on down Multnomah Channel, headed for the Columbia River town of St. Helens, just beyond the downstream tip of Sauvie Island, to moor *The Turtle*. At St. Helens the beaches are whiter, the islands less crowded. The Columbia flows bigger and swifter, bluer and more clean-feeling, than the Willamette at Portland. We took our time, passing houseboat villages and small boats at anchor, fishing. Sauvie Island—flat as Holland—lay on our right. Low hills of the Coast Range rose on our left.

Wind and waves were up as we approached St. Helens Marina. Because *The Turtle* is flat-bottomed and draws less than four inches of water, she is more buffeted by wind than by current. I misjudged the strength of the wind and narrowly missed the Columbia County Sheriff's patrol boat and had to take a couple passes at it before *The Turtle* came parallel to the dock.

This boat would take some getting used to. But I understood right away what it meant to have a boat to share, and a good friend to share it with. Not that I'd been unhappy with life so far, but I could never afford such a luxury as a twenty-foot river-cruiser. And here it was. I felt life unfolding to a new set of possibilities. In the same way a boy goes off to college, say, or a young man becomes a father, I'd been booted up to the next higher station in life.

~~~

I took the boat out almost every weekend that summer, more often than Sam wanted to go. *The Turtle*, with its shallow draft, probed backwaters and sloughs where few other boats could go. It was a boat for privacy, with room to spread out and to read or write. And I could run her ashore, head-on, to a sandy beach. I could off-load a Saharan princess without getting her feet wet. The trick is to throw an anchor astern before hitting the beach. Step off the bow as the boat hits the sand and run a line to a cottonwood tree. *The Turtle* is now secured both bow and stern. Adjust the lines so she's a little off shore, in deep enough water to take the wake of passing ships but shallow enough to wade out to.

That she's flat-bottomed is also *The Turtle*'s major drawback. This boat gets hammered in rough water. Three-foot waves are common at St. Helens when the wind howls. Instead of cutting through the waves, she bangs into them one at a time. I rattled my fillings a time or two getting back to the marina from beach picnics.

By late August—although we were sharing the boat—Sam let me pay for the moorage. I was alone on *The Turtle* far more often than with Sam.

One late-August evening all four of us—Sam and Gail, Donna and I—cruised from St. Helens up the Columbia and poked into Lake River to Ridgefield, Washington. Sam let me handle the boat all the way. He watched without comment how I handled the wake of an ocean-going freighter in the ship channel. We headed that evening for a restaurant run by an elderly Romanian couple at Ridgefield. I docked successfully. The meal was good. And on the cruise home a full moon lit our way across the broad Columbia. The wind had died. The river had settled, and the moony water scrambled in our wake.

I don't know when he did it—whether he wrote the message that night, or visited St. Helens in the meantime—but in *The Turtle*'s log, the next time I opened it, was a message from Sam. To me, from Sam. He had seen how I loved that boat. In celebration of his birthday he had decided to give it to me.

For his birthday, Sam gave me *The Turtle*.

River City

St. Helens Marina is not Marina Del Rey, but it does moor some condominium-sized yachts. The smart set look down their noses as if *The Turtle*—a homemade, wooden boat—is queering their party. Children can't get enough of her, but fishers are baffled by the all-enclosed cabin that would appear to eliminate bad-weather fishing. What I have here is a green, squarish, socially awkward thing that inspires strangers to ask, *What kind of boat is that?* Or, shaking their heads, *That's some kind of boat you got there.*

One time out in *The Turtle* I aimed to tie up for a night at the Gilbert River dock. No other boats were there. My arrival put out a great blue heron who took noisy flight—grawk!—and flapped back to perch at the far end of the dock. At dusk I turned on the cabin light to read, and could no longer see outside. After I switched off the reading light, my eyes slowly adjusted. Optics reversed. The last ambient glow in the sky revealed the heron, right there at my window, peering in as if puzzled.

But what do I care what others think?

Having a boat puts a fresh angle on the joys and contradictions of this place, this river city, this Portland. Having a boat, I find the optics reversed. I am craning out a new window on home, peering at familiar arrangements as if they were marvelous.

~~~

Late on a Friday, out for the weekend, I headed upstream into Multnomah Channel, the west side of Sauvie Island. The island, flat as a pool table, splits the Columbia from St. Helens to Portland. Indians called it Wapato Island, for its potato-like tubers, the starch in their fish-rich diet. To Lewis and Clark, passing in 1805, this was a benign and fertile land, astonishingly green in November. The surrounding waters were thick with canoe-borne natives who lacked the war-like hostility and erect posture of plains Indians. These short fat people lived in cedar plank lodges at permanent village sites and were shrewd at the arts of trade and petty larceny. "Those fellows we found assumeing and disagreeable," Clark wrote. "Those fellows Stold my pipe Tomahawk" and

"One of those Scoundrels Stole a cappoe[coat] of one of our interpreters." The explorers paddled on past dark to get clear of one of the most heavily populated areas of aboriginal America.

Today Sauvie Island is a wildlife preserve at its downstream end, a duck-hunting range at its shallow-lake center. Zoned for farming within Portland city limits, the island is fiercely rural. Residents tolerate weekend bikers and a nude-swimming beach, but they put out their horns to fend off a proposed golf course. From the boat, berry farms and pumpkin patches lay hidden behind a dike that keeps the river in its place.

This was in June, and the river was flooding. In three hours I slogged only ten miles against brown current. On my left, the river sucked at the lowest branches of cottonwood trees. On the right lay dike-protected pastures. The sky had a single cloud formation that issued from the south horizon, expanding, enflamed by the falling sun, as if the San Francisco Pillow Company had blown up. Downy white fluff spread overhead toward Seattle. As the sun dropped, clouds thinned and pinked. Darkness found the trees at shoreline, but the river went bright to its edges, as if sky had dropped into it.

A brace of cormorants arrowed past, low to the water, and I wondered about *The Turtle* as a mood-altering device. Something about the flow of water, the smell of river, can suck the irritation right out of a man.

I tied up at Coon Island, near city limits but worlds away from the hustle and rush of town. Only three other boats—fat white yachts—hugged the dock. Two of them had televisions on, so I was essentially alone. At 10 p.m., curls of river current still mirrored the last light of day. Crickets and frogs began to scritch and croak. A huge yellow moon came up in sections behind strands of breakaway cloud. It's a fact that the moon, when it first gets up, appears larger. Because beams of light have to travel through more of the Earth's atmosphere at that low angle, light rays bend. The moon, as if viewed through the lens of a magnifying glass, appears to be more than it is.

Maybe I was seeing the whole world that way. As I lay in the cabin, waiting for sleep, the moon broke clear and silver and bright. Light from the long-gone sun—in a sensational bank shot—reflections off reflections—bounced from the moon, ricocheted off the river, and rippled the white ceiling of *The Turtle*.

Outside, the river licked at the dock and slipped past the boat, whispering of where it had been.

~~~

The Columbia River rises from springwater and glacial drip into brawling mountain streams all along the west slope of the Rocky Mountains. Gathering itself from Canada, seven Western states and two time zones, the Columbia crosses the high desert, knifes through a cliff-guarded gorge, slides into this low green country, and heaves more water into the Pacific than any other river in North or South America. The river carries ten times more water than the Colorado sends through the Grand Canyon, twice the flow of the fabled Nile.

Here we'd had no rain for two weeks. Sprinklers stitched across dry Portland lawns, but the Columbia was still rising as the top half of the planet tipped. The angle of sun that had melted Wyoming's snowpack, and then Montana's, was only now, in late June, unlocking the icepack in British Columbia. Each major tributary rises in turn. The Columbia keeps coming, keeps spinning the turbines and kicking the flywheels of Northwest commerce, keeps pounding off the continent toward the sea.

~~~~

And so I powered on the next morning against stiff current, dodging woody debris, toward downtown Portland. A steady drizzle muffled the air and ruffed the water to show, like clear swirls on frosted glass, where the current wasn't. Only a few stray boats had ventured out that morning, but many more houseboats crowded the river than just a year ago. Through the mist came the hiss of traffic on Highway 30. The rap of hammers and the whine of a skill saw announced more people coming into this place that is growing at nearly double the national rate. Many of the newcomers, paradoxically, came here looking for the quality of life that comes with smaller cities, clean air and water, and open spaces.

A pile of white thunderheads rolled off the West Hills and turned bruise-colored. After a bolt of lightning, the sky cracked. I tied up to a log boom, cut the engine and ducked into the cabin as pearl-sized raindrops peppered the roof.

And then—presto—blue sky broke through. Out came the dazzling greens of sunlit cottonwoods and alders.

On upstream and into the Willamette River I entered the industrial port, where cross-continental railroads and highways meet Pacific-prowling ships. Commerce took over the river. Yet the view from *The Turtle* was of the natural and the human getting along. Herons and kingfishers worked the water near the growl and diesel whiff of a working tug. Men in small boats, fishing for steelhead, caught and tossed back shad. Along the wharves, ocean-going ships took on lumber, gave up Toyotas. In the foreground, an osprey lifted a wide-eyed shad to a nest atop pilings. Behind that, a crane lifted buckets of gravel from a barge to a hopper and conveyor belt. In the background rose Forest Park, a five-thousand-acre swath of thick woods.

By noon I reached the high-rise steel and glass of downtown Portland. That year's run of spring Chinook salmon already had passed, but one of the great sustaining notions of this place is that salmon and steelhead do, still, surge through the heart of a metro area of 1.8 million people. When the dogwoods bloom, we have one of America's great fishing holes within view of a Merrill Lynch office. Within a few hundred yards of each other are NBA basketball and a heron rookery. I could dock the boat and stroll to Powell's, America's largest independent bookstore.

Where else on the continent—on the planet—do the great intentions of nature and civilization come braided so closely together?

Fifty-three thousand immigrants took the Oregon Trail from 1840 to 1860 seeking a new life in the wilderness. To Oregon's Willamette Valley came families, many of them from failed farms in the pestilent Ohio River Valley. Nearly half the settlers were female. Oregon's pioneers were pious and relatively well educated, headed for the steady toil of homesteading. To California went single men, adventurers, drawn to the gold fields. By way of explaining differences between California and Oregon, nearly everyone here can tell the story—no doubt apocryphal, but perfect—of the directional markers at a split in the Oregon Trail. The trail south was marked by a pile of gold-quartz stones. The branch north had a sign, "To Oregon." People who could read came here.

Grafted to that hardy and literate stock came a shoot of New England merchants who arrived with their goods by ship. Captain John Couch, one of the city's founders, saw right away the commercial possibilities. Portland was as far upstream as seafaring ships could penetrate, far enough to lade the wealth of the Willamette Valley. But what really excited Couch—what he wrote East about—was that he could shoot ducks from his front porch.

Portlanders are now a fully commercialized people, but nature is still the ultimate hero of urban life. After lunch we can get to ski slopes or clean beaches or never-logged forest, and get back in time for dinner. Even when we don't, we could. Natural awareness runs through everyday life as a kind of ongoing muffled hum. Never too deeply buried in the urban ethos is an imaginative truth that not so long ago we emerged to this riverside clearing, the sons and daughters of pioneers, self-selected for rugged individuality.

Oddly, my view from the boat that morning suggested how we insulate ourselves, with bridges and sea walls, from the river. In a darker mood I think we might be as estranged from natural rhythms as any other urban folk. Thanks only to a network of flood-control dams are we able to cling year-around to this habitat. We wrap ourselves in the River City myth but still measure our well-being in economic terms. The danger of a working river rises to consciousness only occasionally, when we have to break out the sand bags, or ludicrously, when a gravel barge swamps a dozen rugged individualists from Nike rowing an unlit dragon boat at night.

As a people we came here busting woods and taming rivers. Now that we've mostly done that, our sense of identity hinges on what we have *left* of woods and rivers.

It's true that Portland has been ahead of other rapidly growing cities in adopting land-use planning laws, saving greenspaces within the city. A larger truth may be that the main reason we have greenspaces to save is we got here too late to completely screw things up. The Endangered Species Act—listing as threatened the wild salmon that migrate through the urban area—put Portland to the test. ESA listings underlined a dawning awareness that we are at a major pivot point in the affairs of humans and the wild. We could lose what is unique about this place. We could submit to the great Western theme of destroying what we love the most.

One irony of the ESA listings is that we have come a long way in cleaning up our waterways. Forty years ago the Willamette River gave off a septic stink. The river in town was so rank you wouldn't think of swimming in it. Fixed-point pollution has been largely curbed, sewage overflow decreased. The encouraging thing is that it's only been in the past decade or so that an awareness of human responsibility toward the habitat really began to penetrate the urban mindset. Kids these days are more alert to the connectedness of things—of woods to salmon, of nature to commerce, of rivers to our sense of spirit and well-being.

We're getting wiser.

Will we be wise enough in time?

More people are coming. Each month, more people immigrate to Oregon than took the Oregon Trail in any year. As my species crowds the Portland-Vancouver metro area, the threat we pose to our rivers is more subtle, more quietly insidious, than bad logging or toxic outflow from a chemical plant. It's the danger of losing in small increments the surrounding wetlands and greenspaces to asphalt and condos, of leaching small poisons from driveways and lawns. From the boat the river looks and smells clean, but I am haunted by recent warnings: don't eat a lot of those suckers and carp, those bottom-fish. In the paper I read sickening reports of one-eyed fish with crooked spines in the Willamette, and of Columbia River otters with withered penises, shrunken testicles.

~~~~~

Another time, on another outing, I anchored overnight at a Sauvie Island backwater, Cunningham Slough. When the morning sun rose high enough to catch the west bank, a small river otter emerged from the root system of a willow and slid down into the water. Then another one belly-slid down the mud bank. And another. Five, in all—liquid black and glossy—climbed back up the bank and went skidding down again, nosing into the water without a splash.

They surfaced for a curious look at the boat. While I sat there the otters started wrestling in the water. They made of themselves an otterball. Heads over tails over heads over tails, the otterball went churning along the surface, throwing up spray. When that got old, they dived and surfaced separately. One little show-off came up near the boat and exhibited a crawdad between his teeth. He cracked and ate the crawdad.

When I glanced up, I saw the otters' parents. They had come out on the bank to watch, and to watch me watching.

Optics reversed. I felt, for my own crowding species, on the spot.

The Animals Changed

River otters have more fun than we do. You think? O.K., maybe I see them only at play. Anyway, bad news about river otters is particularly disturbing. What's this about otters in the Newberg stretch of the Willamette with withered penises and shrunken testicles? I believe what I read in the paper, but how do we know? Who gathers this information? And what induces an otter to hold still for measurement? There must be a story—some drama—in the approach of a human, with tape and calipers, to a river otter.

Kathy Shinn at the Oregon Department of Fish and Wildlife couldn't say, but would look into it. I wanted more than facts. I asked her, "Whose job is it? Is there some plain-spoken, story-telling old sleuth who . . ."

"Oh!" she cut me off. "Joe Pesek. Not about otters, especially, but you have to talk to Joe."

So I called up Joe Pesek, who had retired in 1997 after thirty years as an ODFW biologist. He suggested lunch at a Shari's restaurant, and we met near the confluence of the Clackamas and Willamette rivers, just upstream from Portland. He wore blue jeans and boots, and his brown-graying hair was short and kempt as a colonel's. "Now where are you from?" he said.

Right here, I told him. Grew up on the Clackamas, at Estacada. Pesek, it turns out, graduated from Oregon City High School in 1956. He's only five years ahead of me in the same watershed. And so with just two or three sentences we found solidarity. Before we were even seated, Pesek was telling about his bicycle trips to Estacada and on up to Fish Creek, camping and fishing with a buddy when they were kids, first on one-speeds but then what a difference three-speeds made on the Clackamas River Road.

The waitress led us to a window seat and slapped down a pair of menus laminated stiff enough to paddle a canoe. Pesek was bright as a wood duck. He wore red suspenders over a magenta shirt, open at the neck to a sky-blue T-shirt. His trim beard framed ruddy, bumpy-skinned cheeks, and his glasses magnified eager blue eyes.

Pesek talked about how lucky we were to have grown up with rivers and woods. He talked without prompt or punctuation about those days and how these days he visits schools as a mountain man in buckskins with a muzzle-loading rifle. The other day he visited Irvington School to talk about owls and there were maybe sixty kids and he asked how many of them had ever been camping and only three hands went up—just three!—and when he was a kid he made a boat out of stray lumber and tin roofing that worried his mother because his friend's brother *did* drown on the Clackamas but these city kids' parents must have never been camping either so he asked the kids where they had camped and all three said it was at Columbia Slough but at least you can do that here in Portland no matter that his own background is Czech by way of North Dakota in 1870 his people got moved closer to Fort Lincoln because Sitting Bull was on the rampage and . . .

Our food came. My roast turkey with mashed potatoes and gravy was good. I steered Pesek back to this watershed. How did he get to be a biologist?

"I was the first in my family to go to college," he said. To Oregon State. He hadn't liked high school except a course in advanced biology. He didn't see the point of English, but a teacher badgered him to take her fishing. And he did. "I took the English teacher fishing. She was trying to reach me," he said, as if this were an impossible idea. "I would say something and she'd say, 'You should write that down.' "

Pesek never had the patience to do that, and still doesn't. But he reads. The first books he mentioned were two of my favorites, Don Berry's *Trask* and *Moontrap,* historical fiction on the Northwest frontier.

Edgewise, I put in some words. I told him I'd been hanging out on the river and thinking about otters and others. I was curious about adaptive pressure on native species. "Since we got here," I said. "Since Lewis and Clark. Darwinian change on our rivers."

Pesek set his fork down. His blue eyes got bluer. "I named my boat *The Beagle,*" he said. And then he went off about the distinction between research biologists, who tend toward micro-measurement, and management biologists. The latter deal with farmers and landowners. They take the larger view of a watershed. He'd been a management biologist. He gave me names to contact for different areas of the Willamette and Columbia, and he told me how ODFW is organized by 1) fish, 2) game, and 3) non-game animals such as ospreys and eagles and otters.

I asked him about otters. He said the statistics on sex organs came from otters turned in by trappers, for tagging. Really? I hadn't known otters were trapped. But just for study, he said, not for pelts. And while I turned this over in my mind, Pesek skipped ahead to Darwinian change in the watershed. Species aren't what they used to be. He mentioned Chinese ringneck pheasants, "wild" turkeys, chukars, and California valley quail. None of them are native here.

"Some mink were native," he said, "but most of the mink you see now got turned loose or escaped." Mink farmers, following the fashion for furs, came up with a breed called cotton mink. Those, with white chest-fur, have interbred with natives. "You want gray mink? We can *make* those. Blues? Blondes? The farmers bred those, and threw out the others."

Pesek talked about the nutria scam, a pyramid scheme. Promoters in the 1950s advertised two pairs of animals for $500 and guaranteed to buy back the first litter for $100. Nutria are a fast-breeding rat-like species, big as beavers, supposedly valued in the South for their meat as well as for fur. "Nutria farms sprang up, with rearing ponds full of them," he said. "There were so many nutria the bottom fell out of the market. The scheme collapsed. Nutria swept down the Willamette from the Santiam when a farmer opened the gates and shot himself."

Pesek talked and talked. He talked about exotic plants that colonized the lower Columbia.

"In the old days, ships filled their holds with dirt—for ballast—at Liverpool. When the ships reached the Columbia, they dumped that dirt. With the dirt came seeds. Reed's canary grass. English ivy. Red dead nettle. Purple loosestrife. Because the English love their gardens," he said, his voice rising with the connectedness of it all. "The English had collected seeds from all over the Empire."

He mentioned Himalayan blackberries, which overwhelmed our tastier and smaller-seeded native blackberry. Scotch broom, now, is all over. I pictured my wife Donna's Aunt Eva, the prim World War I bride who never lost her English accent or her way with gardens. Aunt Eva had the tidiest patch of blooms in all of Estacada. I thought of Donna's own not-so-prim garden, strewn with seeds from Giverny, France, and with Canterbury bells from England, via Aunt Eva. Aunt Eva herself, come to think of it, spawned here. I tried to recall which of the cousins issued from Aunt Eva's stock. But then all of us at the family picnic are but three or four generations removed from England or Wales or Germany. And the planet, as I wondered, grew so small I could roll it in my hands.

In the meantime, Pesek had left flora for fauna. Some native life forms are reviving.

"Raptors are back," he said. "Just twenty years ago, bald eagles were having a hell of a time. Eagles and ospreys eat fish. They top the food chain. They get the highest doses of whatever's in the water." The population here had dwindled to fifteen nesting sites, and ODFW set a recovery goal of thirty. "When I left," he said, "there were thirty-six nesting sites. Now eagles are on Coon Island. Five nests on Sauvie Island."

Why?

"We don't really know," he said. "Or ospreys. When I came to ODFW there was only one osprey pair between here and Astoria. Now they're all over the river. Ospreys like navigational aids."

It's true. From *The Turtle* I see osprey nests atop the channel markers. Osprey nests cap the pilings that anchor log booms. Ospreys have evolved toward these artificial perches, away from riverside snags.

We talked about the more obvious toxins that probably led to the raptors' earlier decline—outflow from lumber mills, dioxins from paper plants, oily residue from roads and rails. Pesticides and herbicides. "Even the Indians threw crap in the river," he said. "There's more of us now, and different kinds of poisons. Lead paint, from all the ships coming up the river. Lead is probably still down there, under the silt. Reproduction rates on eagles had dropped to 0.79, not enough to sustain the population. We had no ospreys. Now they're back. And the herons, terns, and cormorants—doing great."

Again I asked why.

The scientist in him just shrugged his shoulders.

"Why do you think?" I said. "You're not working for ODFW now."

Pesek gave me a look. "The river *is* cleaner," he said. "And people would like to take credit." He took off his glasses and rubbed them on his shirt. He put them on again. "But maybe the *animals* changed," he said.

"They evolved to beat the poisons. Take the osprey. Ospreys have a twelve-year life span. They'll raise only four broods in eight years. If just one of those broods managed to survive, it would take a long time for the river to repopulate with others who can live here. It's taken about that long."

While I was digesting this, Pesek nailed down his point. Species adapt to a sudden event of selection pressure. It's the reason last year's flu-shot formula doesn't work this year. It's the same reason my doctor prescribed Septra when Erithromycin lost its potency. Viruses and bacteria evolve to outflank the medicine. Pesek's example was DDT. Heavily used in the 1940s, DDT killed all the mosquitoes at first. *Almost* all. Species adapt. A few—by some twist in their genetic make-up, by some slight variation in the sequencing of bases in a double-helix molecule—survived. And because that variation was heritable, the survivors bestowed on their progeny a resistance to DDT. Later still, whole populations of bugs got by.

"They study fruit flies, you know?" he said. "Fruit flies reproduce so fast. In twenty-nine days you can change the color of their eyes!" I'd finished my dessert, but Pesek was still on his salad. "Ospreys and eagles," he said, "are much slower than bugs to reproduce. Maybe we're just seeing that cycle. The animals changed."

~~~

St. Helens, the town in Oregon, takes its name from the Washington mountain (a flat-top since 1980) that rises in plain view across the river. I moor *The Turtle* there—a forty-five-minute drive from home in Portland—not just because the Columbia at St. Helens is bluer and wider and less crowded than in Portland. Also, I was born there. We moved upstream when I was little, but St. Helens was the family place. Dad and his five brothers and a sister and all the cousins gathered there for Christmases and summer outings. A recent family reunion featured nine sand-bucket holes for barefoot golf on the big island opposite town.

The navigation chart calls it Sand Island. We always called it The Island. Half a mile long and at no point more than a hundred yards wide, the island is ringed with clean beaches and topped with cottonwoods.

Back when my dad courted an Astoria girl who would become my mother, The Island was an escape from the watchful eyes of their Depression Era elders. Long before the divvying up of chromosomes that gave rise to me, Bob and Betty took off for a canoe picnic that turned into an overnighter. A wind came up, and they couldn't—or didn't—paddle back to St. Helens that day. Two of Dad's brothers motored out to The Island the next morning and stumbled upon the overturned canoe that protected the young lovers from blowing sand.

What if their outing had ended in disaster? A kid lies awake at night with the what-ifs.

But my parents did have children. Lodged in my brain from Richard Dawkins's *River Out of Eden* is the notion—blindingly obvious but still astonishing—that *all* of my ancestors, and yours, had children. Not a single one of our progenitors failed to reach adulthood, to find a mate, and to reproduce. Although countless numbers of their contemporaries failed just one of these tests, nobody in our line flunked any of them. Saved, when Dad's brothers stumbled across the overturned canoe, was an unbroken strain of DNA shuffling and redistribution that had flowed for half a million years of human evolution. All the way back to when we came slithering out of the water to try living on land, nobody alive has an ancestor who stepped on an asp or fell young to the plague or drowned swimming from The Island to St. Helens.

A Darwinian view of life extends back to the primordial soup, some four billion years ago, when the chemical elements and conditions fell into place to make the first self-replicating molecules. A double helix molecule managed to build various machines for its own survival, giving rise to the animal kingdom and the world of plants, and later to human beings.

Organisms, over time, inherit stuff that works. That's why salmon are so good at swimming, why herons are so proficient at fishing, why cottonwoods are so good at stabilizing riverbanks, and why viruses are so nasty at spreading. That's how humans developed language and books so I can begin to know about this. It's why we love life and sex and children. Selected, over billions of years, were strings of deoxyribonucleic acids that could replicate another package before Bob and Betty, recent carriers, wore out.

Bob and Betty didn't know this. They didn't need to know. Nature didn't care that Bob and Betty thought theirs was a match made in Heaven. The idea that we humans carry out some purpose of a designing God served Bob and Betty well, and it is slow to yield to the truth. But the truth, too, can be as poetic and inspirational as any of the creation myths. With adaptation and selection comes an elegant beauty, a gospel of wonder that such a clean set of underlying principles could give rise to this bizarre extravaganza called life.

Let 'Er Buck

When Bobby Logue broke his neck at the 1983 Pendleton Round-Up, he was twenty-three—just old enough to ride like a man and still young enough to have no fear. Logue, of Cumby, Texas, was the brash rookie, the kid with the fast mouth and the quick feet, the cowboy who let it all hang out. Going into Pendleton, he was the second-ranked bareback rider in the world, pushing No. 1.

Then came Pendleton. The gate to his bucking chute swung open. Logue's horse dipped its shoulders and came rip-snorting out the chute sideways instead of straight into the arena. The horse—a savage, snake-stomping bronc—tried to scrape Logue off on the row of chute gates. Off balance from the start, he caught his left boot on a cowboy scrambling off a gate. The bronc veered right, stumbled, and pitched. Then it crashed on top of Logue, who went down head first between the horse and the ground. Logue's upper spine bent like a bobby pin.

Broke his neck in four places.

The way it has been explained to Logue, he broke cervical vertebrae numbers two, four, five and six. "If I'd also broke that number three," he says, "I'd never of rode again."

He would have died, that is. Same thing.

~~~

Two years later, in time for the 1985 Pendleton Round-Up, Bobby Logue jockeys a big blue rental car to a gravel-scattering stop in front of Severe Brothers Saddlery, the cowboy bunkhouse. Logue is just in from Abilene, after taking a plane to Spokane and then continuing on down to Pendleton in this midnight blue Chevrolet Caprice littered with empty V-8 juice cans and crumpled Dorito bags.

From the car stagger Logue and five other pro rodeo cowboys, five of the world's best in the rough stock events: bareback, saddle bronc, and bull riding.

Rough stock riders stride with a good wide base, as if expecting an earthquake any minute. The boots, the hat, the Wranglers with a pale-worn circle the size of a Skoal can on a back pocket . . . those could be on anybody. A pro, though, wears a championship belt buckle the size of a hub cap. He lists slightly off-center as he walks because one side of his upper body is overdeveloped and hyper-extended from hanging on to outlaw stock.

With his speckled brown eyes and a crooked grin, Logue is more mischief than Marlboro Man. But give him a bowl of Wheaties and a drop of milk on his brown mustache, and he could testify about what the big boys eat for breakfast. In his first year back since the accident, Logue has won more that $35,000, which puts him sixth in the world at bareback.

"I'll win the world," says Logue, by which he means the bareback world championship of the Professional Rodeo Cowboys Association. The scoring system is simple. One point is awarded for each dollar in prize money earned at PRCA-approved rodeos in the United States and Canada. The rodeo year ends in December at Las Vegas with the National Finals, where the top fifteen money-winners compete in each event.

The tricky part is that 625 PRCA rodeos are packed into only fifty-two weeks in the year. Nobody can do them all. But if a cowboy does not enter more than a hundred rodeos—often four or five a week—he can fall behind the competition. Pro rodeo is booming, with better television coverage and richer purses and more cowboys competing than ever before. To go for the world championship, the modern cowboy will spend about $30,000 in entry fees and travel expenses. Only a dozen or so cowboys in each event end up winning more than $30,000, but the top guy can win three or four times that amount.

Logue is only one of many, of course, who gather in Pendleton each September with plans to win the world.

"There will be three Oregon cowboys in the bareback finals this year," says Ron Parrish, a blue-eyed, barrel-chested cowboy from Bend who really *does* look like the Marlboro Man. "Joe Talburt (of Roseburg), Steve Carter (from Klamath Falls), and me."

Pro cowboys think the Pendleton Round-Up is terrific. The money is good, and Pendleton has a seventy-five-year tradition as a Wild West Show. Big knowledgeable crowds turn out every year, and not just for the rodeo. They kick up their heels and party. It's as if a great seasonal wind scoured the land and swept up every Airstream, Winnebago, and pick-up camper and dumped them all into the brown bowl that holds Pendleton.

Add some good old romp-'em-stomp-'em music, plenty of booze, and the friendliest hosts this side of Mardi Gras, and . . . well . . . let 'er buck.

"Pendleton is definitely in the top three for tradition," says Bruce Ford, the four-time world bareback champion, from Kersey, Colorado. "Others are the Calgary Stampede and Cheyenne Frontier Days."

~~~

Base camp for pro cowboys at Pendleton is this Severe Brothers Saddlery, a former military barracks on the hill above town. Bill and Duff Severe—world famous for saddles and fancy leatherwork—provide wall-to-wall bunks in a two-story, weather-beaten building with creaking wooden stairs and the smell of fresh-cured leather and saddles-in-progress. To a pro cowboy, who learns to sleep anywhere—back seats of cars, hotel lobbies, the bathtub in somebody else's cut-rate motel room—Severe Brothers Saddlery is Cowboy Heaven. They gather here not just to sleep but also to sing and to tell stories, to compare notes about the ornery stock they've drawn, and to gossip about who's hot on the circuit.

One of the hottest on the 1985 tour is Clint Corey of Silverdale, Washington. Corey, twenty-three, is in his first full year at pro bareback, with winnings that already total $52,000 and a No. 2 world ranking from the latest Pro Rodeo Sports News. He wears a black Stetson and a Fu Manchu mustache. With dark, nervous, gunslinger eyes, he looks as if he might open the refrigerator with a Colt .45 or pull out a hunting knife to pick his teeth.

When Corey glides into the Severe Brothers kitchen, veteran cowboys feign no-notice of him. They talk about him. Corey listens.

"That kid Corey, he draws like a thief."

"No, he can ride anything. He don't need a good draw. He makes any rank horse look juicy."

"He's unconscious, is all. Corey ain't woke up yet."

"Hey there, Clint. Zat you? Howya doin'?"

Corey exhales. "Doin' real good," he says. He accepts a can of Budweiser. A broad ivory grin cuts across his formerly sinister face like a beacon of light slicing through the tough-guy façade. He's just a kid—shy, not sinister—waiting until he was spoken to before he dared to speak. A rookie. He is thrilled to hear veteran cowboys talk about him, Clint Corey, as if he really belongs here at the Pendleton Round-Up.

These guys say Corey has all the athletic gifts he will need on the pro circuit. Only time will tell if he also has the mental grit. He'll have to be disciplined enough to keep his head clear of cobwebs, smart enough to juggle computerized registration procedures with airline schedules, and bold enough to risk his own money to make money. Nerves of steel, Corey will need, to survive a lifestyle where all the physical and mental conditioning is funneled, finally, into eight short seconds of competition each time out of the chute.

~~~

David Bothum, the saddle bronc rider from Echo, Oregon, knows about pro rodeo's head games. Bothum, thirty-one, is getting better at an age when many of his contemporaries are wasted. Last year he won $46,588 and ranked fifth in the world. Total earnings in his eight-year pro career exceed $280,000.

Bothum is two people.

Away from the rodeo arena, he has won the Hermiston "Real Estate Man of the Month" award. He grins a lot and looks as if he needs a shot of vitamin E just to get geared up, he's so laid back. His easy blue eyes, reddish brown hair, and freckles at the neck prove that even a young man can be a good ol' boy.

The second David Bothum takes over about two hours before he rides. "I become an animal," he says. "A bad one. A grizzly. If I prepare right, I can make everything else a blank. By the time I get on the horse, I actually black out."

Getting pumped at Pendleton is easier than it would be somewhere else. Pendleton is the big one, his home rodeo. So when Bothum, in his gold Cadillac Seville, enters I-84 from Echo and noses down into the Pendleton bowl, he's in a zone. Bothum *smells* rodeo. Fresh straw and sweet manure, barbecue chicken on outdoor grills, Indian fry bread and coffee . . . Animals and sweat and a festive crowd . . . For Bothum, it's the aroma of competition, as dizzying as a woman's perfume.

After paying the $100 entry fee, Bothum carries his saddle behind the north grandstand. He paces. He thumps his chest hard enough to fell a juniper. He performs isometric exercises against the concrete base of the grandstand. He stretches his legs. He bends his torso backwards and clenches both fists in front of his belt buckle until the carotid arteries stand out on his neck like red nightcrawlers. Although the day is cool, beads of sweat form beneath the brim of his white hat.

Now he shadowboxes. As if trying to rid his boots of a noxious substance, he snap-kicks the air in front of him.

A friend comes by. "Cyd needs to see you," the guy tells Bothum. Cyd is his wife, a live-wire former tennis champ. She's in charge of tickets for friends and relatives today.

Bothum struggles to focus.

"No, really," says the unlucky messenger, reading Bothum's eyes. "She wants to talk to you."

Cyd should know better. She does know better, but in the excitement of the moment—Pendleton is her home rodeo, too—good judgment has eluded her. She has her word with Bothum, who speaks softly, off the record. If his blue eyes were lasers, Cyd would be a puddle of hot plasma and scorched hair on the concrete floor.

When Cyd has gone, Bothum returns to his pacing. By the time he is in the bucking chute, poised over a horse named Three Chicks, his body is wound tight as a steel spring. The announcer emphasizes Bothum's home state roots—*a Silverton boy, come to Echo by way of Blue Mountain Community College right here in Pendleton!*

Bothum barely hears.

The gate swings open, and Bothum rides half a ton of fire-snorting fury into the arena. He spurs Three Chicks out strong and catches his rhythm early. With back arched and chin tucked, Bothum holds tight with one fist and waves the other free and frantic. His spurs rise above the shoulders of the horse every time its front feet pound the turf. Back come his feet as the horse bucks forward and tries to blow him out of the saddle. Bothum is all reflex, flash-quick reaction, in a neck-whipping battle with an outlaw horse.

At eight seconds, a diesel horn blows. End of ride. Bothum leaps from bronc to pick-up horse, then hits the ground with both feet and raises his white hat to the crowd. Grandstanders go nuts.

Bothum scores thirty-eight on one judge's slate, forty on the other's. His seventy-eight (of a possible one hundred) is the day's best, easily qualifying him for the Round-Up finals. He has won the right to compete for the Pendleton championship on Saturday. Today is Thursday. Tomorrow he will rise early in Echo and drive to Portland. He'll catch an 11 a.m. flight to Albuquerque, where he'll ride Friday night. Saturday morning he'll fly back to Portland and drive three and a half hours to Pendleton for the Saturday afternoon finals.

~~~

Less successful this day, which has turned gray and wet, is Bobby Logue. Wearing a white plastic neck brace, Logue spends his eight working seconds just trying to catch up with a wacko horse that bolts straight from the north chute and across the arena, horizontal instead of up and down. The horse finally runs out from under him and dumps him in soft mud. Logue slides toward the south grandstand on his rear and power-glides to his feet and into a victory salute with both hands raised.

Judges, a humorless lot, are unimpressed. His Pendleton Round-Up is finished.

~~~

After the day's disappointments, Logue convenes with former world champ Bruce Ford and Bend's Ron Parrish at a cheap Chinese restaurant. Also here is Randy Taylor from Tulsa, Oklahoma. Taylor, who refers to himself as The Indian, is a chisel-sculpted cowboy whose eyes, hair, and skin tell better than words that he is one-quarter Cherokee. He also is the only one at the table who qualified today for Saturday's bareback finals. Taylor hangs Egg Foo Yung from his chopsticks like a victory flag. The others stare glumly at their food.

Logue, after dinner, allows as to how it might not hurt to drop in at the Let 'Er Buck Room.

"Just for one drink," he says.

The Let 'Er Buck Room, under the rodeo grandstand, is wall-hung and ceiling-draped with wagon wheels and ox yokes, saddles and stirrups, horse blankets and buffalo hides. Three bars cater to Oregon Trail-sized thirst, epic thirst, the kind that calls for hard liquor. By the time Bobby Logue and crew arrive, the Let 'Er Buck Room is an absolute crush of tourists and cowboys and *le tout* Pendleton. Steamy after the day's rain, it's a tropical forest under a canopy of brim-to-brim cowboy hats.

"Howdy, pardner!"

"You know me . . . I'm Jed Bart's ex-wife."

"Bobby!"

"It's Bruce Ford!!"

The men all look like Les Schwab, or will look like Les Schwab in a few years. Trim and athletic women mix easily here. Randy Taylor, the increasingly cheerful Cherokee, sidles up to the backside of a pair of tight jeans on a woman who stands, oblivious to Taylor, near the Let 'Er Buck Room bar. "Ride that!" Taylor suggests, to no one in particular—more like a public service announcement—on his way to snag another whiskey and soda.

When the Let 'Er Buck Room closes, Logue and friends accept an invitation to the rodeo Directors' Room, upstairs. Behind the bar looms Ty Hansell, a swarthy and thick-voiced pillar of community spirit.

"Have a drink," Hansell growls. It's an order, like *Have a drink or get out of town.* "Put that wallet away. Your money's no good here."

Before long, Bobby Logue is behind the bar with Hansell, and it's plenty loud in the Directors' Room. Hansell is telling everyone within earshot— roughly a city block—how Dr. Phil Corbett leaped unbidden into the arena two years ago when he saw Logue's accident.

"He saved your life, Bobby," says Hansell.

Logue, considerably cheered up, leads his group from the Directors' Room and then up and over a nine-foot fence topped with three strands of barbed wire. Real cowboys do not slink around looking for an exit gate. They spill across Court Avenue toward The Relay Station, a country western lounge with refrigerator-sized amplifiers blasting "Louie Louie" into the warm night air. On the sidewalk, vendors offer everything from cowboy hats to fancy belts to fuzzy dice. An art dealer says his best seller is this painting of the moon-silver unicorn and a woman with a phosphorescent tear rolling down her left cheek.

Inside The Relay Station, cowgirls ricochet across the dance floor in calf-skin vests and glow-in-the-dark earrings. It's a great party, a real hoedown. You'd think this is the place to be, but word reaches Logue that Ricky and the Redstreaks are playing at the National Guard Armory.

Ricky and the Redstreaks! Gotta go there.

Outside the armory, an argument about chewing tobacco develops into Logue and Taylor cuffing each other and wrestling on the lawn. This harmless scuffle draws the attention of a couple of brown-shirted Umatilla County sheriffs. One cop grabs a fistful of Taylor's Cherokee-black hair and pulls him off Logue. Cops back off after friends of the accused insist that the whole scene is just horseplay.

But now the don't-fence-me-in mentality kicks into high gear. Baiting cops, after all, is a natural for these eight-second athletes who live by reflex more than thought. Suddenly all four of them—Logue, Taylor, Parrish, and Ford—

are thrashing and flailing in an eight-booted, four-Stetsoned tangle on the armory lawn, cursing, spitting, and rolling into shrubbery.

Here again comes the law.

Bruce Ford deals with the police this time. Ford, tall and languid with a Yosemite Sam moustache, comes on with those beatific blue eyes, and everything is calm. The police do not want to stuff Bruce Ford—the first man ever to win more than $100,000 in a single rodeo event in a single year (1982)—into the Pendleton hoosegow. Ford negotiates his release and that of his three partners.

Inside the armory, Taylor turns his attention to young buckle-chasers on the dance floor. Others search out gambling tables in the beer hall. The cops cruise like slow brown fish and keep a wary eye on these four.

There is no more trouble.

Along toward 2 a.m., the place is closing up. Bruce Ford stands among cowboys who have gathered near the door to share a ride back to Severe Brothers Saddlery. Ford—who has not had a drink stronger than orange juice all night; he never does—has a strange look in his tender blue eyes. I say something totally forgettable to Ford. Ford hurls himself violently backward and crashes into a jumbo galvanized garbage can, raising a terrific racket. He clutches his jaw in agony, as if he's just been sucker-punched. He stares wildly and points at me. I'm just standing there, dumb as clay. Logue and Parrish grab me from behind, as if to prevent further attacks on Ford, and two hulking Umatilla County sheriffs muscle in to help subdue the innocent writer.

~~~~

Back to Severe Brothers Saddlery, back to the smell of fresh-brewed coffee and new leather, back to the music of Bruce Ford, who is not only a world-champion cowboy and vaudevillian but also the finest guitarist to appear here since John Denver showed up at the saddlery two years ago.

And here, somewhere between yesterday and tomorrow, comes the feather-brushed illusion of life without fences, of men around an open-range campfire after a tough but honest day's work. Camaraderie trumps competition, temporarily, in a fickle and hostile world. The stock a pro rodeo cowboy draws is bred for orneriness. Judges are unpredictable. On the job, he's never more than eight seconds away from a ride to the emergency ward, and as soon as he gets famous in one dusty town he has to move on to the next. Unappreciated by the nation's sport press, he's the only professional athlete who can rank in the top ten at his specialty and still have to pay an entry fee and travel expenses. The shared difficulties make rough stock riders an intensely loyal lot. Never will one cowboy bad-mouth another or fail to come to another's assistance. A phrase of Bobby Logue's echoes in the mind, even as the red tail lights on his Chevy disappear off the Pendleton hill toward another rodeo.

"David Bothum is a hell of a rider," Logue had said, "and a hell of a cowboy."

There is no redundancy in those words. To be a hell of a cowboy is to subscribe to an unwritten code of conduct, which is not so different from the code of the Old West. The code has to do with grit and courage and physical competence, of course, but it also has to do with generosity of spirit and helping somebody who is down on his luck. Never whine about bad breaks. To survive, members of this tightly knit, male-bonded road show share travel and motel rooms and meals even as they bust their butts to beat one another.

"What I'd miss most, if I had to leave rodeo," says David Bothum," is the friends."

The way to leave rodeo, five out of five cowboys agree, is the way Jody Tatone left it. Tatone, a bull rider from Boardman, began his meteoric pro career driving a Pacific-blue Porsche and moved up to a Cessna 210 when he hit the National Finals in 1981. Tatone married Miss Rodeo Oregon of 1980, Italy Hughes, a raven-haired beauty from Roseburg who fell for the dashing Tatone when, she says, "He knew how to order wine at the Inn at the Quay, in Portland."

In 1982 Tatone won the Brahma bull ride at Pendleton. He had a good shot that year at the world championship—the very top—when his hand caught in the rope as he fell from a bull in Salt Lake City. Jerked his left arm right out of his socket.

"I didn't even know I was hurt," says Tatone, "until I moved to unbuckle my chaps." His left arm fell vertical like a strand of spaghetti.

Tatone, a former valedictorian at Boardman's Riverside High School and a political science graduate of Oregon State, quit rodeo in his thirty-one-year-old prime. Now thirty-three, he has two blonde daughters and the Dodge City Inn in Boardman. He has set up an arena and rodeo school directly opposite the plate glass windows of his Long Branch Saloon. At the Round-Up, now,

Tatone dresses like a western-wear spread in *Gentlemen's Quarterly*. Instead of riding the bull, he's up in the booth slinging it, over KWHT radio.

Tatone's fame east of the Cascades endures as David Bothum's climbs—another local boy makes good on the rodeo circuit. That Saturday, Bothum returned from Albuquerque to win the saddle bronc finals at Pendleton, for which he won $3,446 in cash, a new saddle by Severe Brothers, a pair of Tony Lama boots, the championship buckle, and the undying admiration of a whole culture.

It doesn't faze Tatone or Bothum that rodeo's boom has failed to touch the so-called sophisticated set, or that sports pages in Portland and Seattle snub rodeo as if it were demolition derby. In the Inland Northwest, rodeo is not only sport but also allegory, a symbol of the open range and rugged individualism.

Says Bothum, coming off sixteen consecutive days of rodeo that put eight thousand miles on his Cadillac Seville: "You meet a lot of people, see a lot of country, and do what you want to do." He takes a deep breath, maybe catching the whiff of another rodeo just over the horizon. "If I was going to change something about my life," he says, "I couldn't think of nothin' to change."

Deaf Basketball

When you referee a deaf basketball team, keep in mind that the players are deaf. Blow the whistle and they just keep going. How would they know? Make crisp visual signals, and allow them a little more touching on defense. You wouldn't think sound helps track a basketball opponent, but apparently it does.

I refereed the Oregon State School for the Deaf, from Salem, at Westside Christian School in Portland. Varsity girls. The deaf girls played basketball with exuberant energy and unthrottled emotion. They had fun. I'd forgotten there isn't much laughing out loud in high school basketball. These girls emitted quick shrieks of surprise or pleasure as they went grunting and careening about the court. They lost badly but cheerfully to the Christians.

The deaf team did have one good athlete, a tall blonde with fine springs in her legs and a bright spark to her eye. Gazelle-like, she moved. She snagged rebounds that weren't meant for her. She fired sharp outlet passes. On offense she had a nose for the basket, but her teammates seldom delivered her the ball.

Late in the game, this gazelle girl got the ball in the key. She took a couple of steps without remembering to dribble, and drilled a sweet hook shot.

My referee partner, Ed Denmark, a well-to-do hardwood dealer in real life, had whistled the play dead. Traveling. The poor girl's celebration at having sunk her pretty shot was eclipsed now as she realized it wouldn't count. She grabbed the ball and slammed it to the floor with sufficient force that—although she right away knew better and tried to smother it—the ball rebounded above her head.

The normal and accepted procedure here is for the referee to blow a T. A technical foul. It was Denmark's call, not mine. What would he do? I held my breath. The kid was sorry. She'd already lost that neat hoop. Her team was getting crushed. Mercifully, Denmark decided just to warn her. He would explain it to her.

But she's deaf.

The game stopped. We summoned her coach from the bench to sign this decision to the girl. She was contrite but thoroughly puzzled, expecting the T but getting words. So you see. Mercy was the wrong call, the same call I would have made in Denmark's spot. When you referee a deaf basketball team, keep in mind the kids are just deaf. They're not stupid. The girl deserved a T.

~~~

After the game I showered, changed clothes, and settled into the deaf section of the bleachers to watch the boys' teams warm up. The gazelle girl was not wearing a cheerleader outfit, but she posted herself among the cheerleaders and joined right in.

Deaf cheerleaders have all the right moves, but they voice no sound. Here they trotted over to the opposite side of the court to face the home team fans. They mimed an introductory cheer that included acrobatic routines and finished with individual salutes—"Hi, I'm Deborah," "Hi, I'm Judy"—you know that one. Each cheerleader, in turn, tried to say her name out loud. In most cases, you could tell what her name was.

When they came back to our side, an American flag appeared at mid-court. We all stood at attention, with hands over hearts. A chubby girl from the Christian school sang "The Star Spangled Banner" into a microphone. She was good. She was so good singing the anthem that a great wave of sadness passed through me. I'm not what you would call a sucker for the national anthem, but this was chilling.

When the anthem was over, the deaf kids knew it was OK to make noise. In fact the hearing-impaired can generate unseemly noise just taking a seat, unwrapping a Snickers bar, chewing potato chips, and signing joy. While our section was preoccupied that way, the Christian fans across the court had bowed in silence. A young man at the scorer's table was reciting a prayer.

Nobody else in my section knew it.

Soon the adult sitting next to me—probably a teacher—saw what was up. Her look of panic must have mirrored my own as our eyes met. We tried to nudge and sign silence through our rude section of the bleachers, but we probably succeeded only in drawing more attention from the prayerful. It was awful. What would these Christians think of us?

When their gaffe finally dawned on the deaf students, the prayer was over. They, too, felt awful. For maybe three full seconds. Just long enough for each cheerleader to face the home crowd and—apparently spontaneously, all at once—slap a palm to her forehead and roll eyes heavenward in a how-stupid-could-we-be-please-forgive-us gesture that would break your heart it was so correct.

Hideaway Slough

Time, on *The Turtle*, ignores the clock. River time is the slow crawl of sun across the arc of early June sky, the sun rising upriver and falling downstream. A day begins with the twitter and quack of the birds announcing the rise of light outside the cabin. A day ends when there is no longer enough light to see the words on a page. Time to eat is when the stomach growls. Time to bathe is a hot afternoon and the river to jump into.

But where time is fluid, space needs definition. I needed a place. I wanted to anchor myself someplace in the maze of islands upstream from Cathlamet, on the Washington side of the river, and Clatskanie, Oregon. The ideal spot would have a sandy beach with a deep enough pitch that *The Turtle* would stay afloat at low tide. Avoid the ship channel, where the best beaches are. Shelter from the northwest wind would be good, as would a far-reaching view. But shelter and view often preclude one another. I poked around for a few days, trying this place and that, experimenting with various anchorages. None were quite right. But then . . .

Crims Island is more like an island group, with tiny sloughs threading through. I circumnavigated the whole business. Upstream on the ship-channel side, two miles of white sandy beach held only an abandoned lean-to with a faded American flag on a driftwood pole. Back downstream on the Oregon side, I passed a pair of osprey nests atop log pilings. The Lewis and Clark party had paddled past here and named it Fanny's Island, for Clark's younger sister, Frances. But the name that stuck came from James Crim, who filed his claim on the island sixty-five years later. Nobody lives here now. A lone bald eagle soared flaplessly above cottonwoods. The only trace of human history was a broken farmhouse with blank windows and sagging eaves, slumping at its joints into a meadow.

I poked *The Turtle* into a narrow Crims Island backwater with jungle-lush shores. A deep-enough anchorage adjoined a grassy dry flat—a little prairie-like plateau. Hmm. Good place, this. A man could get off the boat here and walk around if he took a mind to. Pitch a tent, even. I threw an anchor astern, pitched another onto the grass, and winched the boat into its new place. The opening to Bradbury Slough was just a couple of hundred yards away, near the upstream tip of Crims Island. I could spit a watermelon seed halfway across this little sluiceway. On the other side were low Russian olive trees and a dead cottonwood, bony and leafless as an X-ray of tree-ness. A ridge of sand, topped with thick woods, shielded me from the ship channel.

The wind came up that first afternoon. It barreled through the treetops with the rush of a freight train, but the brush and grasses at my shore merely swayed in light breeze. *The Turtle* lay as calm as a library.

I had found my place. I'll call this place Hideaway Slough.

<center>~~~~</center>

At first light, a beaver comes swimming downstream on my side of the slough. Spying the boat, the beaver veers off. She crosses the channel, ducks into a tangle of roots beneath an overhanging willow, and vanishes.

Songbirds herald the planet's roll toward the morning sun. The sky colors in from rose to blue in the time it takes to roust myself from the sleeping bag, pull on clothes, fire up the stove, run hot water through a coffee filter, and sit on the back deck with coffee. At 5:30 (by clock time, in early June), the tops of cottonwoods direct sunlight. In the next hour, Earth's shadow crawls down from the tree tops to the base, like a reverse curtain to the stage. The boat lies at anchor on the shady side. The air is still, the water flat, mirroring the opposite shore of low bushes and the tall dead cottonwood tree. For all the chirping and warbling, I can't see many birds. But among the singers are the soprano goldfinches, an alto redwing blackbird, a tenor owl hooing deep in the woods. and the bass grawk of a passing blue heron. A woodpecker tattoos a hollow cottonwood, for percussion.

If I don't stir—just sit there—the action at Hideaway Slough becomes visible. A male goldfinch, bright lemon against the green background, alights on the tallest cattail near the boat and poses, as if for his Audubon sketch. Swallows swoop along the water collecting bugs. Another little flycatcher flies directly up the slough as he flaps up to height, arcs flapless down to near water like a spent bullet. Fat carp cruise below the surface, now and then scratching the surface with dorsal fins. A kingfisher flies out from the willow bush on my right, hovers in mid-air over the water, makes an arrow of himself and dives—plunk—spearing a fingerling and splash-flapping to a low limb. He points his beak skyward and swallows the fish in one neck-stretching gulp. He takes a couple of small bows, as if to say *There, that's how it's done*.

Behind me, across the wide Columbia, sirens wail along Washington's Highway 4, mourning tragedy somewhere, not here.

Air on the water is cold. I wear sweat pants under my jeans and a flannel shirt over sweatshirt, yet my fingertips go numb on the pen. But it won't be cold for long. Gearing up this morning is the dominant weather pattern of a Pacific Northwest summer. Some two hundred miles from here, east of the Cascades, a wheat rancher is scanning the clear-blue morning sky and thinking, *another scorcher*. While his fields warm to the rising sun, the air, too, will heat and want to rise. Low pressure created by warm air rising off the skillet of Eastern Oregon draws heavier cool air in off the Pacific. This early breeze will be a stiff west wind before noon, roughing the lower Columbia but fluttering Portland flags and cooling the city. By late afternoon the wind will howl through the Columbia River Gorge—windsurfer heaven—and dissipate out east across the irrigated farm country and high desert.

~~~~

Awakening one morning to rain tapping the roof, I leaned up on an elbow and stared out the window. Rain on unruffled water made tiny blips here and there. Each drop launched circles on the surface that radiated outward and rippled the reflection of the dead cottonwood across the slough. As the raindrops came closer together, their loops interlaced like the Olympics logo gone amok. If you didn't know anything about rain—if you saw rain for the very first time from this low angle—you'd think it's not falling but coming up. Each raindrop was all but invisible compared to the upward *re*-action of river spouting back to the sky. The whole slough began spout-dancing. Some spouts left bubbles that drifted away on the current. The water surface was frosted glass, the color of jade. Swirls marked slower-moving water. The whole arrangement was so beautiful there was nothing to be done about it, no reason at all to get up that morning.

~~~~

On another misty morning, *The Turtle* lay in the company of eight wood ducks, four males and four females, quietly floating the slough. Shy creatures, these, rarely seen up close. The males—bright red eye, orange beak, with flashy green and blue tail feathers, white throat, brown chest—set me to wondering. What's adaptive about that? Their coloring—their sex appeal so roundly trumping camouflage—must enforce shyness, except toward female wood ducks. These boys were way overdressed for Hideaway Slough, as if lost in a bad neighborhood on their way to the harlequins' ball.

~~~~

Spiders love a wooden boat. Spiders colonized *The Turtle* the first summer of its launch, and their descendents know no other habitat. They go where I go.

The spiders who live upwards from the port windows were on a roll the other day. The boat lay at anchor with that window to lee. A downdraft off the cabin roof brought gnats into the spider web, parallel to the window, outside. Each incoming gnat put up a struggle and got stuck worse. Gnat frenzy led to intervals of exhaustion, or resignation, and when the web stopped twitching, a spider emerged from a crack between window and frame. Out *sprinted* the spider, along gossamer threads. I've seen Jason Kidd on the fast break. I've seen Barishnikov on the stage. Katrina Witt on ice. Those were good. But I've never seen more startling quick grace than with this spider tripping eight legs in sequence across the shuddering web. Without a misstep, the spider wrapped its legs around the victim.

I like to place my magnifying glass against the inside of the window and watch the spider's little anus squirt stickum. When it gets too personal, I put the glass down and remember to breathe evenly. Of all possible ways of capturing and socking away food, who would have thought of this?

~~~~

Two guys in a Duckworth with a trolling motor puttered into Hideaway Slough and toward my boat when I was fixing dinner. They were the first people through here in two weeks. They wore duck-hunting camouflage and had fishing poles in their boat. They cut the motor to talk. "Any bass in here?" The talker was a hefty bearded guy. His little buddy was silent at the motor.

I hadn't seen any. I said I wasn't fishing.

The two of them looked at each other. What could I possibly be doing? "Probably too cold yet for bass," the guy said. We shot the bull for a spell. They invited me to dinner at their place, on the ship-channel side. I hadn't known I was sharing Crims Island with others. I had, though, seen a ramshackle lean-to with a frayed American flag on ship-channel side. The American flag on an unpopulated island in America had given me the brief willies, but these guys didn't look like survivalist kooks. "Come on over," the big guy said. "We got spaghetti on."

I raised my salad bowl and said thanks, but I had chili cooking.

He laughed. "We have beautiful women at our place."

Sure you do.

"No, really. Come on over. Half a mile down, you can just walk across the island. Down where the beaver dam was."

I thanked them anyway. The silent partner started their motor again. They slid on down the slough leaving a cloud of blue exhaust on the water. In their wake, over chili, I was thinking *down where the beaver dam was.* I'd seen beaver slides at the slough's narrow outlet. Slick mud chutes led from the vegetation line to water. The February flood must have ripped out their dam. News that beavers had *had* a dam here was worth considering. It would take an audacious creature to try to dam the tidal Columbia River.

~~~~~

On my river chart is a dot labeled "Stella" on the Washington shore. Stella, I thought, might have a store. Groceries and ice. If so, that would be a closer source of re-supply than Clatskanie. Yet I'd never seen a village at that place on the shore. So I pulled anchor and aimed *The Turtle* up the slough and out onto the river. I quartered into the current and crossed the ship channel toward Stella and saw just a small huddle of very old and very new building on pilings at the outlet of Coal Creek Slough. On the deck of a condo facing the Columbia sat two teenage girls in lawn chairs, sunbathing.

I called out. "Is there a store here?"

No response. I was only fifty yards from them. Couldn't they hear me? They faced the river, but did they see me? For a moment I had that feeling—familiar to a man my age—that he no longer registers on the radar of the young. He may not even exist. But how could these young buds not see *The Turtle*?

I cut the motor and called again, louder. "Is there a store here?" The girl on the left was speaking into a cell phone. The other one, I saw now, wore headphones. She saw *The Turtle* and unplugged herself. She nudged her friend, who looked up and saw me but couldn't be bothered. Current drifted me slowly downstream. My rope to the world was unraveling, strand by snapping strand. "IS THERE A STORE HERE?"

The two of them conferred. Without moving the receiver from her ear, the cell phone girl called down the river at me: "NO!"

~~~

Back at my anchorage, there are more patterns to learn. Visible action dwindles to near nothing as the heat rises. Hideaway Slough falls silent. I fall into the same pattern, napping at mid-day, writing a little, reading some, listening to the Mariners on the radio if they're playing a day game or three time zones away. I am less alert to my surroundings than at the edge between sunlight and darkness.

Beavers appear only at daybreak or after sundown, and the days are getting longer. The beaver who comes into view at 5:12 one morning will appear at 5:04 the next. The kingfisher arrows upstream and reappears at regular ten-minute intervals for an hour or so, perhaps doing laps around Crims Island. The raccoon is nocturnal but governed by tide, pawing along the shore for mud-morsels at low tide. If low tide is full dark, I don't see that raccoon, but I can be sure he is making his rounds.

At dusk each evening a little white-tail doe appears at the margin of the brush across the slough. She nibbles at greens and laps up some river.

These patterns are reassuring. The boat doesn't move, day after day, yet the river is alive with pattern. Without changing my place on the river, I am everywhere on it, like the air or the light. I say the boat doesn't move, but only in the sense that I don't move it. The boat rides up and down on the tide. The biggest pattern other than daylight and dark is this lunar-induced to-ing and fro-ing as the Columbia fights to merge with the sea.

Until I read up on it, I thought the Pacific Ocean tide worked like the water in a very large tub. High tide on the Oregon coast must be answered at the same time by low tide in Japan. But no. High tide here is matched, of course, by high tide across the Pacific. The gravitational pull of moon (and sun) draws the planet into an egg-shaped spheroid with greater diameter in a line running directly through the spinning Earth. Low tides are at the poles when it's high tide at the equator.

Tides are the planet's largest wave. A lunar day, resulting from the rotation of the Earth on its axis, is about fifty minutes longer than twenty-four hours.

The pull of the sun and that of the moon sometimes partially cancel each other. Other times they boost each other. The moon—because its nearness cancels the sun's huge mass—more than doubles the draw of the sun. Lunar and solar tides will coincide and be fully cumulative only twice each lunar month, when the sun, moon, and Earth are most nearly lined up. At new moon—or full moon—I'll get higher high tides and lower lows.

There's more to it than that, including the declination of Earth on its axis that gives rise to winter or summer.

This far up the river, at this time of year, the tide brings about a five-foot swing from high to low, dropping the boat so that my view out the bank-side window changes from grassy plateau to a close-up of yellow wild iris on glistening brown mud. At high tide I can loosen the anchor line and pull on the bow line and step off the boat for walking laps through the grass. The lifts and drops of tide occur a little each day. I get hungry a little later each day, eating dinner in the dark.

〜〜〜

Two mink patrol the black-brown mud at shoreline. They come around, not every morning, after the beaver makes its rounds. These mink are about two feet long, half tail, with stubby legs under a long body no thicker than a big sausage. They burrow narrow holes into the shoreline mud, at varying heights. At least one hole is always above the water surface as the tide goes up and down. Lewis and Clark—those sharp-eyed observers and scrupulous recorders—made no mention of mink. Mink are a legacy of ranchers who did well when mink fur was at the height of chic. Some mink escaped the farms. Others went feral when the fur market went bust. Farmers let them go.

Remember Joe Pesek on mink? Pesek said that farmers bred mink selectively. They came up with tan mink and blond mink to meet evolving fashion.

Never, on the river, have I seen a mink in any other color than deep dark brown. You'd think if lighter-colored mink are out here, they would be easier than the dark ones for me to see. I would have seen one by now. I'll bet when the lighter ones got loose they were easier for bald eagles to see and to nab. Fewer pale mink survived long enough to pass on copies of the gene for altered coloring. The mink I see on the river are the color of the brown-black mud-line they patrol.

〜〜〜

Hideaway Slough is too sluggish for a cleansing swim, but a short tromp through alders leads to firm white sands facing the wide blue Columbia. Upstream, in the distance, Mount St. Helens wears a wedding skirt of fresh snow. Here I can swim against the river, finding that place in the water where my strokes cancel current. No need for a swimsuit. Nobody here but me and the wild ones. Still, there's a fearsome vulnerability about sitting naked on a towel to air-dry. Some trickster might burst from the woods and make off with my clothes.

I wished I had that poem of John Daniel's with me. It's not on the boat. His poem reverses a Genesis passage where Adam names the creatures. The animals eye the New One, the walk-upright.

Deer notes the New One's bare skin and says something like, *He'll sleep cold.*

Doesn't see so good, says Eagle.

Clumsy swimmer, says Fish.

Came crashing through the brush, Coyote says. *At least we'll know when he's around.*

Let's watch him for a while, says Heron.

I do, says Beaver. *I watch him. Sits at daybreak and sundown on that green box he sleeps in. His lodge? Both eyes forward on his head. Tiny teeth. Eats twigs and nuts from a blue bowl.*

Wild ones agree. The New One will never make it.

What I have over the rest of them, though, is tools. Lacking claws, humans "evolved" pliers and scissors and blades. Lacking fur, I sleep in a down bag and don cotton protection from cold. My feet, poor things, aren't webbed or tough, but I have shoes. Eyesight poor? I have binoculars. *The Turtle* itself is a tool, a mobile shelter. Not here, but from home I could drive a four-wheeled tool across land at a speed greater than deer. I can fly—hello, osprey—across the continent. Humans have leaped ahead of the slow workings of natural selection, and we make do in ways never thought of by the first riverpeople.

We specialize. I don't hunt or gather my own food. Specialists harvested or killed, processed and packaged, every item of food I have on the boat. Same with shelter and clothing. Somebody unknown to me cut the trees for the plywood that got trucked to the lumberyard where Sam got the stuff for this boat. The motor—made in Japan—runs on fuel that successive specialists discovered and drilled and piped and refined and trucked to Clatskanie. I only hosed the gas into the can. Left to my own survival skills, I would die of starvation or winter exposure. I am of a different species, not just from the other survival packages that creep and fly and swim at the slough, but also different from Lewis and Clark.

What we have over the rest of them, too, is language.

OK, the wild ones chatter about for sex or warn vocally of danger. But humans swap complex ideas from one individual to another and from one generation to the next. A pair of bicycle mechanics on the eastern seaboard solves the physics of flight and within a century the improvements lead to intercontinental—interplanetary—transport. One idea leads to another. Natural selection and refinement of the redwing blackbird took millions of years, but the leap of humans into flight happened in an eye-blink. Good ideas get repeated from human brain to brain, and the best of them survive. The brain is to ideas as habitat is to life forms. Only in the recent millennium did we reproduce language in books. I don't know much more about the habits of beavers than beavers can know of mine, but I can go to the library. Or Google it. I can look it up.

~~~

At 8:35 p.m. on June 20, the longest day of the year, the sun slips down into the far hilltop like a hot coin into a slot. High in a cottonwood grove, two herons get into a raucous fight or have sex. At 10 p.m., enough light still spills over the globe for me to distinguish green on the banks, faint pink in a high cloud. Half an hour later a full moon the color of melting butter slides up into the cloudbank between cottonwoods. Coyotes yowl. I hear three distinct calls, all from this Crims Island group. Coyotes howl back and forth for a few minutes before all fall silent. Their yowls seem less to declare territorial rights than to reassure themselves that there are others like them out here.

Crickets and frogs take over. Moonsplashes bathe the boat in cold light. The sky is so deep I could fall out into it.

Heavenly bodies pull on earthbound creatures. A fearsome memory—not just a chemistry—rolls through all living things. The moon climbs higher in the sky, bright enough to write by. I can scratch words onto a page, which sometimes works when I am lost. Stay up and fight through it. Fire up the stove. Put coffee on. The river lips the shore. The river laps against the boat.

Pretty soon I am just shy of dead and wishing that time, like the river, felt the pull of moon and went back on itself now and again. Instead, time flows only in one direction and leaves a man wide awake and lovesick, feeling short.

A beaver sounds—ka-PLOOM—and scares me half way to Astoria.

Maybe it's all right to let the river get the upper hand like this. The world is good. It means us no harm. But a mind can wander too far from itself. That's probably as good a reason as any for towns and cities, where people can forget how large the world is. A man wants to stay out here only so long.

Miss Ivory Broom

I am in love with a six-year-old. Ivory Broom is in the first grade and rides in a wheelchair on my school bus to a special education class at Sitton Elementary School, far north in St. Johns, Portland. She is the first child I pick up each morning and the last I drop off in the afternoon. We have some quality time together.

Ivory has *spina bifida*. I'd heard of that before I met her, but I couldn't have told you what it is. A bus driver is given too little information about a child he will be with for a couple of hours each day. The student information sheet just said "severely disabled, brittle bones." So I looked it up.

The trouble—*spina bifida*—starts in embryonic development. Researchers in London have identified a genetic mutation in mice responsible for the birth defect that derails the formation of the neural tube, the part of the developing embryo that will become the central nervous system. The mouse gene in question is more than 98 percent the same as its human counterpart, so this is probably what happened to Ivory Broom before she was born. The neural tube begins as a flat plate of cells that during normal growth folds down the center. The two edges loop to form a tube. The tube then develops into the brain and spinal cord. Unless it doesn't. Something goes haywire in the unfolding of genetic instructions about how to make and run a human.

If the upper end of the neural tube (near the brain) stays open, it's fatal.

If the lower end stays open, surgeons can repair it soon after birth. But what you get is an incomplete child. Ivory Broom. Only her top half works.

Knowing this, I was a nervous wreck before I even got to Ivory's house the first day of school. You can practice the hydraulic lift and tie-downs on a spare wheelchair at the bus yard, but you never know how a fragile child will fit securely. And "brittle bones"? Yikes. What if I have to brake suddenly? What if some idiot runs a stop sign and hits us broadside?

Anyway here she came, that first day, wheeled out from a low green house by a gorgeous young mother in purple bath thongs. Ivory herself was not the pathetic broken creature I'd prepared myself for. She was fair-skinned with freckles and big fearless blue eyes and light brown hair that her mom had fixed into a complex French braid. No bigger than a large Chinook salmon, Ivory came rolling toward the bus strapped tightly into her wheelchair. She wore an eager lopsided grin like this was a yellow amusement park ride and she was the luckiest girl in the world to get on it. Ivory waved her little fingers at me as the lift took us up, and I thought, *Uh-oh, she lacks arm control, too.* But no. She was showing me—so proud—her two-tone manicure.

Can you see this? I had focused so hard on what's wrong with Ivory that she just floored me with what's right! Her tiny fingers. Her pretty hair. Her spirit. Turns out this kid has huge spirit.

She also has the lungs and brass voice of a squad sergeant. Although her brain works slowly, Ivory has language. She bellows it out one syllable at a time. The other day I told her she was lucky to have a mom who loves her so much, and she said, "YOU . . . GOT . . . THAT . . . RIGHT."

I told Ivory I love my own daughter, and my daughter's name is Heidi.

She thought that was funny. Ivory thinks almost everything is funny. When she was through laughing—one har at a time—she said, "BUS . . . DRI - VER . . . YOU . . . ARE . . . A . . . CHAR - AC - TER."

Well, I guess that's not exceptional, now that I write it. Maybe you had to be there. You had to hear the life-loving relish with which she belts it out. Or just the other morning we were almost to school. I had a full load of six broken kids on the bus and Ivory back there said, "OOOH . . . GROSS!!!"

What's gross, Ivory?

Never, on this run, is everyone's attention beamed in one direction. But here she'd nailed all of us. We waited. The dramatic tension was exquisite.

"MY . . . SNOT," she said.

Because, you see, when Ivory has the sniffles but fumbles a tissue onto the floor she cannot pick it up. She was just letting me know so I could stop the bus and let Jacoby get up to assist her. Oh, that's the other thing. Jacoby. Jacoby is (or was, at the start of the school year) a sullen fifth grader who got kicked out of his neighborhood school for violent behavior and for not trying. Jacoby is self-pitying and resentful at having to ride this short bus "with the retards" to his own special ed program. He can foul the air inside my bus just sitting there if he chooses to. At first, he chose to. Or maybe, I think now, he was just scared. Lost. But anyway, Ivory's daily greeting—"JA . . . CO-BY . . . I . . . AM . . . HAP-PY . . . TO . . . SEE . . . YOU"—began to coax a smile out of him.

With time, Jacoby began sitting opposite Ivory's wheelchair and talking to her.

And just the other day—this really got me—I saw in my overhead mirror they were holding hands across the aisle back there. Jacoby now has a spring in his step to the bus each morning. He is teaching Ivory her numbers. He also helps Ashley (brain-squashed, from the car wreck that killed her mother) and Anthony (developmentally delayed) fasten their seatbelts, which they cannot do themselves. His teacher tells me Jacoby is doing his schoolwork. (!) The little ones recently elected him President of the Bus.

So you see. Ivory would not let Jacoby brood. What we have here is a busload of children who have every reason to feel sorry for themselves. But despair? Ivory Broom won't have it.

~~~

So anyway. You've seen school buses. Mine is a short one, a special ed bus with never more half a dozen kids aboard. You get to know them. This bus has five seats and two wheelchair spaces. The lift folds outward from the right rear. What I do is I drive these birth-damaged or world-beaten children to schools often far from where they live. I make several runs and put ninety miles on the bus each day. It's not all candy and balloons like on the Ivory Broom run. Some kids are "special" because their behavior was too disruptive at their neighborhood schools. I glimpse some home lives that reek of desperation. Every day I see despair. I hear it in the children's voices.

"My daddy's in jail."

"We're not having Christmas. Mom says we can't afford it."

"My mom didn't come home last night."

When I asked one girl her plans for the weekend, she said, "We're canning." *That's nice,* I thought. *Putting up preserves.* She meant scavenging the neighborhood trash for aluminum cans.

I've seen sadness I never could have thought of. One middle-schooler was so increasingly hyper on the ride home I called his mother out to the bus. She was too empty-eyed zonked to make sense of me. The boy's teacher, later, explained to me it's not unheard of for a parent to be taking a kid's medications, to be downing the meds herself.

Not that I can say for sure that's what happened. But boy . . .

Despair is when you're Devon and you're twelve and you have a slow brain and bad teeth and the wrong clothes and got kicked in the nuts by those girls on the playground and told you are dirty because you are black, and YOU got in trouble because you fought back. The teacher wrote it up—fighting with girls—and now your dad will fly into a rage when you get home. You're the last rider on this route on a demeaning short bus. You rock in your seat and your eyes are wild with fear and your shoulders begin shaking. Your eyes meet those of the bus driver in the overhead mirror, and it all comes gushing out.

"My dad won't believe me," Devon sobs. "I'm always in trouble. I'm stupid. I'm ugly. It's not fair," Devon wails, and this is the rock-bottom truth. It's just not fair. He hopes nobody will be at his home, and I will have to deliver him to Children's Club. Try to imagine. How would you like to be terrorized at school and afraid to go home? Devon is not a bad boy.

Suck it up, Devon. I'll talk to your dad when we get there.

〰

But hey. You have kids? Hug your children. We can beat back despair on my Ivory Broom run because those children come from loving families. They get a kiss good-bye from somebody and smiles when I deliver them home. It just goes to show you. What a difference to the damaged ones a warm family makes.

Now here comes Samantha, a late addition to my Ivory Broom run. Another wheelchair girl. Samantha is twelve, with breasts and makeup. Belligerent, self-absorbed and foul-mouthed, she came wheeled out that first day from a squalid house by an unwashed uncle with mean dull eyes. Right away Samantha informed me, "I have an attitude."

Not on my bus, you don't. Consider these sweet other children.

Ivory adored Samantha from the start. Little girls look up to big girls. More so, here, because Samantha's wheelchair is motorized.

One morning on the sidewalk, before loading, Samantha threw a feeble punch at her uncle and kicked off a wheelchair footrest and—with Ivory watching, wide-eyed—screamed obscenities skyward. I closed the lift and drove off and left her there. And because she would much rather go to school than stay home, her behavior improved in succeeding days. But then another morning Samantha told me, as I was lifting her, that she was tired of living.

She didn't want to go on living. Think of this. Your heart goes out to a young person so desperate, so despairing. And so in the privacy of the lift I whispered to Samantha that if she comes out with the F-word one more time—just once—I am going to wring her neck.

Not really. I didn't say that. You can't threaten a student. Schools have psychologists for this sort of situation.

But what I was going to say was I took this bus-driving job just hoping for routine. Routine, I'd thought, might kill dread. I'd had some experience, myself, not with despair, exactly, but with a dreadful flatness. I was through teaching and stuck at writing and I couldn't remember why I should get up and at it. And there is, for sure, a lot to be said for scheduledness. But the real deal here is story. You've got all these little characters, and each of them is a story. You can't help thinking who, or how much, they are.

Story, it turns out, is the assassin of despair.

This began to dawn on me on a different run. I had a busload of five little autistic K-1 boys who had no words in common except "Uh-oh," and "No." There was a brief, one-block descent on that run where I turned from S.E. Sacramento Street and dropped off the Alameda ridge on 60th. As the bus nosed down, Eddy Lavares said, "Uh-oh" and the boys screamed bloody murder until the bus found its proper elevation and I announced, "We made it!"

This is a story. It's a very short story, but it is. The boys never tired of it. Day after day. "Uh-oh." Followed by screams. And then, "We made it!"

What I'm saying here is these boys didn't have words, but they had story. We were our own story. This story brought them great joy. Still, I didn't quite realize what we had there until the children on my Ivory Broom run—with more complexity because three of them are what you might call verbal—came up with the same story. Yes.

We were cruising west on Lombard in the pre-dawn dark. Light rain. Mushy leaves lined the street.

"Bus Driver!" said Ashley, in high alarm. "Car behind us!"

All except Ivory—who cannot turn—turned to look. "WHAT!?" Ivory said.

"Car behind us!"

Well, on Lombard there is always a car behind us. But now Hurricane Lee, as rear gunner, aimed over the back seat and made machine gun sounds. The others (who could) formed pistols of their fists and forefingers and blasted away at the offending vehicle. As a rule you don't want guns on the bus, but I let this go. It was a story. My little desperados and I were one step ahead of the Federales. "Ditch them," Jacoby said.

I have to stay on my route, always, but coming up was a turn off Lombard onto Charleston Street. And there—sure enough—as I wheeled to the right, the Federales sailed on down Lombard and away.

We ditched them. *We made it!*

~~~

One morning I was messing with their heads. *OK, kids. No school today. We're going to Dairy Queen.*

This was not automatically a welcome idea. These kids love school, they really do, and they expect to go there. Ivory looked at me as if I were developmentally delayed. But we loaded Samantha, the last passenger, and I "phoned in" to Dairy Queen our orders—seven Oreo Blizzards, six Cokes, and a senior coffee—on the intercom. Yes, I have an intercom. It echoes inside the bus like the voice of God.

"He's kidding," Samantha assured Ivory. "See, we're still going to school."

I stopped the bus at Pier Park and opened the door and "took in" our orders and napkins from the woods. Jacoby distributed the imaginary treats, and we had a good lip-smacking time of it. Story is powerful to these kids. Anthony got so happy he wet his pants. Continuing on, I scolded Hurricane Lee for eating too fast and warned Ashley not to spill any. By the time I got them to school, Hurricane Lee was faking the dry heaves, and another rolled off the bus claiming a tummy ache.

~~~

Ivory tolerates, but does not relish, foolishness. What Ivory likes are the classics. Snow White. Joan of Arc. On Glisan Street at 39th is a traffic roundabout with a statue of Joan of Arc on her horse. I told the kids the story of this brave girl soldier who saved France from the dirty rotten English. If we're not running late I drive around and around the traffic circle so they can admire Joan of Arc from all angles—her glittering golden armor, her raised lance, her squared shoulders.

Ivory loved Joan of Arc. I brought her a picture book, from Donna's school, about Joan of Arc. Ivory was thumbing through it one morning and fumbled the book onto the bus floor.

"BUS . . . DRI – VER.   PICK . . . IT . . . UP."

I can't, Ivory. I'm driving.

"PICK . . . IT . . . UP!!!

Ivory. Not now.

"PICK . . . IT . . . UP . . . PLEASE. . . . I ASKED . . . NICE."

You did, Ivory. But I'm driving the bus right now. I'll pick up your book when we get to Treasure's house.

I felt her smoldering silence back there.

OK? Ivory?

At a stoplight, she and I locked eyes in the overhead mirror. Ivory bit her lower lip and raised a little finger at me in the mirror. "BUS . . . DRI – VER," she said. "YOU'RE . . . FIRED!!!

～～～

This boy called Treasure? He has a real name, but his mom and teachers call him Treasure. He's a first grader with knees and elbows that don't work right. He is not a wheelchair boy. He can walk stumblingly along a flat surface. His mom carries him up and onto the bus to his seat. He has a bad speech impediment but can say a couple of halting syllables at a time. When he's had a good day at school, Treasure will say to me, "Go Cowish." He has big pleading eyes, and he says with some urgency, "Go Cowish."

Tell me, Ivory. What's Treasure saying?

"GO . . . CAR . . . WASH."

Aha! So when his mom came to carry Treasure off the bus, I asked her. What's this about Treasure and the car wash? She said when he's been a good boy they drive him through a car wash. He loves the car wash.

So anyway, the other kids on my bus began to pick up on Treasure's "Go Cowish," and when he goes into that mode they chip in with Treasure-like utterances of their own. If they've been good, that is.

"Go Cowish," Treasure says.

"Go beach," says Hurricane Lee, on the way home from school.

"Go Mexico."

"GO . . . PAR – TY," says Ivory Broom, like let's rock!

Others pick up on that, and I have a busload of hilarity. It's "Go party" and "Go party" and this is the funniest school bus in the world until Ivory Broom, in high alarm, says, "BUS . . . DRI – VER. . . . TREA . . . SURE . . ."

Poor grunting Treasure back there is repeating, "Go potty," and trying to squeeze it out.

Treasure, No!!! Go parrrrrr-ty!

~~~

I said Ivory Broom likes the classics? After Joan of Arc, her favorite character is Snow White. Ivory asks for that story when the other kids have been dropped off, when only she and I are bound homeward. But Snow White gets tiresome, and her story has too many characters if you ask me, and so I tell her "Snow White and the Beanstalk." "Snow White and the Three Bears." Ivory gets into that one. I tell the story slowly enough that she can repeat the best lines. When the bears come home and the tension builds, she just listens, rapt. I get to the part where *Somebody has been sleeping in* my *bed*, and Ivory goes, "OH . . . MY . . . (deep breath) . . . GAAAWD!!!"

Now. Explain this to me. I've taught *King Lear*. I taught *Sometimes a Great Notion* to sharp sophomores. Yet I can't recall any classroom experience more satisfying than when Ivory Broom breaks into "Snow White and the Three Bears" with "OH . . . MY . . . GAAAWD!!!"

I get the willies, you know? The good willies.

~~~

Now this Hurricane Lee whom I have mentioned once or twice is a turbocharged seven-year-old in flashy athletic gear who sprints across the lawn and leaps onto the bus each morning while still getting dressed, swinging his backpack, papers flying in his wake. I thought at first Lee spoke a squeaky language all his own. In fact he just talks unintelligibly fast. He has a smile that can light up all of February, but the boy cannot sit still. Ivory keeps an eye on him for me. "BUS . . . DRI - VER . . . LOOK . . . WHAT . . . HUR - RI . . . CANE . . . LEE . . . IS . . . DO - ING!!"

On the ride home, Hurricane Lee sleeps.

One afternoon my nerves were shot. While loading the kids at school, I suggested that Hurricane Lee drive the bus today. I would go in the back and sleep.

Ivory, stern as royalty, said. "NO!!! . . . *YOU* . . . DRIVE . . . THE . . . BUS."

So it's not exactly true, what I said before, that Ivory thinks everything is funny. In the story that is our bus ride, nonsense is not funny. We each have our roles to play, and Ivory keeps us straight.

Oh, Ivory, I was just pulling your leg.

Now that, to her, is funny. Hilarious.

"PULL - ING . . . MY . . . LEG!!!"

Ivory loves the words. She takes the full flavor of new ones and makes them her own. She doesn't miss much unless the words go too fast for her. She does struggle with words that come over the two-way radio, and will ask me for clarification. But she never complains. That's the thing. Her flamboyant lack of self-pity. Can you imagine? I pick her up at 6:53 a.m., and we don't get to school until nearly 8:00. She is six, and she can't move on the bus. At school she takes nourishment through a tube straight to her stomach. She is only now learning to eat. On the way home Ivory is often exhausted. "I . . . AM . . . *NOT* . . . TIRED." But then her eyes don't track, and her little hands won't work right. Even then, she will not complain.

Are you comfortable back there, Darlin'?

"TEN-FOUR. . . . THANKS."

〜〜〜

See, I try to explain this and my eyes get watery just on their own. This is Ivory Broom's story, but it is my story, too. I can't wait to get up and get going each day. Fire up the bus. Hear what Ivory has to say. Head for the library at midday. Some days I can write as well as ever.

I told you how Ivory loves "Snow White and the Three Bears" ? Well, there's a problem with the ending to that story, and Ivory knows it. I didn't know it until she kept giving me that puzzled no-reaction, a baffled silence, when I finished. Like, is that all? Snow White just ran out of there and fled through the woods? Because if you think about it, Snow White should never have gone into the three bears' house in the first place.

So then what? I asked Ivory. *What happened to Snow White?*

Ivory thought it over. "AND . . . THEN," she said, "SNOW . . . WHITE . . . SAW . . . A . . . BLUE . . . BUT - TER . . . FLY."

So you see. Now we have a satisfactory ending to that story.

Killed in the Woods

The phone rings, and you pick it up. You hear that a friend got killed in the woods, and those four words—*killed in the woods*—plunge down your spinal cord like a cold steel blade.

They can't tell you right away how it happened, but getting killed in the woods is different from, say, dying in the woods. It doesn't happen to old men, and most likely the funeral will be closed-coffin. You recall others, friends or a relative, who got killed in the woods. *Tree split on him. Log shifted. Cable snapped. Truck backed over him.*

John Keller was a logger, a good one. John's early specialty was climbing and topping. With spiked boots and a climbing strap, his cutting tools dangling from his belt, he would climb the tallest and straightest tree in a stand. Limb it on the way up. Buzz the top off. Rig the tree as a spar pole for high-lead logging. Cables will then haul newly felled logs to a central point near the spar pole, to be loaded onto trucks. There are other dangerous jobs in the woods, but none where success or failure is quite so visible. Toppers are exaggerated people. A tree-topper has to be strong and athletic, cool enough to apply a power saw at dizzying heights and quick enough to counter gusts of wind while at work. He doesn't have to be a deep thinker, but he must be brash and decisive. It doesn't hurt if he likes to be the center of attention.

John Keller combined all of these traits. But his career as a topper started backwards. He began by falling.

~~~

Although John came from a family of loggers, he was not yet a logger at the time of his fall. Six years out of high school, he ran a filling station in Estacada, often slipping off from the gas pumps to climb the spar pole at the Timber Festival site. He was what we called crazy. John so loved the world that he tried to drink it all of one gulp—booze and fast cars. He survived rear-ending a school bus with his motorcycle. You'd have thought he wouldn't live twenty-seven years, much less the forty-seven he finally put in.

In 1969, on a dare, John entered the speed-climbing competition, novice division, at the Estacada Timber Festival. It was a sizzling day in July, and he addressed the spar pole in a beery haze, without having slept the night before.

Up the tree he went, boots spiking bark, his climbing strap skipping ahead of him around the tree. Seventy feet. Ninety feet up.

People who saw it—I didn't—will tell you he fell as if he were unconscious. But John insisted, later, he remembered falling. He remembered, at the top, thinking *this is a very bad time to black out*. He blacked out long enough for his spikes to lose their grip on the bark. Both feet flipped out to one side, above his head, initiating the hundred-foot drop to the base of the tree. John says his life passed before him, just like they say it does, and he remembers bouncing at the bottom.

The bounce is what they still talk about in Estacada. At the base of the tree was fresh sawdust over plywood, and John bounced six feet in the air or a third of the way back up the tree, depending on whom you talk to. Back on the ground, he wiggled a toe inside his boot. He shared the surprise of those gathered over his body when they confirmed that he was—incredibly—alive.

The line between fool and hero in a small logging town is as fickle as anywhere else, but maybe easier to cross. Having already established, as he lay there, a shining place for himself in local folklore, John faced a dividing future. He could become enormously foolish. Or, given his tools, he could be heroic. That is, he could become a logger. And he did.

Backwards—from the fall to the climb, from exhibition to work—John Keller carved out a sober and lasting reputation for himself among Estacada woodsmen.

~~~~~

Twelve years passed between John's fall and the next time I saw him. Telescoping metal spar poles had all but silenced the call for tree-toppers, and 1981 was a bad time anyway to find work in the woods. John was a cutter, a faller. And he had a bum back. On his down time, he sold real estate. Real estate was all wrong for John. He was too agreeable and trusting to be a seller. Clean clothes didn't fit him, and he belonged in the woods

When I caught up with John at his low, humid house on Springwater Road, the wild man I'd known was someone else. He had just finished, out back, shearing a sheep. In the front room, on a wall above his wife's loom, was a glowing portrait of Jesus Christ. John handed me a beer and popped open a can of Pepsi for himself. He'd married Janis Salyers, a clear-eyed, no-nonsense, Earth-mother beauty I'd never have paired up with John. They had a kid. John could still laugh at himself—on the stereo was a raucous bit called "Loggin' and Lovin'" by the Cascade Mountain Boys—but he had left foolishness behind. If the woods picked up and his back straightened out, John said, he might get back to logging.

In a few years the woods did pick up. He began gyppo logging. John would gather a crew and clear your back forty, or bid on a salvage job the big outfits had passed up. Just when he began to make ends meet, his second child was diagnosed with cystic fibrosis. Then his business partner bailed out on him, leaving John with debts and back taxes he'd thought were paid.

Bad luck and good stories came to John Keller like iron fillings to a magnet. He bought a used Caterpillar D-4 and posted signs—CAT WORK—around town. His first call was from a lady whose cat was stuck in a tree. John scaled the tree and rescued the cat.

In May 1992, some Estacada friends gathered at our house in Portland after my novel, *Ricochet River*, came out. The book features a larger-than-life Indian kid who fell from a spar pole at a small town Timber Festival. John and Janis came. They brought the kids. He liked the porch better than inside, although he wasn't smoking. He held a 7-Up can with two hands between oaken axe-handle wrists. John stood there with an easy-going grin and calm brown eyes and the serenity of a man who knows who he is. He didn't have much to say. Men on the porch stood a little straighter. Women gulped.

When people left, Donna and I talked. She, too, has known John Keller since back when he was crazy, and she didn't know what it was about him. Janis and the kids had it, too. What was it? But the hour was late. We forgot about that until the phone call.

～～～

In September 1992, John Keller ran his Cat along a steep grade, clearing road. A stand of vine maples bent beneath the uphill track. When he shifted direction, the physics of it favored the maples. The cocked trees sprang up beneath the track, lifting that side of the Cat and throwing John to the ground.

The Cat rolled and crushed him.

John had been working some distance from his crew, and they didn't miss him for half an hour or so. When they did, and went to look, it was clear he got killed instantly.

"John was a logger," says Norman Christensen, a logger. "If you got close you could smell the sawdust, the work. His rigging truck looked just like him—run hard and put away wet. In summer he ate dust. In the fall he was wet from morning 'til night. In the dead of winter he was cold to the bone and worked fast and hard to keep warm. John loved it," Christensen says. "Logging gets in your body. At first light, when the sun comes up behind Mount Hood and the birds start chirping and the air is cool, you can feel it go down in your lungs. The smell of the woods as it's being logged."

"You couldn't find a better man to work with," says Mike Perry, a logger. "Things break down. You get screw-ups. John shrugged it off. That's logging, he'd say. And he loved those kids. If it wasn't a school day, he'd take his little ones to the woods with him. They must have got up at three o'clock in the morning. *You kids stay in the truck.*"

"John knew what he had," Christensen says, "and it was enough. It was a lot. He had his family and his work. When he shook your hand, you knew you had a man on the other end of it."

Another Way the River Has

Up at daylight, I poked my head out of *The Turtle*. Sam McKinney, in his boat, had coffee ready. "Lots of dew," he said. He drew a finger across his cabin roof. "She'll be a nice day."

Sam met up with me yesterday at Clatskanie, sixty or so river-miles downstream from Portland, on the Oregon shore of the Columbia. We'd poked around Bernie Slough on Puget Island, dropped in on Tom and Sherry Vaughan at Skamokawa, Washington, and tied up for the night here at Aldridge Point, back on the Oregon side. His boat was another twenty-footer. He'd salvaged the Fiberglas hull of a sailboat and built a wood cabin with a forward hatch. Sam could stand up, shoulders above the roof, to pilot it. An eight-horse Honda outboard fit forward of the stern. The boat was freshly painted light blue over true blue above the white shell. He'd had this vessel in the water only a month, and he had not yet christened it. When I called it *The Nutshell*, he feigned injury but had to nod.

We headed downstream before eating breakfast under clear skies on a flat river. There was so little breeze I could smell Sam's pipe smoke as he led us between Woody and Horseshoe islands, past a line of fish shacks. We crossed the ship channel and cruised along near the steep rocky Washington shore. A freighter churned upstream. The following waves, no trouble in deep water, lifted us up and down. At Altoona, a boarded-up fish station listed riverward, as if a kick to its shins might send the whole sad business toppling into the water.

Past Harrington Point, the rocky shore slumped away. The Columbia River, as Grays Bay, broadened to an expanse easily mistaken—as Lewis and Clark mistook it—for open sea. In cold rain and wind, low visibility, they confused the breakers and saltwater in the estuary for the Pacific itself. "Great joy in camp," Clark wrote on November 7, 1805. "We are in *view* of the *Ocian*, this great Pacific Octean which we have been so long anxious to See."

Sam slowed, for a look at my navigation chart. The chart showed sand bars scattered across Grays Bay toward Rocky Point, three miles distant. But no sand bars appeared.

"Take it slow," Sam said. We headed across the bay, two boats abreast. The river spread wide and ruffled silver across its unsettled bed. Black snags poked through the water, and others might lurk just below the surface. I plowed a furrow into the sandy shallows only once as we crept across the bay. To the left of a lighted buoy off Rocky Point, we anchored in a small deepwater cove, tied the boats together and fixed breakfast. I floated a fistful of granola in a blue bowl of cold milk. Sam spread peanut butter and cheese on rye crackers.

Grays Bay takes its name from Robert Gray, the Boston captain who crossed the bar in May of 1792 in the *Columbia Rediviva*. Gray's motive was trade, not exploration. Robert Boit, the best writer aboard Gray's ship, wrote in his journal, "This would be a fine place for to sett up a Factory," by which he meant a trading post. Beaver and otter abounded. Gray had his eye on the America-to-China fur trade through the Sandwich (now Hawaiian) Islands.

I asked Sam. Did he know where, exactly, Gray had anchored in the bay? It had to be close to the northwest shore, in deep enough water.

"I don't think anybody knows," he said. "It could have been right here, where we are."

Just a little west from here, too, Lewis and Clark's Corps of Discovery had been pinned down by driving swells and torrential rain. Drift logs rode the incoming waves and threatened to crush the canoes. "From the 5th in the morning until the 16th is eleven days rain," wrote Clark, "and the most disagreeable time I have experenced confined on a tempiest coast wet, where I can neither git out to hunt, return to a better situation, or proceed on."

From this "dismal nitch," where could they hunker down for the winter? Should they retreat up the river and seek protection from the raging coast? Or should they stay close to the river's mouth, here, where they might hail a trading ship? On November 24, 1805, the commanders put the matter to a vote. York (Clark's servant) and Sacajawea voted with the rest. "A vote," said Sam, shaking his head. "What kind of leaders were these? Lewis and Clark could have dictated the choice." It had to be the first time a black man and a woman ever cast their votes in a matter of official consequence to the United States of America.

No human dwelling rose within sight of our mild June cove. Up close we had dark woods, big sky, and broad blue bay. The Oregon shore was eight miles away. Not visible from here, but just beyond Tongue Point, was Astoria, the first permanent U. S. settlement west of the Mississippi River. Yet probably not one in a thousand people in the Northwest today has laid eyes on this roadless notch in Grays Bay, this place so rich in history.

I'd never seen it, even though Astoria is part mine, part me. My mother finished high school at Astoria. When I was growing up, the mouth of the Columbia River was our family's summer getaway destination. We caught the Megler ferry from Astoria, on the Oregon side of the river, to launch salmon fishing trips from the Washington towns of Chinook and Ilwaco, and for clamming on the Long Beach Peninsula. My sister Sue still lives in Astoria, and her daughters graduated from Astoria High. Dad had his fatal heart attack on a fishing boat near Buoy 10, and I had my appendix out at the Ilwaco hospital.

"I once lived here," Sam said.

Wait. What? "Where?"

"Right here. When I was twelve, I spent a whole summer at Frankfort, here. A fishing village. These broken piers?" He pointed out stubs of evenly spaced black timbers, the remains of a wharf. "Just before World War II."

I eyed the shoreline, reclaimed by fifty-year-old firs. Thick underbrush reached down to the water. A pair of buffleheads cruised near shore, diving and disappearing, popping up again.

"My friend and I came on a little steamer from Astoria. Two boys, alone, on our first summer away from home. I don't recall my friend's name," he said, after a pause, "but his grandmother met us at the dock. I can see her now. Gray hair in a bun. She wore a faded dress with a flour-dusted apron around her waist. At one end of the dock was big red fish station. Under the dock, fishing boats were tied stern-to-pilings. The steamer landing was the village center. A row of wooden houses stood back from the beach. A plank walkway angled from one house to the next. A roadless fishing village."

You stayed with the grandma?

"She laid down rules. Stay out of the kitchen except at mealtimes. Wash on the back porch. Keep the wood box filled. For a bedroom she showed us the hay loft over the barn. *Good enough for boys*, she said. It was perfect. We slept in the hay under deerskins. There were no beds to make, no floors to sweep. Nothing to pick up. Bats overhead. Mice in the straw. Cows and chickens made the first soft stirrings each morning. Mornings were cold. Colder still was the tap water into a gray enamel wash pan on the back porch. And then to the warmth of the kitchen, its wood stove."

A narrow black cormorant topped the buoy, its wings spread wide to dry. Caspian terns patrolled the high sky. And Sam had disappeared inside himself.

"By day we were Indians," he said. "We gathered berries and licorice root from the woods. We built a raft of old fish boxes. The grandmother, busy with canning and sewing, left us alone. We were expected to be nothing but boys—half savage, dirty, always hungry. I think we were the last generation of boys to be trained as fishermen. The village didn't last another generation."

Trained? As fishermen?

"The grandmother put us in the hands of Fred, an old Finn. We went out nearly every night in his gillnetter. With the net out, we drifted. Fred instructed us in sex and swearing. In Finnish. The hours of the first drift would pass and the sun would drop where the river meets the sea. Sometimes there was only starlight, or the tiny light at the end of our drift line. The work began when Fred started hauling in the nets. By hand. Nets with fish in them, you can't imagine. Heavy. Gather the net into the boat. Those early gas-engine boats needed a squarer. Someone on the opposite side of the boat had to row, to keep the boat square to the incoming net. That was my job. I pulled at the oar and kept the boat square to the net. I kept the boat steady as these great gleaming salmon flopped into the well. Salmon piled up on our bare feet, to our ankles, to our knees. Usually we made two runs on the outgoing tide. The second haul came in the cold dark hours before dawn. My friend and I fought over who got to man the sweep. Rowing kept you warm. All I had was one wool sweater."

I'd seen at the Astoria Maritime Museum such a sweep, such an oar, on a gillnetter. This was some sixteen feet long and thick as a lodgepole pine. The breed of people who plied that oar in bad weather must have had long limbs and industrial-strength hinges at the shoulder.

Astorians of my mom's generation *were* long and strong. Before basketball became an urban game, Astoria High School Fishermen won six state basketball championships from 1930 to 1942. These boys issued from three or four generations of Swedes, Finns, and Norwegians before gas engines made the river accessible to people of normal dimensions. The University of Oregon Ducks, then known as "The Tall Firs," won the first-ever NCAA basketball tournament in 1939. Three of the five starters came from Astoria. Cause and effect is illusive with human subjects, but imagine the offspring of oarsmen swapping chromosome for a few generations with the sisters of their like-bodied friends.

"When the boat filled with fish," Sam went on, "we crossed the river to Astoria and unloaded our catch. Fred collected his cash and left us in charge of the boat. He headed for the saloons. Later he'd come staggering down the ladder to the boat and fall asleep. This was our glory time. I was in command of the boat. Run it back across the river to Frankfort! I'd lay a course that would clear the sand banks, the seine nets, the ferry crossing, and then around the point here.

"I can close my eyes now," Sam said, and he did. "A small boy is at the wheel of a fishing boat. A moon lights the water. Another boy sits at the stern with bare feet hanging over the side, swinging to the motion of the boat's passage through the waves. An early experience," he said, "becomes something you go to find but can't quite get back to. The sense of possibility keeps haunting the mind. Those events shaped my life."

～～～

Sam wanted to head up Grays River to visit Bob Pyle. "I called ahead," he said. That was the first I'd heard of it. But sure, I said. Bob and Thea Pyle—a writer and an artist—live up the valley here. I know them a little, not well. So we pulled anchor and cruised the shoreline looking for Grays River, a small one, emptying into the bay. An unbroken line of green rushes marked the bay's shore. Sam slowed for me to catch up. "You have the chart," he said. "Lead the way."

I did, and in half an hour the rushes slowly parted to reveal the last meanders of a tidal inlet. Grays River wasn't much, twisting this way and that. Sun shone now on my back, now on my face. A harbor seal raised his puppy head between Sam's boat and mine. A trio of turkey vultures hunched on a fir branch, black eyes in bright red heads. The road to Altoona came near the water, and we passed a chateau-sized gray house facing the river behind grass high enough to hide a horse. On the left rose a parcel of virgin forest, a rare thing to see this close to water. Towering Douglas firs rose among western hemlock and Sitka spruce. Gray beards of lichen hung from the lower limbs.

The head of another seal crossed in front of my boat. But no! This one had tall ears. I put the motor in neutral and pointed out the deer to Sam. When I looked ahead again two more small heads were following her, swimming across the river. We drifted and watched the doe climb the bank. She froze to wait for her young ones. The two fawns climbed the bank and vanished without a sound into the brush.

Less than a mile farther along, I heard a shout from Sam, behind. He bent over the gunwale of *The Nutshell*, banging cold tobacco from its bowl. Then he went into the cabin. He wasn't coming. I kicked the motor into reverse and idled back to see. Sam poked his head up and said something unintelligible, with the pipe clamped between his teeth. He lifted a floorboard and looked up, wide-eyed. "I'm sinking," he said. He lit his pipe and puffed on it.

I positioned *The Turtle* to tow him ashore. Sam snagged the line I cast him, and I swung *The Nutshell* toward the right bank. We secured both boats, and I looked into his. Water in his boat was ankle deep in the cabin, shin deep in the stern. "I can't figure it out," Sam said. From the cabin he emerged with a small battery-run pump. When he got the pump going, its hose issued a faucet-sized stream of water over the gunwale. "It's coming in faster," he said, "than it's going out."

I considered where we were. It could be worse. We'd seen the road to Altoona not far back. I saw a house upstream with a telephone line leading into it. The slope of the shore here was too severe for me to step off the boat and check the hull from the outside. I could swim, though, beneath his boat. Visibility would be poor in thick water, but . . .

"I think I've got it," said Sam. He was bent over the floorboards near *The Nutshell*'s battery/gas compartment. He said something I didn't get about the daggerboard. It's hard to understand Sam with his pipe in his mouth. But whatever the problem was, he'd found it and soon corrected it.

The water level in his boat stabilized.

"In an emergency," Sam said, "the first thing you want to do is light your pipe."

While we waited for the pump to drain the boat, we talked about how rivers hate plans. Something always comes up. Sam said that his mother, well into her nineties now, had called the Coast Guard when he didn't show one night. "All she could tell them was I was out in a boat. *What sort of boat, Ma'am?* She didn't know. *Where was he headed?* She couldn't say. *We'll watch for him, Ma'am*, the Coast Guard told her."

〜〜〜

Little Grays River kept going and going, off the navigation chart. From the bay
we'd traveled a couple of hours, not counting the near-sinking and pumping
time. We crossed beneath a country-road bridge but not the historic covered
bridge that the Pyles live close to. Dull-eyed cows looked up from pastures. I
got antsy about gas. My five-gallon tank was nearly empty. The three-gallon
spare would get me back to Cathlamet from here. But Grays River kept twisting
into the lowlands, with no sign of village or store. We kept going.

"Maybe the Pyles," I said, "can drive us to a gas station."

"If they're home."

If they're home? "You said you called ahead. They're not expecting us?"

"I phoned," he said. "I left a message, but I couldn't tell them when."

Sam.

We were near the limit of navigable water when the Grays River grange hall,
on Highway 4, came into view. A roadside restaurant was closed. The general
store was boarded up. Across the highway, though, stood a phone booth. I
stayed with the boats while Sam crossed the highway to call the Pyles. When
he returned, Sam said, "Thea sounded hesitant. We'll stay only a bit. She's
coming to pick us up."

We wolfed down sandwiches and climbed up the bank with empty gas
cans. Thea drove up in an ancient Honda Civic the color of mush. "I hope I
didn't sound unhappy," she said. "We're glad you came, but it's been a horrible
morning." The Pyles' cat had died at the vet's after a lingering illness. She and
Bob had brought the carcass home just an hour ago. "We were about to bury
the cat when you called."

To me, the world is no less rich when somebody's house pet dies, but Sam
expressed sympathy enough for both of us. Thea drove the river road and pulled
up a driveway with grass between the tire tracks. She stopped at a grand old
dowager of a farmhouse with a view across Grays River Valley. Rhododendrons
bloomed. A brilliant red maple contrasted with the dark green Douglas firs,
hemlocks, and several trees not native here. To the right of the front porch
rose a monster tree that Bob—when he met us on the porch—identified as
the second-largest white oak in Washington. "Planted here by the Swedes who
built the house," he said.

Robert Michael Pyle is a scientist and nature writer, the author of scholarly
books on butterflies and the excellent *Wintergreen,* about Grays River Valley
and the Willapa Hills. His silver hair falls in lush locks to his shoulders. He'd

trimmed his beard and shed thirty pounds since I'd last seen him and looked glad for a distraction. He put tea water on. Thea quartered apples and sectioned oranges and set them on a blue plate. It was nice. We sat on wicker chairs on the verandah and talked.

"Where's Donna?" Thea said.

"Donna isn't crazy about the water," I said. "She and a friend are in Europe. They're touring Hapsburg capitals—Budapest, Prague, Vienna and . . . I forgot what other."

"I can understand that," Thea said. Thea Pyle is an artist. She paints plants and birds really well. Thea looks, and probably is, younger than the rest of us, with straight brown hair to her waist. She's shy. I asked what she was working on, and she said not much. Thea felt like she needed a break. Younger people often feel like they need a break. I sat there trying to remember what that was like while Bob talked about the demise, here in the valley, of small dairy farms. Since dairy farming moved toward larger consolidated operations, locals can't afford to transport milk to market and make a profit.

The smell of scorched metal reached the porch, and Bob raced to the kitchen. When he returned, Sam told the heart-rending story of the final nuzzles of Gray Bear, his and Gail's deceased cat.

I wondered about the tide going out. "Could strand our boats. Don't you think, Sam?"

Sam looked surprised, as if he'd forgotten we came by boat. The four of us squeezed into the Honda, and Bob drove to the gas/grocery store at Rosburg. We filled the gas cans. I wandered about the store in a daze at all the good things to eat. Bob, a country squire, leaned against the doorsill and chatted up the owner like *Give my guests anything they want.* The U.S. Postal Service rural delivery lady gassed up her Jeep Cherokee and visited for a spell. Then we drove back to the boats.

Tidewater had slipped right out from under them. *The Nutshell* perched dry on a gravel bar. Only the right stern corner of *The Turtle* touched water. Bob went joyful over the strandedness of these boats and drove back to the house for a camera. Thea shed her white Keds and toed down the bank and through the mud. She washed her feet and climbed all over *The Turtle,* which made me happier than it should have. The river we'd come up—a lazy tidal backwater—had become a shallow bounding stream, urgent, gurgling beside our boats. Through crystal-clear water, rocks in the streambed ranged in color from pewter to yellow. Grays River was colder on my ankles than the Columbia. It looked like, but ran smaller than, the upper Clackamas. There would be crawdads here, and smooth flat stones to skip on the green pool below that riffle. You couldn't ask for a better place to be stranded.

It was 3 p.m. The tide table called for low tide at 3:50, but when would the river push back to here and float our boats? We would be here a while, and nobody was unhappy about it.

When Bob returned he snapped photos from the bank and came down to the boats. Thea, wading around, picked up a pretty-grained piece of dark wood in the shape of an eye tooth, hard as stone. "What is this?" she asked. A river tooth had caught her artist's eye. River teeth are what's left after a river eats a tree. Knots—the indigestible parts—tumble downstream. When you find one, a river tooth is something to keep.

The Pyles remembered they had a cat to bury. When they left, Sam settled into *The Nutshell* for a nap. I tried to nap but was wide awake, thinking about dropping in. My folks used to drop in on friends. People dropped in on us. O.K., it could be awkward or embarrassing to be dropped in on. The house is a mess. Underwear is on the line. We're having macaroni and cheese. But there's something to be said for dropping in. If they'd known we were coming, the Pyles might have been different people. The drive to the gas station helped us more than it put them out. And we'd relieved their mournful day. Donna and I seldom drop in. Nor do our friends.

Four boys—none of them more than twelve years old—came down on two bikes to the gravel bar for a look at strange boats in a weird position. One boy, evidently slow-minded, pressed his nose against the window of *The Turtle* and asked me several times, at five-minute intervals, "Are you going?" The others overturned rocks, ski-jumped their bikes off the gravel bar into water, skipped stones, and harassed crawdads. In jeans and T-shirts, they were dripping wet and kept at it until a sound of metal banging hollow metal called two of them to dinner. The other two soon left. Those boys got a lot done here, just them and the river.

~~~~

When Sam woke up I cooked Pasta-Roni. He tossed a salad and we ate dinner on *The Turtle*, still on the gravel bar. Not until 7:45 could we push off.

We motored back out Grays River to the wide bay and wheeled around into the twisting Deep River. Running lights on, we tied up to an abandoned set of fishing docks at 9:30. The croaks and screes of frogs and crickets filled the air, but the sun hadn't yet pulled all light from the sky. The dock adjoined a higher platform, also abandoned but sturdily built. Big enough for tennis, it had a hot tub-like structure at one corner, like half a barrel, its staves dried and separating. "The bluestone tub," Sam said. "Fishermen soaked their nets to preserve them. This is a net-mending dock." Sam found a tangle of left-behind net and fingered it. "Linen," he said. He picked up a wooden float—sun-cured so the grain stood out—and handed it to me like a gift. "Now they use plastic floats and nylon nets. This is the original stuff."

Bluestone?

"It was blue to look at. Copper sulfate, I think."

Clouds swept across the warm night sky. Between them, timid stars peeked through. The river was a perfect mirror of the dark Coast Range and a lighter fog bank above it. Only two lights—one across the river and its reflection on the water—shone through, and we watched the river move through the night.

What got me was how much was here, and now it's not. Just two hundred years ago people were running around here barefoot, chugging seal oil straight. They were a plump sleek people, short, their low centers of gravity well adapted to canoeing. Centuries after Gutenberg's printing press, they had a rich store of stories but no written language. Where in the world, I wondered, have humans adapted so rapidly and radically to a place? Sam McKinney overlapped the steamship era on the Columbia. Sam and I might be closer contemporaries to Robert Gray than Gray was to Christopher Columbus. I ran it through my head, and that was true. Three centuries passed between Columbus's landfall and Robert Gray's crossing the Columbia River bar. Since then, in only two centuries, the animals changed. The people changed.

~~~~~

I awakened at graylight the next morning. Five o'clock and foggy. *The Turtle* didn't budge as I stepped off her, onto the dock. Uh-oh. The boat hadn't moved because it rested on mud, not water. We'd come in on a high tide, near dark, and now both boats were stuck fast in muck. The dock, too, sat at a wonky angle to riverbed. Deep River. At a place called Deep River, you don't expect to be mud-stranded when the tide goes out.

I brewed coffee and carried the cup to the fog-shrouded net-mending platform. Between our dock and the far shore of Deep River lay a mud bar, like the broad back of a brown whale. Sam poked his head out and gave the situation a whatta-ya-know shrug. Stuck again. He ducked back inside his cabin.

The new day began working its way through a pink slot in the gray sky to the east. On the water, not a breath of wind. Tiny air bubbles wobbled up through the shallows like reverse rain, the riverbottom giving back air to the sky.

A beaver slipped under the end of the dock that was still afloat. I walked over to see where it had come from. The beaver's hole was under water, in flat mud, shaped like an airhole in oatmeal. His "lodge" must be in or behind the dike. The beaver reappeared downstream but took a wide turn and came back beyond the mud bar. Sea gulls trod the glistening mud. A raccoon prowled the foot of the dike, pawing at clam holes with little human hands. A mole slithered into the exposed roots of riverside grass. A cormorant cruised along the channel surface and ducked under water—ploop—to "fly" in a different medium. Beware, you slow-moving fish.

Wisps of vapor danced across the river, and the songbirds were just a-going it. I walked back to the net-minding platform, newly attuned to an orgy of life and death at the threshold. Life at the border between water and land is richer than elsewhere. All along the wet mud bar were tiny air holes for little breathers taking on tinier fuel. Here in the back-and-forth wash of salt and fresh water, noiseless mouths and claws and filters were at work on the business of life. An aroma of rich rot filled the still air as the sun broke above the ridge to the east, powering up the whole haunting and wondrous system.

Three gulls began squawking over a reddish morsel on the mud bar. A heron swooped in and scattered the other predators. I couldn't tell who won the prize, or even what the prize was, but the birds' set-to raised a savage racket.

I'd lost sight of the beaver. But when I walked to the upstream edge of the platform, he was idling in shallow water. The beaver and I eyed one another. Just a pebble-toss away, he was pointed toward me and had nowhere to go. He couldn't sound. The water here was too shallow. The beaver wore a loose coat, shaggy and thin, having shed the thicker dark fur in favor of light summer wear. The beaver's winter pelt had changed the course of history here. Fashion at the turn of another century prized the beaver's soft underfur, the best felting material for top hats.

An osprey came whistling over the fir tops at the far shore, and when I looked back toward the beaver he had vanished.

I walked down the dock and up a plank ramp to the dike. Two farm houses held the high ground. At sea level, behind by the dike, lush hay grew between irrigation ditches. Atop the dike ran a one-lane road, paved. I walked upstream until a shaft of sunlight hit a big gray doe, a mule deer, at the woodsline. She stood frozen, watching me watching her.

A short yellow school bus took on children at a farmhouse, and I walked back toward the dock thinking my heart might break. What is it? Morning sun lights up an unstartled deer. Children step into a yellow school bus. The wild and the human commingle here in an astonishing array of survival packages, the inventive *variety* in ways to live on a swampy bottomland. I'd read somewhere that I am seventy-something percent water. H_2O. The human body, by volume, is mostly water. A kid mounting a school bus. A beaver emerging for its morning rounds. The heron terrorizing gulls. These riverside willows, too, all these collections of fiber and rising sap . . . Each life form is just another way the river has of getting up out of its banks.

By the time I got back to the boats, I was liquid inside my skin. Sam sat on his deck like a boy in his tree house, watching the river fill.

"If we'd had our way," I said, "we'd have left at daylight. We would have missed this show."

"That's it," he said. "That's just it. A river has its own ideas. What we see of a river is not ours to choose."

Surf Savvy

Eighteen-to-twenty-five-foot swells slammed the mouth of the Columbia River and broke all the way across the winter bar. From Buoy 11, inside the river, to Buoy 4 in the Pacific, the surface boiled with whitewater and angry spray.

Chief Petty Officer Steed of the U.S. Coast Guard, at the helm of a 44-foot motor lifeboat, had to navigate from the Washington side of the river toward South Jetty, where the breakers of Clatsop Spit, on the Oregon side, had trapped a 40-foot trawler. Steed's lifeboat is built for heavy surf. But to reach the imperiled trawler he had to take it straight south, across the river, while keeping the bow of the boat pointed west, into the oncoming breakers. No boat is designed to do that.

The boat slipped sideways in the trough between the breakers and then turned to hit each oncoming wall of water, three to four seconds apart, head-on. Safety-strapped upright to the open bulkhead were Chief Steed's three crew members, immobilized and willing to be blindfolded and shot where they stood. Through darkness, rain, wind, and cold—all the worst conditions—it took Steed more than an hour to zigzag and chop his way across the river.

While he maneuvered to pass a towline to the disabled trawler, a breaker caught the lifeboat broadside. The boat did what it is designed to do in overpowering conditions. It began a 360-degree roll. Steed yelled to his crew, "Take a deep breath!" thereby emptying his own lungs.

It can take up to fifteen seconds for the lifeboat to right itself. In the refracted and conflicting breakers, the inverted lifeboat lay as if undecided whether to swing upright to port or to starboard. The hesitation left plenty of time for Chief Steed, underwater, dangling upside down and strapped to his helmsman's chair, to think what bad luck it would be to run aground in this position.

The lifeboat did right itself, motors still running. Steed reoriented the boat to the "midnight sun," a searchlight on a rescue helicopter hovering close by. His radar console was gone. Because both whip antennas had snapped off, he had no communications system. Distributed evenly among his three crewmen were one broken nose, one charley horse, and one dislocated shoulder. Steed was unhurt, and two of his crewmen still could function.

Steed hooked up with the disabled trawler, but immediately to his south rose the rocks of the jetty. He could not pull away north, parallel to the waves, without flipping again. And to head away from the breakers would risk having the trawler lifted and tossed onto the lifeboat by another wave. The only alternative was to tow the trawler straight into the breakers, seaward, and wait for the storm to abate. That's what Steed did, finally tethering the two boats to the Columbia Lightship outside the bar.

By late afternoon the next day, the bar lay down. It was possible to tow the trawler to Ilwaco and safety.

Chief Steed and his battered crew then returned with the lifeboat to the whitewashed buildings and manicured lawns of the Coast Guard Station, Cape Disappointment, which is (jump back, Miami Beach; step aside, San Francisco) THE BUSIEST MOTOR LIFEBOAT STATION IN THE WORLD.

~~~

The fishing port of Ilwaco (pop. 604, and declining) bills itself as THE SALMON FISHING CAPITAL OF THE WORLD. Within five miles of Ilwaco's lone stoplight, in the southwest corner of Washington, begins THE WORLD'S LONGEST BEACH, and therefore, each summer THE WORLD'S LONGEST BEACH RUN. In August, tourists will help locals launch THE WORLD'S LARGEST KITE. Gone are the days when the nearby village of Chinook could claim THE GREATEST PER CAPITA INCOME IN THE U.S., but in Long Beach sits Marsh's Free Museum, which boasts a shrunken head, Jake the Alligator Man, and THE WORLD'S MOST UNIQUE COLLECTION OF GLASS BALLS.

Don't be numbed. It's OK. Upper-case thinking is the style here on the Long Beach Peninsula. And amid all the razzmatazz and boosterism arising from this land of natural and unnatural wonders lie some perfectly real distinctions.

We have here THE GRAVEYARD OF THE PACIFIC. Ilwaco is the closest outpost of civilization to the conjunction of ocean and river that has wrecked, beached, or sunk some two hundred and thirty ocean-going vessels since the day someone arrived with a dry enough scratch pad to keep score. The Columbia River Bar and its surrounding sand traps—Peacock Spit, Clatsop

Spit, and nearby shores—have beached the big ones at a rate of better than one a year since 1792.

Thanks to electronic navigational aids and engineered improvements to the bar, the wreck rate for ships has dropped. But sportsfishers who ply these productive and dangerous waters still keep things exciting. Emergency calls come into the Operations Center at Cape Disappointment at a rate of two a day in the fishing season. The station will rescue four hundred boats a year, and it will lose a few. One lifeboat goes out on a daily patrol in the summertime, with two more standing ready. At night another boat crew sleeps in quarters near the docks, where the crew can roll out of bed and into a rescue mission in less than three minutes.

Having graduated from daily duty saving lives, Chief Petty Officer Steed (no first name; just Chief Steed, as he is known in these parts) is now senior instructor at the Motor Lifeboat School, **THE ONLY HEAVY SURF SCHOOL IN THE WORLD.** Foreign governments send their people here to study search and rescue under Chief Steed.

A lifeboat student will learn here to never take a breaker broadside, and to stay out of the curl. The curl in a green wave is trouble. One cubic yard of water weighs nearly a ton. A twenty-foot swell about to break can bring fifteen thousand tons down on the deck unless the lifeboat is pointed straight into it and can surge through or climb over a wave before it breaks. White water is less dangerous. Its energy is mostly expended, and it is full of air coming up from underneath.

Steed calls on twenty-three years of lifeboat experience up and down the Pacific littoral, nine of them here at Cape Disappointment. His knowledge of local hydraulics, topography, and weather conditions, along with his experience on a motor lifeboat, contribute to what is called surf savvy, not all of which can be taught. With his students—most in their early twenties and all with at least one year of experience on the lifeboat—Steed issues detailed instructions in practice sessions and lets the kids find out some things for themselves.

A former student recalls a winter training session near South Jetty, where incoming waves, deflected off the rocks and the shallow sands of Clatsop Spit, churn the surface like the agitator in a big washing machine. The student sat at the helm reacting to frequent and detailed urgings from Steed, barking over his shoulder, until the instructions stopped. A huge green curl came at the lifeboat forty-five degrees to starboard. Too late to hit it square. As the wave loomed over the boat, the student glanced over his shoulder for Steed. And there was his cool instructor, hands cupped in front of his face to light a cigarette.

"Aw, it wasn't that dangerous," Steed recalls. "I had an eye on that wave all the way."

~~~

Steed can seem disoriented on land. "What's the name of this little side street we live on?" he asks his wife, before giving directions over the phone. But the house is easy to find. It's the only residence on the block behind the fire department and the police station. Mock-ferocious dogs bound across the neglected yard, and a driftwood sign—Jerry & Briita—hangs above the weathered gray porch.

Chief Steed (Jerold L., for the record) is living testimony to the military distortion of the aging process. Eligible for retirement now, and with a reputation that should have left him weather-whipped and wobbly, the old salt just turned forty-two. Blond with a puckish grin, he looks even younger in a Superkid T-shirt and jeans. Tattoos of anchors and dragons decorate both arms. He has the build and demeanor of a formerly gifted halfback, kicked off the team for disregard of training rules.

Briita, a sturdy and attractive blonde of Finnish stock, is a native of Ilwaco. Not at all reluctant to think of her man as a hero, she pulls out a photo album stocked with shots of the lifeboat at perilous angles in foaming surf. While Steed is content enough to grin and scratch his ear at some of these impossible pictures, Briita cues him. "Tell about the time . . ."

Steed will get going later about some of the morons on boats he has rescued. But first he'll talk about the river, his gifted dancing partner. The Columbia River gathers its momentum from as far away as the Selkirk Range of the Rocky Mountains in British Columbia, twelve hundred miles from Ilwaco. By the time it collides with saltwater on a summer day, the river is surging seaward at a rate of four hundred thousand cubic feet per second. MORE THAN ANY OTHER WATERWAY IN THE WESTERN HEMISPHERE. The ocean is anything but pacific in accepting this freshwater contribution. Ocean swells, like the winds generating them, are predominantly from the west. Twice every twenty-five hours, the Pacific takes over and pushes against the river, raising water levels all the way back to Bonneville Dam, a hundred and forty miles east.

These conflicting forces of the Columbia and the Pacific meet in a constricted and shallow arena. The bar is an accumulation of shifting sands between the two jetties that define the mouth of the river. At an average depth of only twenty-five feet, deepened by dredging to forty feet in the channel, THIS IS THE ONLY PLACE ON EARTH, as far as Steed knows, where the swells can rise higher than the average water depth.

~~~~

One of Chief Steed's protégés, Petty Officer Pat Newman, twenty-five, drives a red Z-28 Camaro to work in the pre-dawn morning and takes command of a 44-foot motor lifeboat. Newman's pencil mustache, tanned good looks, and jaunty cigarette are appropriate for a man who reasonably expects to save a life or two today. Newman grew up in Longview. He regards his crew with a no-nonsense squint and issues clipped and quiet orders. He brooks no backtalk, no whining, and no discussion about how to ready the boat for patrol.

His three crewmen on the boat today are well-drilled kids with an expensive and powerful toy. Seaman Pat Chase, a shy hayseed from Tacoma with an ingenuous grin, is the engineer. Carlos Herrera, twenty, from Van Nuys, California, is so excited to be doing this job this morning he can hardly contain himself. Cliff Cabrera, from Tampa, Florida, is soft, cheerful, and a step slow in responding to Newman. He thinks before acting.

Though this August day is just breaking—with mauve, lace-like clouds over Astoria to the southeast—a procession of fishing boats from Ilwaco harbor already has grown thick and steady. "No Wake, Please" reads the sign above the Coast Guard docks. Fishing boats throttle down and glide by quietly, like guileful salmon past a drowsy bear. Diesel fumes rise wisp-like behind bigger boats and dance lightly over the gun-metal-green water. There is not a whisper of wind. Gulls loop and dip boatward as if looking for a breakfast handout, and the smell is of salt and mud flats.

Newman blasts a warning on the air horn before wheeling the lifeboat into this stream of outbound boats. His craft is the sleek white enforcer, and is treated as such. From a nearby boat, wide-eyed youngsters ogle the lifeboat as if regarding the Lone Ranger up close.

Over the radio crackles a message from the Operations Center. Already! Newman is not yet a quarter mile from the docks. Eager crewmen gather at the radio to get this first hand. " . . . 24-foot trawler with green trim. Do you see her?"

Do we see her? We're still in the access channel between Ilwaco and the Columbia. Open river is a mile away.

Newman peers back over his shoulder, toward the docks he just left. He mumbles a disgusted affirmative into the transmitter and cuts a tight U-turn. Crewmen groan. Eyes roll heavenward. First call this morning is about a cabin cruiser, powerless, not two hundred yards from the Coast Guard Station. The boat lies at anchor in fifteen feet of gentle backwater.

Newman and his crew go about the "rescue" as if they were Green Berets called in to remove an offending tricycle from a driveway. They are nevertheless solicitous of the downcast owner-operator, addressing him as "captain." They instruct him to pull anchor and fix the towline.

To Francis C. Whitcomb of the *How-Du-Do*, the mortification is near complete. A veteran of fifteen summers in Ilwaco, he normally charters. But this Saturday he invited his wife and friends from Yakima to go out. Some of the folks in passing boats, gawking, are friends of his. Whitcomb has had to call the Coast Guard before—hit a log, once; steering went out another time—but rescue is more tolerable when an element of danger is involved.

Newman's lifeboat tows the disabled *How-Du-Do* to its berth in Iwaco. Whitcomb would clearly rather duck his head into the engine compartment and work out his problem—a severed gas line, he thinks—than fill out papers. But regulations call for a "boarding" after each mission. Newman conducts a sympathetic safety inspection. He dings *How-Du-Do* only with outmoded emergency flares and abandons Captain Whitcomb to his private shame.

~~~~~

On his way once more toward the river, Newman passes the sleepy Coast Guard station. At the docks rest three more 44-foot lifeboats. A 41-foot utility boat, faster but not so surfworthy, is on standby, along with a couple of smaller boats for light towing. Cape Disappointment is THE WORLD'S TESTING GROUNDS FOR NEW MODEL LIFEBOATS. Under repair here is an experimental 30-foot speed burner with the agility to sprint laterally through breakers and pluck survivors out of the surf. Still working the bugs out of this model, the Coast Guard has discovered that the boat's high-strung engine, at full surge, will leap free of the motor mounts.

In dry-dock at Ilwaco is a monster 52-footer.

But the workhorse of the fleet is the 44. The one we are on is twenty years old, with no sign of aging. It's been torn down and rebuilt every year of its life. Upgraded, lubricated, and repainted, the lifeboat emerges better than new, incorporating changes in the model since the first 44-footer hit the water, in 1961. More powerhouse than speedboat, the lifeboat can tow vessels of up to twenty-five tons through surf. Self-righting and self-bailing, the boat has nine watertight compartments to ensure that a roll will result in it popping upright like a giant metal cork. Everything from the engine compartment to the whip antennas is standardized by type, size, color, weight, and proper storage place for ballast. Even the contents of a crewman's lifejacket pockets are standardized. Mirror and whistle, upper right. Day and night flares, lower right. Strobe light, upper left. Pencil flares, lower left. No surprises. Everything in its place.

Leaving the station behind and running late, Newman has an excuse to open 'er up. A deep-throated rev of the twin 185-horse diesel engines pushes the boat high in the water as Newman swings a wide right onto the Columbia, blue under cloudless sky. Still a full hour before "max ebb"—at 0826 hours—the river flows in the same direction as the lifeboat. Buoy 11, leaning heavily westward and trailing a V-shaped gash of whitewater, is the only reference to the speed and power of current.

There will be no dramatic rollovers this morning. The bar lies smooth and docile, undulating lazily.

About six miles off the bar, just south of the Columbia River entrance buoy, fishing boats congregate as if in a small and poorly zoned city. If there are five hundred boats out today—from Ilwaco, Warrenton, Hammond, Astoria, and Chinook—four hundred of them are gathered over a patch of the Pacific no larger than downtown McMinnville. Private boaters trust the experience and fish-finding skills of the charter captains. The boating community sticks together.

Fishing is slow. Newman and his crew see only one pole bent to battle as they cruise slowly through this congregation, although one bright fall Chinook is lifted proudly for Coast Guard inspection. The morning air warms to the point where shirts in fishing boats come off. A Columbia River pilot boat, loitering between jobs, has fishing poles extended. The 210-foot Coast Guard cutter *Resolute*, a floating helicopter pad out of Astoria, drifts idly. Newman and his crew consider boarding a fishing boat for safety inspection, but decide against it. On a day like this it would be rude, like breaking up a lawn party.

A call does come in from the station. An 83-foot commercial trawler, blue, has been out two weeks and is one day overdue returning to port. The wife is worried. Newman promises to keep an eye out for this boat, but he's not likely to find an overdue boat disabled near the bar itself. The Coast Guard will launch a search by aircraft out of Astoria.

~~~

THE OLDEST OPERATING LIGHTHOUSE IN THE PACIFIC NORTHWEST sits on the southwestern-most rock in the state of Washington, above the station at Cape Disappointment. From this green-capped promontory, the white column emits alternating red-and-white flashes of light to aid ships at sea. Before the lighthouse was complete, in 1856, Native Americans conducted a messenger service to the trading post of Astoria, paddling fifteen miles to the east and across the river to give notice of a ship on the horizon. A white flag or a fire blazing on the rock at Cape Disappointment then guided vessels to the mouth of the Columbia.

Paths to the lighthouse and surrounding viewpoints twist around mossy concrete bunkers and overgrown emplacements for cannons that stood guard through World War II.

At the foot of the lighthouse squats a glassed-in observation post, equipped with high-powered telescope, radios, and direction-finding gear. On a gray August weekday, Chief Petty Officer Jim Caldwell, thirty-two, of Portland, will rush to this viewpoint to coordinate a rescue operation. But when the call first comes in over FM radio, he's down at the station's Operations Center.

Saddle Tramp, a 26-foot cabin cruiser, has a broken crank shaft. The boat drifts in the river half a mile inside North Jetty. The captain is not panicked. There seems to be little immediate danger. Caldwell orders the 44-foot lifeboat out. By radio he directs the captain of the disabled *Saddle Tramp* to drop anchor, which he already has done. It will take twenty minutes or so, aided by the flow of the river, for the lifeboat to get there. As a matter of routine, Caldwell alerts Astoria—for possible helicopter support—to monitor radio communications with the crippled boat.

Not five minutes after the first call, another message arrives from *Saddle Tramp*. The anchor is not holding. The current is very strong, and he is closer to the rocks of North Jetty than first reported. An edge to the captain's radio voice spurs Caldwell to further action.

Dispatch the 41, he orders.

Sirens wail at Cape Disappointment.

Caldwell jumps into his pickup and charges up the nearly vertical eighth of a mile to the observation post.

In the meantime, the smaller but faster 41-foot Coast Guard boat rips away from the dock and unzips the access channel to the Columbia. It passes the 44 near Buoy 11 in the river. Caldwell sees, with relief, that the speedier rescue boat will get there in time. He relays this information to *Saddle Tramp*, and instructs the captain how to ready his boat for rescue.

Through the telescope, Caldwell watches the 41 approach *Saddle Tramp*, now dangerously close to jagged boulders at the jetty. The tow rope is passed successfully, but the deck cleats screwed to the bow of *Saddle Tramp* are too small to accept a thick towline.

On the third try, with the tow rope gripping something other than deck cleats, they hook up. But *Saddle Tramp*'s anchor, ineffective earlier, is now deeply entrenched and holding *too* well. The 41 cannot pull the boat and the anchor free. Caldwell radios the captain of *Saddle Tramp* to cut his anchor line.

The 41 appears to have *Saddle Tramp* in tow.

Now it doesn't. Caldwell, from his distant observation post, can't tell why. He can only watch as the current slips *Saddle Tramp* around the tip of North Jetty and into the worst possible water—over the shallow sands of Peacock Spit, just outside the jetty.

The slower 44-foot lifeboat arrives on the scene. While the 41 collects its towline, the 44 follows *Saddle Tramp* into rough water. From Caldwell's observation post, *Saddle Tramp* is hidden behind the jetty, close to the rocks, and he can see only the superstructure of the lifeboat. He second-guesses himself. Should he have ordered a helicopter out earlier? But now that the anchor is cut and both rescue vessels are on the scene, a lifeboat has the best chance of rescue. And as Caldwell watches from the observation post, the 44 emerges from the far side of the jetty with *Saddle Tramp* safely in tow.

~~~~~

Chief Steed worries more about little sport-fishing boats than about Ilwaco's commercial and charter operators. Weathered and riverwise souls, the people who make their living around the bar have the equipment and the knowledge to meet or to avoid the dangers, Steed says.

But the sportsman in his own boat may not know Peacock Spit from a light beer. There is no law saying he must have a powerful enough motor to bring him back against an ebbing tide, nor must he have a radio aboard or wear his life jacket. The prudent sportsman will. But a fisherman with a fish on is oblivious to anything else in the world. Wife overboard? Liberian freighter bearing down on his port side? Dark funnel-shaped cloud off his bow? First he will land this fish. A salmon on the line erases a guy from the roster of capable and clear-thinking adults for up to half an hour, after which he may look up to find his position quite changed. If a fog rolls in, he's apt to point home toward Guam instead of Ilwaco.

Chief Steed, who has MORE UNDERWAY TIME ON THE 44 THAN ANYONE ELSE IN THE WORLD, has seen some dingalings.

He tells of intercepting a 12-foot aluminum dinghy with a blissful young couple rowing seaward. "Rowing! They had their baby strapped to the thwart," he says.

Rubber rafts, kayaks, canoes . . .

"I thought I'd seen about everything," Steed says, "until one day we had a wooden raft out there. Crude planks across poles. A raft, with a party of jubilant city folks in lounge chairs, cold beer, riding the ebb tide toward the bar. I couldn't believe it. No motor. No oars. These idiots had no idea where the hell they were. So we go out and pick them up, and they get *belligerent* with me! I saved them from floating out to sea, and they're all bent out of shape."

Steed could file his retirement papers any time now. But then what? Buy a boat? On vacations he'll take off on the motorcycle with Briita riding tandem, but how invigorating is that when the government will pay him to ride the 44 and test new lifeboats? He will stick around Cape Disappointment for a few more years. What's a man to do? Steed can't ride his motorcycle into the sunset from Ilwaco.

A Stranger in Town

At daybreak on a misty June morning, I pulled anchor at Hideaway Slough and headed downstream for food and re-supply in Clatskanie, and *The Turtle* unzipped the top four inches of a placid Columbia rolling out to sea. A white furrow of my overturned wake folded back into gray and sent the reflection of near shore into wobble. No houses mark these shores. Blur your vision—ignore the wharf of an abandoned World War II ammunition dump—and it's easy to imagine you're seeing this place the way the Corps of Discovery saw it, two hundred years ago.

But no. Not quite. The river and its shores have changed. The Lewis and Clark party noted here how the hills on the left receded from a "butifull open and extensive bottom" that extended a good three miles from the river. In the marshy flats grew nettles and grass, rushes and cattails.

On *my* left, a tall dike keeps the river in its place. Beyond the dike, hybrid cottonwoods grow in rows as ruly as corn. These trees rise to varying height from field to field but of uniform height within each field. Genetically engineered, they sprout fast enough in this rich bottomland to be harvested for paper pulp when they're only nine years—but fifty feet—up from the seed. Pink wild rose along the bank would have been familiar to Lewis and Clark, but not the Himalayan blackberries, reed canary grass, and purple loosestrife—all introduced since Euro-Americans arrived.

The habitat changed, and with it the kinds of plants and animals that make a living here. Cougars and coyotes have scattered, although they still prowl at the edges of human activity. Where cultivated land replaced woody swamps, many of Oregon's geese adapted to grain fields and golf courses. They don't bother to migrate anymore. Farther downstream on the Columbia, Caspian terns have colonized a sand pile in the river that didn't exist until the U.S. Army Corps of Engineers piled dredge spoils to create Rice Island.

Yet the river still hides the Crims Island group and my Hideaway Slough, barely touched since Lewis and Clark. Thankful for *The Turtle* and Gortex, I cut the motor, let the boat drift, and ducked into the cabin for a look at the journals. Clark had noted here how the explorers, all "wet and disagreeable, had large fires made on the Stone and dried our bedding and kill the flees."

I left the broad Columbia for Wallace Slough, and then took a sharp left at Beaver Slough. Banks on each side came in close. A slough wants to meander, but dikes keep this one straight as an Iowa fencerow. Engineered turns came at unharmonious right angles to the rise of hills ahead of me. Then U.S. Highway 30 appeared on my right. I cruised past the public boat launch—deserted at 6:30 a.m.—and floated on into town like into the sleeping inner ear of a place. Fog-trapping hills surround Clatskanie, and downtown lies pinched among a jumble of sloughs and the slow brown Clatskanie River. I passed BJ's Dip and Dunk, Jim & Suzy's Head-Quarters and Mr. Fultano's Pizza, all with their backs to the river. Past Mini Mart Gas and Groceries, I tied up at the courtesy dock below Hump's Restaurant.

I mounted a steep ramp from the boat dock to the parking lot. The earth swayed, as it does when you haven't been on it for a while. Keep a wide base, or you might carom off a building. A yellow vending box outside held *The Sunday Oregonian*. So it must be Sunday, I thought. I scrambled back to the boat and returned with quarters to liberate a newspaper. Inside the restaurant, at the horseshoe-shaped coffee bar, I nodded good morning to the waitress. "Coffee?" she said.

"Please." The place was a bit dark. When she poured the coffee, I asked, "Lights?"

"We're not open," she said.

Hmmm. I'd walked through an open door and been greeted and served coffee. The waitress—a stout blonde of childbearing age, well tanned, with a formidable jaw—turned on her heels and disappeared into the kitchen. When she reappeared, she said, "We open at seven." She handed me a menu and topped off the coffee. At 7 a.m. sharp, lights came on. She stood ready to take my order. Sausage and eggs.

"How do you take your eggs?"

"Over easy."

"With hotcakes or hash browns and toast?"

"Hotcakes."

Men of mixed ages came in one by one and began topping the stools around the bar. Some had scuffed work boots and calloused hands, as if on break from Sunday chores. Others could have gone straight from here to church. There was an evident authority as they gathered, like around the *Stammtisch* at the *Gasthof*. They had in common a cheerfulness, and they were all men. But then a florid man with wet-combed silver hair came in with his blond, fiercely blue-eyed wife. When they took the two stools to my right, I placed my thick Portland paper on the stool to my left, to give them room. The others greeted this couple as if they could be counted on for news.

Sure enough, "We went on a ride," the woman said, "over at Mossy Rock. Five hundred seventy-three horses. It was for muscular dystrophy."

"That's a lot of horses."

"And more people than horses. We camped at the gun club."

More stools around the coffee bar took on customers. Booths, too, began filling up with families and couples on their way to the coast. When I was little, we did that. If we were good, Dad would stop at Hump's for milkshakes on our way to Astoria. The regulars, now, on stools around me, ignored these aliens in the booths. "Got your hay in?" someone said.

"Got 'er down and turned, not baled."

A slim old man with straight-up bristle hair and brown suspenders came in and sat down and took greetings. "What're you up to, Clyde?"

"Not a dang thing," Clyde said.

I learned that hay in the fields was late but looked good this season. Some had sold off their cows after the February flood, so the price of hay should go down. But maybe not. "They'll still charge a dollar for hay in the field. Cut and bale it yourself."

"I saw in the paper they were askin' a dollar fifty."

A low whistle. They weighed the relative merits of alfalfa versus grass hay.

"Them cows go for alfalfa like kids after a pie. It don't last."

My breakfast came on two plates: one for the sausage and eggs, the other for three hubcap-sized hotcakes. This was a thumping good change from granola on the boat. All the stools around the horseshoe bar were now occupied except the one holding my paper, on my left. My gaffe dawned on me when someone said toward a booth behind me, "What're you doin' sittin' back there like an aristocrat?" I removed my paper from the stool and set it on the floor. The regular came up and took that stool.

Note to Thomas Jefferson: *These fellows are an erect and dignified people, perhaps of Nordic stock. Clean-shaven and frugal and light of complexion, they speak the same language as ourselves but follow social conventions not quickly*

deciphered by a stranger. They have domesticated animals, and the talk is of
agriculture and weather.

"What's it supposed to do today?"

"I heard rain this afternoon," said the waitress, pouring coffee. "Thunder showers Monday and Tuesday. But that was on the Longview station."

"What do they know?"

A tall, trim-bearded fellow with a cast on his left hand came in and took a stool that someone had vacated. The plaster was bright new white, with green cloth at the wrist. Everyone stared at it. "Busted my finger," he said. I thought this was an incomplete explanation. But the others, satisfied with it, asked him about fishing. He hadn't had much luck. "Ain't no fish in the river."

"That's not true. They're catching steelhead off Adams Point."

"Seen a bunch of boats anchored off the ammo dump the other day."

"That would be sturgeon fishing," said Busted Finger.

"How small can you keep them?"

"Forty-two inches."

"No, that's what it used to be. If it's less than forty-*six* inches, they don't let you keep it. Or over six feet, you got to put it back. Breeders. And you can only keep one."

"Slicker'n goose shit how they measure them sturgeon in the water. They got a tape head that runs down your fishing line, stops at the nose of the sturgeon. Then you run 'er out toward the tail to see if it's a keeper."

"What's'isname, works for PGE, was out off Port Westward and his son got one seven and a half feet long. Had to put it back."

"Time was, them big ones was all over."

"My brother-in-law was bank fishing up by Richland and hauled one ashore. He went and got a tape from the truck, but it was only an eight-foot tape. Spread his arms past that, it was eleven feet. He's got pitchers. Says it took two of them with a coupla oars to push that fish back into the river."

On my right, the horseman eyed my breakfast, having finished his own. Maybe he was just looking for a way to be friendly. I hadn't, so far, given anything of myself away. My Portland paper was on the floor, and I hadn't said a word. The Turtle was down at the dock, out of sight from inside the restaurant. Nobody would know why I lingered over hotcakes instead of hurrying on along Highway 30 as a visitor normally would.

"Are those hotcakes cooked good?" the horseman asked.

"They are," I said.

As if he owned this place, the horseman nodded approvingly. He dropped three quarters on the counter for the waitress and stood up with his wife to leave. His stool at the horseshoe bar was taken by a crooked-grin man in a red-plaid shirt. The regulars evidently hadn't seen him for a spell. "What have *you* been up to? Workin' hard?"

"Hardly workin'. Same old tricks. Over in Longview, selling trailers."

"When are you going to put in an honest day's work?"

A red-bearded fellow with a black cowboy hat and glasses came in. He took a vacated seat at the far end of the horseshoe and lit up a cigarette. He was small and lumpy but alert as a deer, with quick eyes. In reply to someone's what-are-*you*-up-to, he said he had to jack up a friend's trailer house today and put the wheels on. "He's got aluminum wiring," the cowboy said. "They came in and condemned him. Now he's got to move the trailer."

The waitress, hearing this, was furious. "Why does everybody go and help him?" she fumed. "He gets somebody to house him. Somebody to feed him. He doesn't even work."

"He's got three little kids up there," the cowboy said.

"So do I!" she said.

"I just thought I'd give him a hand."

"He'll hire out for a day or two," the waitress said, "and go home! That's not work," she said, and she stalked away toward the kitchen.

The air in the coffee bar went still. Men stared at the walls or peered into their coffee cups. To everyone's relief, a woman in a stylish black dress walked in and looked around and asked if there is a Catholic Church in Clatskanie. Yes, there is a Catholic Church. "Where is it?" she said.

"Up on the hill. Take your first road past Highway 47, to the left, up where it's houses. That's where the Catholic Church is at."

She said she was in town for her daughter's volleyball tournament at the high school. Everybody watched as the city woman walked out. My neighbor said he'd been to Portland the other day and tried to escape during rush hour. "All them cars, bumper to bumper at high speed, I thought I'd never get out alive."

"I wouldn't live there if they paid me," said another.

"That's why people *do* live there. That's why you're poor."

"Coffee in Portland costs a damn dollar."

The waitress emerged from the kitchen with an order of biscuits and gravy. The regulars eyed her as if she might detonate. But she delivered the meal and went around with the coffee pot, topping off cups and smiling, as if nothing had happened. She was extremely tanned. Somebody asked her, "Been lying around the beach?"

"Lying at the tanning salon," she said.

"They say that's bad for you. Bring those cancers up from under your skin."

"That's what my kid says. But I do it anyway," she said. "I just do it a little bit at a time."

"That's like me," said the cowboy. "I only smoke these cigarettes just one at a time."

〜〜〜

Concentrating hard—full to bursting of language—I forgot *The Sunday Oregonian* but paid my bill and hurried back to the boat to write down what I could remember of all this. I thought I had something here, though I couldn't have said what it was. Words. Nor can I ever be sure that the words, if I take them home, will be any good. Like out on the river sometimes, you pick up a wonderfully river-sculpted piece of driftwood? *Wow, I'll take this home.* At home, later, you stare at it. The light is different, or you are different. You can't remember why you saved it. It's just a hunk of driftwood.

〜〜〜

Ice for the cooler. Beer and pop. Groceries for the next four or five days on *The Turtle*. Fill the five-gallon gas can. I didn't have to walk far or stay long in Clatskanie to take care of all that. But the library wouldn't open until tomorrow. I thought I might as well poke around town. Sleep on the boat tonight at Hump's dock.

Across Highway 30 from the restaurant, at Clatskanie's only stoplight, the green highway sign reads:

Astoria 37 →

← Portland 61

Nehalem Avenue crosses Highway 30 at the light. I walked riverward on Nehalem, past two taverns and small storefronts, Hazen Hardware and a grocery store/deli/bakery. Across the narrow Clatskanie River lay a three-house piece of transplanted Holland with windmills and geraniums on balconies. A curious cop in a black-and-white cruiser watched me retrace my steps, cross Highway 30 at the light, and walk up the hill on Nehalem. In the first block I passed Judy's Fashion Outlet, a low cinderblock city hall, and the police station. The Methodist Church is a white clapboard beauty with square white steeple. Homes included Victorians without gingerbread, sturdy modest structures with neat lawns and bright flowers.

The earth felt good under my feet, so I hiked west along Highway 30, past the Safeway and the public boat launch. A well-tended kids' baseball diamond flanked the road at the edge of town. Close on the left rose cliffs of heat-forged rock. On the right, low fields of hay and hybrid cottonwoods. The road had little shoulder. Watch your step here. Keep an eye on the stream of oncoming cars. Sunday afternoon traffic raced back from the beach toward Portland. Many of these vehicles were jumbo high-clearance four-wheel-drive rigs you'd take elk hunting, but they were no muddier than a Lexus sedan.

Note to Meriwether Lewis and William Clark: The new frontiersmen come rocketing back east in Ford Expeditions. They drive Explorers and Blazers. They drive Forerunners and Pathfinders.

~~~~

At the coffee bar early for breakfast the next morning, I ordered the biscuits and gravy. Before the meal came, the black-hatted cowboy—yesterday's Good Samaritan—took his seat at the unoccupied far prong of the horseshoe. It was misting outside but not windy enough to wet the windows. More regulars came in while I went to work on my biscuits and gravy. In the army we called it S.O.S. But here it featured home-made biscuits and honest-to-gawd sausage gravy, heavy enough to fork. The first few bites were excellent. I ate and listened.

In Clatskanie, as in Estacada, people know each other from way back. Friends grow thick, and their roots intertwine like a grove of cedars. People know their place—their place in the natural world—and small-town Oregon is right at the edge of it. The talk this morning is of coyotes preying on a farmer's lambs. And not long ago a cougar had attacked an aging Appaloosa gelding grazing peacefully in its pasture, close to a house on the Quincy-Mayger Road. Cougars almost always avoid people, but still . . . There's a blood-quickening proximity, here, to the wild.

A kindly faced white-haired gent in a short-sleeved pink shirt took the stool on my left and howdied. I said hello. "You with the dodgers?" I thought he asked.

Huh? When he repeated "dredgers" I recalled the Port of Portland dredge crew I'd seen on the river. I said no, I was just poking around the islands on a 20-foot boat. He said *he* had a 20-foot boat, an old Reinell with a four-banger Chevy engine, and what did I have? We got to talking. Turns out he works at PGE's Beaver Plant, a gas-fired generator, and lives at Mayger, just upstream from Bradbury Slough. He has a view down the river, he said, which made us practically neighbors. I didn't catch his name, but he was a talker. He ordered breakfast when the waitress came out, but it barely interrupted his friendliness.

A tall bald regular came in and said, "Something died in the fucking wall at my place. Up behind where the TV is at," he said. "You don't smell it other places, but in that room it could nigh drive a man out."

My pink-shirted neighbor said he liked to trailer his boat up to Neah Bay, but last time he blew a manifold, cost him four hundred and fifty bucks. "One time I took my daughter up there and we saw Orcas up close. It does make a man feel small. I told her we might see a nukie, too. She didn't believe me but the next day a Navy pilot boat came out and I thought, *That boat's leading a sub.* Sure enough the nose—just huge—busted right up outa the water. And then came the conning tower," he said. "The pilot boat swang upside the sub and a coupla men got on. And then that sub just disappeared down under the water! That was some trip, all right," he said. "We saw Orcas and a nucular sub!"

The horseman and his wife came in, helloed, and took two stools opposite my bend in the horseshoe. They were a handsome couple. Give him a hat and a rope, he could be the Marlboro Man. And she had those curious blue eyes. The others called her Pat. I introduced myself. His name was Vern. When he asked what I was up to, I said I'd been poking around the islands by boat.

"Where do you keep your boat?"

I pointed toward the window, and down, and he and his wife about sprained their ankles getting off their stools to go look. "It's that green one," I said. A couple of sailboats were also moored at Hump's dock.

My neighbor, still talking, said, "At Neah Bay those Indians take canoes— or not canoes, really, they're *big*—out on Puget Sound. One time the Indians rescued a bunch of Japanese off a wrecked ship when even the Coast Guard wouldn't go out. It was too stormy. "How do you think they did that? Have you seen the canoes they have?"

I had, and we shook our heads about it. He said he'd read in a book that Indians prized seals better than salmon. "When I was growing up you didn't hardly see any seals at all up the river this far. Now seals hang out at the mouth of the Cowlitz like boarders at the table."

I told him this year we had seals at Willamette Falls, at Oregon City. And sea lions all the way up to the fish ladder at Bonneville Damn. Easy pickings there, for a sea lion. "My cousin Kit," I said, "lost a spring Chinook right off his line to a sea lion. Or somebody did. Kit was in the boat."

He said, "Did you know one of the deepest spots in the whole Columbia River is right across the river at Stella? Over a hundred and fifty feet deep. A guy in a small boat threw anchor there last spring and got tangled in something. Took him down, and that was all she wrote."

Vern and Pat reclaimed their stools. "If you're out on those islands," Vern said, "Watch out for them hogs." His wife nodded pleasantly.

Hogs?

"Wild hogs," he said. "They can be something fierce."

Nearly everyone at the coffee bar had a hog story. Somebody long ago had raised hogs on Wallace Island but gave up. The hogs stayed and went feral. A hog had recently attacked a guy at his duck blind. "What do hogs do in the flood?" someone wondered. "There's no high spots on Wallace Island. Hogs don't climb no trees."

"Hogs can swim."

"One went after that kid on his bike, remember? Out the dike road."

"Them hogs don't back down none," said my neighbor. "I came across one the other morning when I got to work, sleepin' against the building. Gave her a nudge and she reared up snarlin' and I put my butt right back in the truck."

I said I hadn't seen any feral hogs.

"Take care not to," Vern said.

Driving Tunnel

Pat Zosel sits at the controls of his tunnel-boring machine, a colossal rock-eating snake—one-third again longer than a football field, weighing a hundred and twelve tons—grinding his way through the bowels of Harry's Ridge, near Mount St. Helens. Zosel, forty pounds heavier than when he was a defensive end at Linfield College, sits in his yellow rubber raingear like a great ripe pear in the constant cold and humidity and noise and nostril-clogging dust of the tunnel his mechanical monster is carving. The earth rumbles and quakes with the conflict, man and machine against rock.

Zosel grins through his rock-dusty black beard. His brown eyes flash. Here's a man who loves his job. He would just as soon drive this sucker into Longview next Sunday if he could find a parking space.

Zosel wants to tell all about it, but he can't make himself heard over the deafening roar of the tunnel-boring machine with its four four-hundred-horsepower electrical engines and the amplified blackboard-scraping screech of the cutter head's tungsten steel blades biting basalt, punctuated by the thunder of a diesel train arriving from the rear to carry out another load of rock. The train rumbles into the hollow tail of the snake, where its headlights cast long harsh *film noir* shadows. Over it all hovers the pungent smell of hot piston-juices cutting the chalky stale air of the hole as Zosel's great snake grinds steadily forward, chewing hard rock.

Soft rock, oddly enough, means trouble. Shortly before 8 p.m. on the swing shift, Zosel's crew meets a patch of rock that flakes off the ceiling behind the rotating cutter head. The boring machine stalls. Zosel, a ponderous bear of a man, lurches down from his operator's console to join the rest of the ten-man crew in clearing the rubble with picks and sledges, shovels and fingernails. Men's bodies bend to the curve of the narrow tunnel walls. Some crawl on hands and knees to scratch out waste rock and make space for steel ribs, shoring up walls and ceiling.

When the pre-cast steel ribs don't fit, it means the concave tunnel walls have "squeezed" inward, an event that drives the adrenalin and heightens the already furious pace of activity. Zosel's yellow raingear, which protects him from the cold ooze of spring water gurgling from tunnel walls and the tunnel's forty-two-degree chill, becomes instead a rubber sweatsuit. He digs out rock and pounds cold steel into the walls. One false step among moving men and heavy metal and four hundred and eighty volts incoming can kill a man, quick.

The harder the men work, the less they have to think about the isolation and ever-present danger down here, some four hundred feet beneath the hogback crest of Harry's Ridge. Instead of musing on the madness of it all, Zosel and the swing shift pound this narrow hole ever-deeper into Mother Earth. Their immediate mission is to punch it farther and faster than the last shift drove it toward Spirit Lake. That's where the great earth-serpent will break through in March, if those wimps on day shift and graveyard can keep up the pace.

~~~~

On May 17, 1980, Spirit Lake was a pristine, postcard-perfect emerald nestled only three miles north of the rounded white cap of Mount St. Helens. On the next day, May 18, that mountain cap came hurtling toward the lake with such suddenness and force that an epic splash lifted a wave eight hundred and fifty feet—twice the height of Portland's tallest building—above the original lake level.

After the settling of boulders, broken trees, pyroclastic mud and ash, the bottom of Spirit Lake lay two hundred feet higher than it had been. More importantly, the avalanche of volcanic debris had blocked the lake's outlet to the North Fork of the Toutle River. The lake now had the potential to hold three times as much water as it had previously. Its capacity increased from one hundred and sixty thousand to five hundred thousand acre-feet of water. If allowed to fill without restraint, the lake might breach its unstable debris dam and unleash a catastrophic flood down the Toutle, Cowlitz, and Columbia rivers.

Just how catastrophic? According to a U.S. Geological Survey "worst-case" scenario, a breach in the Spirit Lake embankment could launch a flow of five hundred and thirty thousand cubic feet of water per second. The numbers boggle. Imagine twenty-two times the flow of the Willamette River at Salem. The flood could carry with it 2.4 billion cubic yards of sediment and result in mud flows to a sixty-foot depth at Castle Rock and forty feet at Kelso.

So . . . What Spirit Lake needs is a drain, like the grated drain two-thirds up the side of an old-fashioned bathtub. The tunnel through Harry's Ridge will be that drain. Overflow lakewater will slip through the tunnel, drop down a back-stairs gully and rejoin the North Fork of the Toutle River downstream. It will bypass the unstable—and in places still hot—debris dam. The U.S. Army Corps of Engineers awarded a $13.5 million contract to Kiewit Construction Co. to drill the tunnel and to flush the first water through it by April 1, 1985, in time for spring runoff.

Kiewit needs to drill this hole in a hurry—get in and get out—pushing three shifts around the clock, six days a week, in some of the nastiest terrain and weather imaginable. Harry's Ridge, the objective, is under assault from two sides. In a pincers movement, ground troops punch the tunnel through from its downstream (outlet) end while the airborne Special Forces shuttle each day by helicopter and then by tugboat across the lake to the inlet portal—a fifty-foot vertical shaft protected, temporarily, by a berm of earthen lakeshore that keeps lake water out of the hole.

Lance Stwolinski, the project manager, is a ruddy, no-nonsense, every-hair-in-place Stanford-educated engineer. In mid-November, now, he is satisfied that the tunnel is progressing on schedule, half way through its eventual mile-and-a-half length. But Stwolinski is worried about the inlet portal. October snows came in heavier than projected. Work there lags behind. Yesterday a log boom broke. East winds pressed a mile-square mass of broken logs—floating on the lake and in some places forty feet deep—against the portal, blocking the tugboat's access.

"We're going to airlift barracks and a cooking crew over the ridge to the lake tonight," he says, "to cut down on shuttle time."

~~~

At midnight, Pat Zosel and the swing shift, relieved by the graveyard crew, ride the diesel train to the tunnel outlet, three-quarters of a mile back. It's been snowing. Now a bitter rain blows horizontally beneath eerie blue-green arc lights at the tunnel mouth. The crew splashes silently—raw-knuckled, grit-bearded, sweat-soaked, exhausted—onto a mud-spattered four-wheel-drive International Harvester troop truck that bounces them down the rutted access road toward base camp, four miles away. Inside the truck, the heater is up. Windows fog. The only light is the on-again, off-again orange glow of cigarette tips.

"Tough . . . shift," says a weary voice in the darkness. It's a six-word sentence.

But Zosel, the talking bear, is warming up now. "Well, sure," he says, "I don't like that tunnel-squeeze business. You get rock flaking off the ceiling into your lap. What it does is it makes you think," he says, as if thinking is the worst thing that can happen to a man driving tunnel. "Or I worry about fire in the hole, with all that electrical equipment and wiring. One time I screwed up and cut the power. All the lights and the noise went off. Man, that was like *death*.

"But like tonight," Zosel says, "it's not that dangerous when the rock flakes off in front of the machine. The soft spots behind us have been reinforced. The gut-buster tonight was our shift got slowed down."

The competition, accompanied by big pressure and rewarded with big money, drives these men and can break them. Tunnel work takes over a man's life.

~~~

On Zosel's one day off each week, he gets down the hill to his wife and three kids at 3 a.m. on Sunday to be husband and father, his head still reverberating with tunnel thunder. The barge carrying the Zosels' household goods and cars was late reaching Seattle from his last job, a hydroelectric tunnel near Kodiak, Alaska. In the meantime the family rented a place up the hill from Kelso and just recently got their furniture. "Look for the house with the U-Haul truck in the front," says Rhonda Zosel, by phone. "You can't miss it."

The house is a split-level number in a new upper-income development carved fresh out of the woods. Lawns have not yet taken root. Nor have the people, who probably won't. Rhonda Zosel, a bright-eyed former schoolteacher with short dark hair, has deep reservoirs of patience. But she does not like this moving. "Matt (her oldest, a first-grader) was ready to start long vowels at his school in Kodiak," she says. "Here in Kelso they just finished long vowels."

Rhonda is too young to know that settled people, too, have doubts. She has escaped the flat comfortable angst of being in her early thirties with three kids and enough money and of knowing exactly what's going to happen tomorrow—and the next day, and the day after that. Pat, now thirty-five, was going to be a lawyer when she met him in college. Both of them are from small-town Oregon. She's from Elkton. He is from Drain. Pat started his own gyppo logging outfit that made them a pile of money just as quickly as it went belly up in the slump of 1982. To pay off their creditors, the Zosels sold their

$158,000 house with ten acres and took off to Alaska with five suitcases, no job, two kids, and a third one on the way. It was the American Nightmare.

Rhonda's brother, with Kiewit, got Zosel hired. He worked big cranes for a while until Kiewit needed an operator for one of these tunnel-boring machines at Terror Lake, near Kodiak. Would Zosel be interested?

Sure would. "My dad was a chrome miner," he says. "I guess it was just a matter of time before I got back in the hole. The pay is good and you can see the results. It's just a good feeling," he says, "to be with men who really work." But he is aware, too, of the uncertainty, down there driving tunnel where the red clothesline of a laser beam whizzes above his left ear through the tunnel dust and the roar of his machine. That laser points the way to the end of this job and whatever comes next. Maybe another tunnel job. Maybe not.

"Yeah, he says, after pausing for reflection. "I guess you could say all miners are a little crazy."

Some men, sons of miners, have it in their genes, like an extra chromosome that makes a man nervous and jumpy when he is not underground. Zosel wonders if he really has it, if he has what it takes.

~~~~

On another day at the mountain, the troop truck drops Zosel's swing shift at base camp, a huddle of thin-walled pre-fab barracks set against the howling midnight wind on a flat-graded stretch of volcanic rubble next to Coldwater Lake. Miners file off the truck. They trudge to the shower unit, shed their grime-slaked raingear and rubber boots, and clean up for breakfast, served at 1 a.m.

Adjacent to the mess hall, the aroma of bacon and sausage penetrates to a bare-walled room with a pool table and a set of dominoes on an otherwise empty shelf. The men gather here before breakfast to shout at one another, their heads still ringing with tunnel noise. This society of the near-deaf is a rough-hewn exhibition of gristle and grit and horn, hands gnarled and fingernails outlined in black. One guy could walk into a tavern and hold up all the fingers on his right hand to order three beers.

"We've had about one accident a week," says the cheerful medic, Don Hanes. "Mostly fingers," he says. "A crushed foot. Nothing serious. Actually we've *saved* two and a half fingers on this job," he says. A helicopter delivered that miner and his ice-packed severed digits to Longview's St. John's Hospital.

John Smith, the swing-shift boss, posts an eighteen on the slate scoreboard above the pool table. Eighteen is the number of feet his crew extended the tunnel in the last eight hours. Footage is the name of the game, and eighteen is a bad score. Soft, flaking rock and tunnel-squeeze caused tonight's slowdown, and that scrawny eighteen on the board burns them. The scoreboard displays what each shift—day, swing, and graveyard—has done for the last week. And rivalry between shifts will lead a miner to question another shifter's birthright, I.Q., and sexual credentials.

"We're the best crew," says the bumptious Zosel. "We topped the board on this job. Eighty-four feet on one shift."

"Swing shift told you that?!!" says Dave Rodgers, the graveyard shift boss, later. "Ask them who cleaned up their mess," says Rodgers, outraged. "And at the end of that day, the numbers came up five feet short. Who do you think the super docked footage from? *My* shift."

"Buncha crybabies," says Zosel.

"Doesn't matter to me what graveyard does," says John Smith, gritting his teeth. He leans over the pool table for an easy corner pocket shot and miscues. He scratches. He misses everything.

The men like John Smith, twenty-eight, even though he's a boss. He is Kiewit's only salaried employee on the shift. His job is to push hourly wagers. They like him because, like most of them, he is the son of a miner. He works harder than he has to, and he hates to lose. And if a miner has eight hours on Sunday to find a loose woman in Portland, he knows to head down the hill with John Smith, a doe-eyed rogue with dark curly hair and an air of lost-in-the-city vulnerability about him. Smith can find women. Women find him.

"Tunnels are the future," says Smith. "Cities will need subways. Underground parking garages. We'll put I-5 underground." Outer space has been co-opted by post-doctorate engineers and NASA computers, and the land is all surveyed and owned. The only thing left is making space underground. Tunnels are the new American frontier. This makes no sense at all, but Smith gets away with it by speaking softly and seldom, unlike the shouters around him. When he utters a simple declarative sentence like *Tunnels are the future*, the men nod sagely and consider him deep.

Another reason Smith passes muster is that he knows the boring machine down to its last wingnut and gasket, and he gets down and dirty with the men in the hole. Social status, in the hole, is inverted. Down is up. Although an untutored observer might think Zosel, the boring-machine operator, holds a prestigious position, Zosel's rank within the tunnel is a significant notch lower than that of the miners, who grovel at the machine's periphery. The most demeaning labor is the most admired, and many of the old-timers harbor some resentment toward the tunnel-boring machining itself. In their view, the machine robs tunnel work of its drill-and-blast dignity.

"I'm not a real miner," Zosel admits between pool shots. He twists his ample face into a hopeful expression, waiting for a shift-mate to contradict him.

"Never will be," sniffs one. "You're a heavy-equipment operator."

It's as if Zosel had contracted an embarrassing social disease. A miner belongs to one of the most exclusive clubs in America today. Only three hundred or so full-time tunnel men exist on the West Coast, and they all know one another. A tunnel man calls himself a miner because his father was a miner. He likes the grubby, armpit-smelling, black-fingered, tougher-than-the-next-guy sound of this word. A miner is one mean, hard-working hombre. Miners are tougher than iron workers, a miner will tell you. Tougher than loggers.

"Some men can't do it," says John Smith. The men nod sagely. Zosel stares through the ceiling, or into his own inner space.

~~~~

There are two kinds of miners on this job. Tramp miners and locals.

Tramp miners come from Alaska and they come from New York and they come from Montana, wherever the last tunnel job was. A tramp miner's eyes glaze over when asked about their homes. "Home? Why, this is home," meaning the current camp. They have an expensive van and a trailer and two ex-wives apiece. They get down the hill to a motel and a bar on Sunday to watch the Pittsburgh Steelers and to get—slowly, steadily—plastered. They talk about that great sporting house in Kodiak where Quick-Trigger Cally earned $200 for half an hour's work and was so busy she had to take appointments. Tramp miners can bust $100,000 a year, no problem, if they want to put in the overtime. They plow through big money like an auger through butter. Tramp miners.

And then there are the locals, plucked by Kiewit from the hiring hall of a Vancouver construction-workers union for this job. A local, chances are, has a house and a wife and a voter registration card. In real life he's a carpenter or an iron worker or a locomotive operator who may or may not have seen the raw guts of a tunnel before. It's all right with a local to work this hard for twenty bucks an hour and no place to spend it, even if it does mean eating breakfast after work at 1 a.m. The locals.

"This camp's real good," says Jack Rodriguez, a local from Yakima. "They got lots of good food, clean rooms, and warm showers. Satellite TV. They make your bed every day. Take out the garbage. I got no complaints."

"On a scale of one to ten," says Dick Fillippe, a feisty tramp miner who is tearing into hotcakes and eggs, sausage, hash browns, and sweet rolls, and chugging a tall glass of cold milk to clear his speaking apparatus, "I'd give this camp, oh, say, a minus one."

"There was green mold on them sandwiches today," says one tramp.

"Four hundred channels," says another, arriving from the TV room, "and I seen that movie last Tuesday."

"I'm gonna tramp this place," vows Fillippe, alarming only the non-miner here who does not know that he simply means to leave soon, for another job in California.

Complaining is as ingrained in a miner as the inch-wide permanent indentation his hard hat leaves around his forehead. But the mood here is aggravated. These men have spent more than two months together in tight quarters, with poor mail service and no telephone and tense work and (officially) no booze. No booze, because at any moment the big siren could blow. They would have to evacuate the red zone. That slumbering monster of Mount St. Helens looms just six miles away—when the clouds open up and they can see it—like the open end of a gigantic horsecollar.

Miners are a high-strung and cantankerous lot even under normal circumstances. Here, they are at one anothers' throats. Little things become sparks near a gas main. Ignition might come when someone tracks grit into the shower stall, or a field mouse takes up residence in barracks B, or a door slams while a day-shifter is sleeping. Arguments rage over the choice of TV programs. The hard-porn channel is like the mirage of a gourmet meal to men stranded and starving in the desert. A missing Pepsi from one miner's room causes such a wild-eyed threat against the unknown perp that you'd think the bottle contains – and maybe it does -- something other than Pepsi.

Dave Bessette and Ron Weasea of the swing-shift crew arrive late for a serving in the mess hall. Weasea—a square-shouldered derrick of a man with wire-rimmed glasses and long brown hair—is called Ichabod. He looks as if he could receive MTV straight from the transmitter, without a set. Weasea stalks the serving line, rolls a sausage in its puddle of grease, and bellows that he wants a salad.

"No salad," says the cook. "It's breakfast."

The mess hall grows silent, as saloon doors in the Old West swing on their hinges. Cowards look for the back exit. The question of whether the 1 a.m. meal for swing shift would be dinner or breakfast has long since been settled by democratic means. But Weasea, here, is beyond majority rule. Any fool can see that. He'll have a salad.

Weasea, against the cook's protestations and abetted by Bessette—a smaller man, with Popeye forearms and a gold earring and the see-through blue eyes of a reformed drug addict—heads for the food-storage locker to liberate a salad.

He emerges holding up two thick frosted T-bone steaks.

"OK, then," says Weasea to the beleaguered cook. "Roast us these steaks." He plops two thick slabs of red meat on the hot grill.

"I'll get fired," says the cook, terrified.

"You won't get fired," says Weasea. He hovers with his sidekick Bessette beside the grill to supervise the cooking of steaks. It's Weasea and Bessette who will get fired for this episode, only to be forgiven and reinstated ten days later because they are, after all, good workers just blowing off steam. Heh-heh. Boys will be boys. And now the two of them retire to a table to devour more steak and eggs and hash browns in a shorter amount of time than would seem humanly possible. But then these men are not quite human. They are miners. They are the toughest, meanest, hardest-driving hombres on Earth —or under it.

The Magruders of Clatskanie

The roots of Euro-American culture spread close to the surface in Clatskanie, even closer than elsewhere in Oregon. The railroad didn't reach town until 1898. Not until 1918 did a road connect the town with Portland, inland, and with Astoria, seaward. And not for another ten years was that road paved all the way. At Hump's for breakfast I talked to a guy whose grandfather was the first to log the surrounding hills. Another's ancestors pioneered gillnet fishing, drawing nets to shore by horse. Another one's grandfather diked and drained the lowlands for farming. The Scandinavians and Scots who settled here go back only three generations.

People shape the place. The place, in turn, shapes the people. It's an evolving—not yet settled—relationship. The trees and plants are different from those Lewis and Clark recorded at riverside. The animals are different or behave differently. But the river and tide and weather are still active characters in the drama, the challenge of learning to live in balance with the land and its other living things. Oregon is a kind of test case for environmental protection, not because its people are more enlightened or farsighted but because we non-natives arrived too late to completely screw things up. Our impact has been sudden and pronounced. It's also been less thorough. Because we have a lot of nature left, the damage here is more reversible than it is on the eastern seaboard, say, or in California. And Clatskanie is like Oregon only more so.

With time, I got to know some people in town. John Lillich is a friend of Sam McKinney. When he saw a McKinney-made boat at Hump's dock, he came by to talk. He offered the use of a shower and washing machine at the Lillich house, the house with the windmills. Later, he introduced me to Margaret Magruder at the dock in front of his house. He was about to take her on a boat trip up the Clatskanie River to monitor water quality, and he invited me to go along.

Magruder heads up the Lower Columbia River Watershed Council. She is a part-time but paid coordinator of volunteers who monitor—and make improvements in—the quality of streams from Scappoose to Astoria. She also is the granddaughter of the man who more than any other shaped the place here. Richard B. Magruder built the dikes. He had big dreams and the audacious idea that this huge lowland swamp near the estuary of the Columbia River could be reclaimed from spongeland to productive farms. The tight symmetry of it—from Grandfather the Changer to Granddaughter the Preserver—sparked my curiosity.

Margaret Magruder is a cheerful, short fifty-something lamb rancher with a round face and glasses, a mop of curly dark hair, and a self-effacing sense of humor. To Lillich's boat, a sixteen-foot runabout with an outboard Johnson, Magruder wore a red down jacket, jeans, and rubber boots. She blanched when Lillich introduced me as a distinguished visitor from Al Gore's team, here to observe stream monitoring. She was jumpy, too, about where to be in the boat. "Where should I stand?" she asked. Magruder was not a boat person.

Just sit down.

"Ah," she said, and she sat as if shot.

We took off upstream. I said I was not with the government. Just a writer, curious about how things work on the river. This struck her as even more nerve-wracking. I thought she might hyperventilate before we came to the first stream-monitoring station. Turns out she had given up cigarettes a week or so ago, but I didn't know that.

Lillich cut the motor. We drifted in toward a pillar beneath the highway bridge, and Magruder pulled from her jacket a spiral notebook and pen to note the readings. Stream monitoring is about water temperature. The colder the better for steelhead and salmon. No factories or mills lie upstream from town, but logging and farming expose the water to more direct sunlight because there are fewer trees along the banks. Magruder pulled a temperature gauge from the water. "We're reading 14.3 [degrees Celsius]," she said. That's well on the healthy side of her charts from state biologists. The readings will help determine which streams are most damaged and which can be gainfully repaired.

Lillich gunned the motor and powered upstream, beyond the tidal slackwater. The Clatskanie River began to look more like a mountain stream. Kingfishers fled before the speeding boat. The water sprang from dark woods and swirled into deep pools, where we checked more gauges. The Clatskanie is barely a river, if you ask me, but it's big for a creek.

Zipping back toward town, we saw how a recent flood had cut away a good twenty feet of bank from a trailer park. The next flood threatens to make an oxbow of that community, cutting it off from the road to town. And again, in town, an undercut threatens the bend around the library. If left to its own prowling, a river is a bank-shifting, organic thing, but for eighty years, rip-rap and pilings have solidified the banks through downtown, where the river makes an S. The flood of 1996 barreled out of the canyon and arrowed straight through town and made a dollar sign of the S. Water topped the barstools at the Conestoga Tavern. Now the riverbanks need shoring up. That's always been done with boulders and piling. Margaret's watchdog group will have to mediate between locals who favor such "hard-point shoring" and the Oregon Department of Fish and Wildlife, which favors willows and natural vegetation.

By the time we returned to Lillich's dock, Magruder was exhaling regularly. I hoped we could talk about her grandfather, the land-shaping R. B. Magruder. Could she join me for dinner that evening at Hump's?

She blanched again. She stared into the middle distance. "I can't remember," she said, "the last time I was asked out."

~~~

Margaret has no memory of her grandfather. He died in 1930, long before she was born. But she arrived at Hump's that evening with a packet of yellowing news clips and loose photos about the making of Clatskanie. Before our orders came, she thumbed through the packet and showed me an article from the *Clatskanie Chief*, written in 1942. R. B. Magruder, I read, *did more to put Clatskanie on the map than any other man before or since. He was small of stature, but great of courage and vision. Can't you just see him smiling as he approached you? He wore diamonds that sparkled like his dynamic personality. He saw flowers in those mosquito-infested swamps.*"

"Maybe he wore a diamond tie clasp," Margaret said, "but he was from a poor Quaker family and sold pens."

She shuffled through more news clips and picked at her salad when it came.

Born in Sandy Springs, Maryland, Richard Brooke Magruder was a salesman who headed west and saw the reclamation of lowlands along the Sacramento River before he got to Portland in 1900. He sold cable to loggers. Trooping up and down the Columbia, he saw the potential of all this land lying fallow, the accumulation of centuries of rich soil deposited by the Columbia River.

In 1905 he quit sales and brought to Clatskanie a load of self-confidence and three big ideas. He would (1) use other people's money to (2) dike and drain the tidal lowlands, and (3) market this place as "the New Holland." In twenty years he snatched from the river 14,500 acres—more than the acreage of Manhattan—of swamp. He changed forever the equation between people and nature.

After dinner, Margaret left me with the packet of news clips and a pair of publicity brochures—one by her grandfather and another by the Clatskanie Chamber of Commerce. I took them to the boat and read until dark.

First, R. B. Magruder went after the financial backing. A photo shows him with a clutch of San Francisco investors, in Clatskanie to look for themselves. He's a smug little fellow wearing a felt hat and boots. Investors, in city shoes, tower over him. These dandies took options on Columbia River bottomland between Clatskanie and the river. With blueprints in hand, Magruder was hosting their lunch when news of the San Francisco earthquake and fire, 1906, hit town. The investors scuttled home to find their businesses burned. Options expired. Magruder had to start over. This time a pair of local big shots—lumberman E. S. Collins and tug boss J. P. Brix—came on board.

Having secured other people's money, he went to work on the second of his three big ideas. Dredge and drain. In 1910 Magruder shipped a pair of barge-mounted long-boom clamshell dredges from the Sacramento Valley up the coast and across the Columbia River Bar. The dredges deepened sloughs and dug new ones. The excavated material formed dikes that rose seventeen feet from the mean low-water mark, three feet higher than the highest known flood, of 1894. The tops of the dikes were wide enough for wagon roads.

"You'll have fifty miles of the best-drained roads in the state," Magruder wrote, in a paper delivered to the Oregon Irrigation Congress in 1913. He'd been at it three years and built thirteen miles of riverside levee. "River boats will navigate to the very door of the farmer." he crowed. Drainage districts, administered by property owners, would manage the upkeep of levies, drainage system, and pumps.

Marketing had begun with his pitch to investors. Now he had to sell the project to immigrants. Come one, come all, you farmers and dairymen.

His 1917 publicity brochure for Columbia Delta Gardens promises, "When you cultivate, it is so easy that the 'sweat of your brow' never runs." A farmer will find five vertical feet of amazingly rich soil. He can expect an irrigation system and pumps that in emergencies can empty out every canal in one-two-three order. He'll raise "perpetual crops, in or out of season." The only mention of rain is that the precipitation is warm in winter. Rail and steamship lines will compete to lower transportation costs, as they have on the Mississippi and the Nile deltas. But the Columbia delta is not *too* much like those places. There is no malaria in these lowlands. Columbia Delta Gardens is the return to Eden.

Plenty of farmers and dairymen bought the pitch. In 1924 Clatskanie had a population of fifteen hundred, about the same as today, with four hundred more families on rural mail routes. Fraternal lodges included the Masons, Elks, Odd Fellows, and Eagles. The town had two banks, three hotels, three mercantile stores, two ladies' furnishings stores, four restaurants, a moving-picture house, and a newspaper.

~~~~~

Today Margaret Magruder sits on the Oregon State Board of Agriculture, as did her mother and brother before her. Her business card reads Oregon Lamb Company—a highfalutin' tag for a one-woman farm nine miles downstream from Clatskankie, off Highway 30. She has a big sheep barn and a one-story house and outbuildings at the south edge of her grandfather's reclamation project. Magruder has been away and come back. After graduating from Willamette University, in Salem, she lit out for graduate school at Syracuse University wearing a beaver coat cut to jacket length.

"I was on track to be a college professor, to teach Russian," she said, over lunch another day at Hump's. "But the closer I got, the less I liked it. They were all theory. City people don't have a sense of ownership, or belonging. I was living in an apartment. I missed the land. And somebody broke in and stole my beaver jacket."

She catches herself. She pauses. "Am I sounding too much like a literary heroine?"

Magruder is highly regarded in Clatskanie, not just because she's a smart cookie and came home. She's also had a string of bad luck that would turn Pollyanna sour. Her brother died at age thirty-one in a tractor accident. Her marriage fell apart soon after that. Her house burned down. These are endearing credentials in Clatskanie for a big-hearted lamb rancher with mud on her boots and a baffled smile, scratching out an honest living from the place. And so when this part-time job popped open at the watershed council, who better than Margaret Magruder to represent local interests? She would sooner be roasted over hot coals than be called an environmentalist. Magruder understands her job as defensive. Now that the idea of removing some upriver dams is fathomable, removing dikes could be next. She'll rally local energy toward the repair of streams, but let's do it with common sense, for Pete's sake. Let's not wipe out a way of life.

After lunch she drove me to the farm in her blue Dodge Ram 1500 pickup, its straw-strewn bed encrusted with mud. This would have been only a ten-minute drive on Highway 30, but Margaret veered out onto a dike road for a look at the New Holland. The dikes had held, through the big floods of 1948 and 1964 and 1996, but there was no sign of prosperous vegetable farms. Cows and horses grazed on the flat grasslands, and much of the terrain was given over to big corporate hybrid-cottonwood spreads. "Columbia Delta Gardens" it was not.

At first there was plain bad timing, Magurder explained. On the heels of her grandfather's project came the Crash of 1929, and then the Great Depression. Bankers pulled out their money. Portland customers had none to spend. Then gas engines and highways trumped the plan for steam ships to the doorstep of family farms. Portlanders got their milk and vegetables from the closer and just-as-fertile Willamette Valley. Worse still, the reclaimed delta lowlands proved devilishly hard to farm. Boggy soil caught and held horses, buried plows, and swallowed tractors to the axles. A farmer got his seeds in the ground too late, or failed to harvest the results on rain-soaked fields.

"Today we grow grass and trees," Margaret said, as she sped across the dikes. "Things you don't have to replant every year."

She stopped the pickup. We got out where a dike road cut across—rather than paralleled—a former slough. Magruder's river council has proposed opening up the berm between Westport Slough and Beaver Slough. A huge culvert through the dike would convert sickly yellow slackwater into a working tidal waterway. "We're working on it," she said. "Remove this berm, and it will open up migration routes for salmon and steelhead."

We drove on, past a pumping station that comes alive only in flood season, and left the dike road for Highway 30 to her house. We bumped across the train tracks and bridged a ditch to her house and were met by a yelping clutter of young sheep dogs. Margaret's son Mac—home this summer from college—came striding from the sheep barn to see what was up. Mac had a firm handshake and the mischievous Magruder grin. But unlike his mom and granddad, he's tall and thin. The only bulge between his boots and cowboy hat is a round packet of chew in a rear pocket of his Wranglers.

Mac joined us at the house, a one-story red new home with a deck on stilts overlooking wide pastures and distant cottonwood plantations. Margaret once owned three thousand acres of diked farmland here. She couldn't keep up with the work or the debt. She sold most of it to Crown Zellerbach for wood-pulp plantations and kept seventy-five acres for raising sheep. We sat on the deck with a beer and talked about what it was to live at the edge of the wild.

It's a constant battle, is what it is. The wild keeps spilling into her lap.

Take the bald eagles, the eagles that hang out on Columbia River islands. "I've had problems with golden eagles, too," Margaret said. But bald eagles are the worst. They swoop in on a lamb, poke holes in its lungs, and leave it lying there," she said. "One year the eagles were so bad I lost forty lambs before I quit counting. I called Fish and Wildlife. I said I have to get rid of this eagle. They said, That'll be $5,000 or one year in jail. I was desperate. I said, *Come get the eagle or come get me.*

"So they came out with a net and laid it on the ground with a sick lamb for bait. They're going to trap this eagle in a net? An eagle is going to fall for that? Hah! So I kept having these lambs with punctured lungs. I'd drive out in the truck with my hammer to kill a broken lamb. I'm not good with a hammer. Mac, here, can kill a lamb with one blow."

"It's easy," he said.

"But me, I had lambs with crushed skulls, still breathing. I cried so hard I couldn't see. Some I had to strangle. It was awful. I read somewhere that if an eagle flies back to the nest with a wound, or even a feather missing, other eagles will kill it. I don't know if that's true. But it's possible, although I am a bad shot . . ."

"She's terrible with a gun," Mac said. "She closes her eyes. She flinches before she shoots."

"Oh my God," she said. "You'll write that I shot the National Bird."

Mac spat into his snuff cup. "Maybe she shot *at* an eagle. She never killed an eagle."

~~~~

Magruder selectively breeds sheep. Eagles move off the river to prey on the lambs. A cougar attacks a horse less than a mile from downtown Clatskanie. Nutria—beaver-sized, rat-tailed diggers, introduced from Louisiana—burrow into the dikes and weaken them. Beavers don't have to make lodges anymore. They, too, carve dens in the dikes. There is vector control for insects. Feral hogs have colonized Wallace Island. Ospreys nest atop transmission towers and wing dams. Salmon and steelhead, too, get human-engineered help. The view from Margaret Magruder's deck is of grasses and trees, similar to the flora Lewis and Clark would have seen here but selectively bred as crops. We get pasture and hybrid cottonwoods, massive square acres of fast-growing cellulose for paper pulp. Scotch broom and purple loosestrife and Himalayan blackberries move in. The diked and slower-moving backwaters are perfect habitat for the invasion of Eurasian milfoil and carp.

Evolution of species unfolded over unimaginable spans of time—thousands and millions of years—way too gradually to have been observed. But here we have a raging new world of species adapting, through natural and unnatural selection.

Aside from rogue eagles, coyotes and dogs are the most troublesome predators nipping at Magruder's purebred sheep. As killers, coyotes and dogs are quite different, although you might be hard put to tell the DNA of one from that of the other. "Coyotes are efficient. You'll see the slash right here," said Margaret, lifting her chin and sliding a finger across her Adam's apple. "They kill to eat. Coyotes are born to kill."

Mac said at college they showed a video about how sheep react to the threat of predation. "They bunch. They are flockers. Coyotes will pick out one sheep for attack. Maybe not the closest, but it could be the weakest. They zero in on a single sheep. Once the attack starts," he said, "coyotes will jump over other sheep to get to that chosen sheep."

"But dogs," said Margaret, "will play with a sheep, like a cat with a mouse, and leave it all messed up."

"Dogs aren't killing for food," Mac said. "They don't know what they're doing."

Before humans domesticated coyote-like animals, they no doubt strengthened the gene pool of their prey by culling the easiest of them to kill. Now humans cull the coyote population. Coyotes get wilier and wilier. Leg traps have been banned as inhumane, too cruel. The solution now, administered by a neighbor adept at coyote control, is a device called the M44, or the getter. Punch an M44 cylinder in the ground, Mac explains. It has a spring that you compress and cock. The bait lies there on the ground. A coyote disturbs the bait, triggering the cocked spring and driving a rod through a cyanide capsule and up through the roof of the coyote's mouth.

Mac is a ranch mom's dream, quick-thinking and slow-talking, polite and self-assured. By his own admission he blew off high school. But at Linn-Benton Community College he "got some partying out of the way" and buckled down to studying. He chose Oklahoma State University for its Animal Science Program. Margaret said Mac was a kid who never wanted to go to town. "He played in the creek. He shot nutria. He liked making ditches. Diverting water. It must be in the genes," she said. "I'd say *Let's go to town for this or that*, and he'd say, *Do we have to?*"

"You'll find a dead coyote within twenty steps of the getter," Mac said. "I've seen two coyote carcasses on top of each other, three strides from a pair of getters."

As we talked on the deck I noticed a llama—shaggy brown, staring witlessly from a wedge of pasture, separate from the sheep. Wait. A llama?

Magruder laughed. "The llama was supposed to bond with the sheep," she said. "He was supposed to protect them from predators. Like I said, we tried everything."

"That llama is a pervert," Mac said. "He bonded too well with the sheep. The vet said he could fix that. With surgery, he could adjust that llama's attitude."

The llama chewed sideways on river grass. Here's a high-altitude grazer, bred to carry burdens, now a guard-beast to fend off coyotes. No wonder he's confused. I suggested they breed shamas, baby lleep, and they looked away.

Mac stood up to leave. Chores waited at the barn. "You want that llama?" he said. "You can take him home."

Birdman in the City, 1987

Mike Houck inflicts terrible punishment on a brand-new silver Vanagon—just 356 miles on it, "picked it up two days ago," he says—lurching across puddled access roads and through a corridor of overgrown blackberry vines to follow the Columbia River slough past industrial alleys and under concrete pillars supporting I-5 near Portland's Jantzen Beach. The Vanagon's windows are down so Houck can listen for birds. "Whoops! Kingfisher!" he calls. His neck whips sideways. "Whoops! Meadowlark!" He slams on the brakes and unlatches his seat belt all in one motion, like Butch Cassidy unholstering a sidearm. Houck bounds from the Vanagon. The western meadowlark—the Oregon state bird—is not all that common here. Long limbs flapping, blue eyes ablaze, Houck scatters seedpods and collects burrs as he stalks a meadowlark that fortune has cast in his way. "What luck, huh!?" he says.

Easy does it, big fella.

"Did you see it?" Houck pants.

No, but I'll take your word for it.

"Outrageous," he says, breathing heavily. "A western meadowlark."

~~~

Urban Naturalist is the title at Audubon Society of Portland for this turbocharged, Lincolnesque birdman in the city. Houck, thirty-nine, carved out his own ecological niche as defender of bird habitat in the Portland metropolitan area. He's the guy who persuaded the Portland City Council to adopt the great blue heron as the city bird. Compiling wildlife inventories, monitoring the city's greenspaces, and testifying at public hearings on behalf of wordless creatures, Houck documents the dynamic give and take among the city's many species.

"Mike makes sure things don't go along quietly," says Brian Lightcap of the U.S. Army Corps of Engineers. "Without that intensity he brings to the job, urban boundaries could keep expanding without limits. No one would know. Growth can be steady, quiet, insidious."

At Portland Audubon, Houck is one of many young staffers and volunteers who share his obsession with preserving wildlife habitat. When the executive director slot came open, Houck wanted no part of it, although his knowledge of local natural history and his credentials—B.S. in zoology at Iowa State University, M.S. in biology at Portland State—made him a prime candidate.

"I'd rather run around and be crazy," he says.

In the Vanagon now he slogs around behind a golf course where luscious landscapes disavow any kinship with the nearby primordial muck. The Columbia Slough slinks quietly, covertly, past cinderblock industrial properties with crumbling asphalt and empty tractor-trailer components and—"Whoops! Yellow-breasted chat!"—used tires. A Goodrich carcass is post-modernist habitat for suckers, and a great blue heron perches atop a G.I. Joe's shopping cart.

"They don't care how it looks," says Houck. "Birds love this place."

This slough, this skid road of waterways, this turgid lazy snake of backwater that parallels the mainstream Columbia from the confluence of the Willamette and Columbia rivers, is of high interest these days to Houck. "We lost 90 percent of the habitat in these wetlands," he says, driving on. His mission is to awaken Portlanders to what remains: an important wildlife habitat near the heart of a major metro area.

Portlanders are urbanized and commercialized, but nature is the ultimate hero of life in the city. Salmon and steelhead surge through downtown. Mountains and forest rise close by, and the Pacific Ocean is within easy reach. Occasionally the people-in-nature theme will rise into real life, such as the election of a canoe-poling, duck-hunting mayor with no prior experience in elected office. The eruption of Mount St. Helens, too, gave a nice boost to Portland. Our most beautiful, most precious, and most dangerous ally here is nature. And nowhere does this theme come into more vivid focus than with Mike Houck, who feels in his bones the imaginative truth of this place.

～～～

At the wheel of the Vanagon, Houck surprises an urban squatter who has stretched a canvas-and-plastic lean-to across the trail. He's cooking a breakfast of crappies on the assumption that no one—ever—would try to drive here. Houck throws the Vanagon in reverse and turns around—"Ooh, look at these goldfinches!"—and back toward a conventional residential area. "Ash-throated flycatcher!" he says. Houck's auditory sense is so acute he's like a blind man leading a sighted person through a darkened room.

He whips his head sideways and shouts, "Whoops! Parrot!" Houck should have a volume knob to turn him down.

Parrot?

"Parrot," he says. "Somebody's got a parrot around here. You'd think we were in Nicaragua."

~~~

The Urban Naturalist has always had a crackling energy, like branching lightning. Classmates at Estacada High School were lucky to have survived association with him. In football, Houck played defensive end and fullback, the two positions for agile bruisers with the least finesse and most demolition on impact. Houck terrorized people, and not just the opposition. Howard Durand, the quarterback, recalls practices where Houck came snorting from defensive end, scattering bodies like tenpins and ending up at the bottom of the pile, face-guard to face-guard with his friend and teammate.

"It's . . . just . . . *practice*, Mike."

In track, he excelled as a miler and half-miler. Houck turned down an appointment to West Point and rode a track scholarship to Iowa State University. After picking up degrees there and at Portland State, he taught biology at Oregon Episcopal School and directed the Community Research Center at Oregon Museum of Science and Industry. But teaching never gave him the freedom to rev it up and *go*, as he can for Audubon.

When Martha Gannett, a volunteer at Audubon, answers the phone and says, "Mike's not here—he flew down to Tucson," I picture Houck winging south without a plane, skimming over Willamette Valley rooftops and soaring above redwoods and flapping into sunny Arizona to address a national bird conference. They know him in New York and Washington, D.C., too, as a leading naturalist from the left coast.

~~~

A narrow band of cottonwoods flanks the Columbia Slough, where river water leaks in from the Willamette and drains out again as tidal action flushes the slough twice daily. Houck, after dismounting from the Vanagon, stands absorbed in the evidence of a beaver-gnawed branch. In the background clacks a grain elevator's conveyor belt. Slowly, it dawns on him that nary a bird is within sound or sight.

No birds anywhere.

Houck, like an embarrassed host, begins calling birds in. He whistles and warbles and chirps, and here they come. Black-capped chickadees appear. Then a bewick's wren. A pair of mourning doves pokes through the surrounding thicket. A downy woodpecker warily checks Houck out. More wild specimens come right down and talk to him, Houck still gurgling and screeching and cooing, speaking bird.

~~~~

Beyond personal happiness, beyond the accumulation of wealth, there should come a sense that a person's time on the planet is well spent, and somehow lasting. Family, for some people, satisfies that yearning. Religion, for some.

Houck, divorced, is fairly sure his mother lives in Kentucky. His father is "somewhere in Rhode Island," and his brother died in a Boring mill accident. His bright cohorts at Audubon are family. As for religion: how should he say this? "Religion," says Houck, "is a raven cruising Kiger Gorge in the Steens. Natural history is my religion."

Houck has avoided the skin of indifference that adults of the species tend to acquire. And by temperament and grit, he could have fit right in with the Natty Bumpos and Daniel Boones who rode point in the great westward movement. Manifest destiny and an untamed wilderness gave us the American Woodsman, the archetypal frontiersmen who carved the way West. Woodsmen and dam-builders set out to tame these rivers and woods, and they mostly did.

When things got tame for Huckleberry Finn, he could strike out for the territory. Houck was born about a century too late. How could he light out for the territory? He was flat up against it. Estacada *is* the territory. The New American Frontiersman becomes the mirror image of the Deerslayer as American hero. Houck finds himself square in the path of the advancing blade of twentieth-century development and civilization. *Stop*, shouts Houck, who is too smart to think he's actually going to stop anything that has two hundred years of momentum and the cumulative weight of expansionist culture behind it, shouting *stop*, as he retreats in front of the advancing blade. If anybody hears him over the sound of the engines, maybe he can at least make the culture *slow down and think* before it plows right on past what he stands for.

A damn nuisance, is what he can be.

~~~

"I've seen Houck show up at a hearing," says Tim Hayford, "and people turn nine shades of red before he even says anything." Hayford works for Multnomah County Drainage District No. 1. His concern is to make land available, usable. Pump and drain. That's his job. "*Wetlands* has become a charged word," he says. "But that's what this area was. Two-thirds of it lay under water great periods of the year. We were clear-cutting, spraying pesticides and defoliants, using heavy equipment to drain and clear. No more. Mike makes us think things through. He'll ask, 'Why do you have to do it this way?' "

When it came time to draft the environmental impact statement for the $15.3 million Airport Way Project—a four-lane extension to the east of I-205—Houck served on the city's technical advisory committee. Others represented the Corps of Engineers, the Environmental Protection Agency, Oregon Department of Fish and Wildlife; Houck was the expert on inventories of birds and wildlife in this sensitive strip of land between the Columbia and its slough. At committee meetings, the mud on his boots testified more eloquently than if he were to scream firsthand knowledge of the territory.

Less and less does he have to wrangle. He's learned to cool the old engine, when that's what it takes. Jane McFarland, an environmental impact analyst for the city, says Houck's strength is twofold. "He knows how organizations operate, how a system is legally supposed to run. And he can mobilize support from other groups."

"I've seen Mike fly off the handle," says Lightcap, of the Corps of Engineers. "But now he knows *when* to charge."

"Maniacs can't participate," Houck concedes. "You can't let them stereotype you as a radical extremist. But compromise can be a cop-out when so little habitat is left. I've tried to cut down on the emotion," he says, "and make the arguments more persuasive. I think the whole environmental movement has turned a corner that way."

~~~

Force Lake—a pond, really, no larger than a softball field—adjoins West Delta Golf Course not far from North Marine Drive. Houck reins in the Vanagon and dismounts to watch lesser yellow-legs, a pied-billed grebe, dismembered truck parts, Michelob bottles, a lesser scaup, spotted sandpipers, coots, a half-submerged vending machine, and ruddy ducks. Beyond the pond, retirement-age golfers shuffle in slow groups. Beyond them, a magnificent stand of cottonwoods contains a heron rookery.

This scene is coherent to Houck. "Golfers and herons get along," he says. "Coyotes and weasels live here. It works."

What is not coherent to Houck is the use of this pond as a race course for remote-controlled motorboats with their ear-shattering whine. More than once Houck has run the racers off. A more permanent threat comes from plans to shoot a new road through here. The project will cost more and be less convenient for industry if it bypasses the cottonwoods.

"Highway engineers have a linear view of the world," says Houck, who lacks peripheral vision himself. When he says, "I'm for birds *and* for development," it's nonsense. In the next breath he forgets himself and refers to developers as "the Forces of Darkness." He watches a young hawk wing in on the morning light at Force Lake. "If you can save just an acre," he says, "some of these species could last another hundred years. What could be more important?"

Now that development and population growth have the upper hand and people can do with nature what they will in the Portland area, the guts have been sucked from the old people-in-nature theme. The metaphor no longer fits. Something went wrong. The titans of commerce in a nature-busting America were the Fords and Vanderbilts and J. P. Morgans, real men. Today's commerce is dominated by anonymous initials—IBM, AT&T, CBS—with lawyers and spokespersons. The cowboys dress like Indians, and the Indians dress like cowboys. Stranger things have happened. The true hero of this place called Portland might turn out to be the Audubon freak.

"If he can excite local officials about what they have right under their noses," says Claire Puchy, director of the Audubon Society of Portland, "Mike's doing his job. He's a great naturalist because he just loves it. And he never wavers."

A desk at Portland Audubon's headquarters, adjoining Forest Park, has Houck's name on it, but you'll seldom spot him there. "I don't know where he is," says Puchy, who has quick brown eyes and fine, bird-like features. "He was here a little while ago." She checks a back office. He's gone. "Mike will hear something in the sanctuary," she apologizes, "and out he'll go."

Huckleberry Houck—*Whoops! Urban Naturalist!*—has lit out for the territory again. The territory is right here in town.

Further and Beyond

Ken Kesey, 1936–2001

If the house caught fire tomorrow, the first book I'd rush to save is a dog-eared and water-stained and margin-scribbled copy of Ken Kesey's *Sometimes a Great Notion*.

It's the best big book we have. No Northwest writer before or since has outdone Kesey's massive novel, which strikes to the very soul of what it means to live here. It's a shame *Great Notion* is lesser read than Kesey's more accessible and also-great *One Flew Over the Cuckoo's Nest*. That one, along with Kesey's personal odyssey as the charismatic bull seal of the Merry Pranksters, catches the spotlight. But over here in the shadows lurks this HUGE work, a book that doesn't invite you in, a book that's better the second and third times through, a book that is wildly experimental in craft but also—surprise—good old-fashioned literature, a classic.

The better the book, of course, the harder to say what it's about. What we have here is a fine story, the saga of four generations of the Stamper Family, stubborn loggers, scrambling for a foothold on the Oregon coast. The rugged individualists are strike-breaking woodsmen, and civilization closes in. More to the point, it's a book about place. To the extent that nobility is achieved or heartbreak rendered, it happens in relation to the big-woods country and wild rivers and raw landscape that used to—and in some places still does—set the Pacific Northwest apart.

In the context of American frontier literature, Kesey's is the next best book after *Huckleberry Finn*. Huck Finn, earlier, could light out for the territory when things got tight. But in geography as well as in literature, we are smack up against it. This is the territory. There's nowhere West to go.

The best Northwest books between *Huckleberry Finn* and *Sometimes a Great Notion* are about the last wild place. They're about nature-busting. Nature is fearsome. Nature is to be brought to its knees. Heroes are the woodsmen and homesteaders and dam-builders who tamed the American Wilderness. H. L. Davis's *Honey in the Horn*, the only Northwest book to have won the Pulitzer Prize (in 1936), is a big reckless novel about a country as raw and unformed as its hero. Stewart Holbrook, in *Far Corner*, gets woods and loggers right. Nard Jones's *Swift Flows the River* stars a steamship captain on the yet-to-be-tamed Columbia River.

And so here comes Ken Kesey cruising that same deep channel with *Sometimes a Great Notion*, a book that rings with the exaggerated language, humor, and vitality of an authentic native tale. Waterways and landscapes are so central to Kesey's story-telling art that nature becomes a character, even the main character. Place is alive. Before we even meet a person we hear a watershed. Soon we get the earth sprouting malignant plants, rain rusting a barrel of nails overnight, and the river sucking at the foundation of the Stamper house. Surf laps at a car. A sand dune—yikes!—swallows Leland. A falling limb dismembers the old man. A newly felled tree pins Joe Ben under a rising tide. Nature is one tough customer.

Rich stuff, these riffs on man-against-nature. No big Oregon book could be without them. And if it were just that—if it were just "Never Give an Inch," the Stamper family motto—we'd still have a good man-vs-the-elements story. But Kesey grapples with much more than that.

Nature is also a healer in *Sometimes a Great Notion*. Nature nurtures. Nature cradles as well as assaults. Kesey understands the continuous scripture of rivers. The book opens with the hysterical crashing of tributaries merging into his fictional Wakonda Auga River. It ends on the same broad river, with Hank delivering the goods on an outgoing tide. And in between, the river not only separates the Stamper place from town but also carries the narrative line. Joe Ben's empathy for wild geese and small animals is why we care so much, why we are left breathless at his drowning. Hank's bell rings at the whisper of wind through tall firs. When things get too tight for Hank/Huck, he finds that place in the river where he can swim hard against the current and stay where he is. There's nowhere West to go.

I get goose bumps at this stuff.

It's not just me. A few years ago the *Seattle Post-Inteligencer* polled contemporary writers, asking what is the Northwest's all-time best book, fiction or not. Guess what lapped the field. No other book was close.

Kesey's genius is that he managed to bridge the chasm between what we were, as a people, and what we are. In Hank Stamper, the logger who loves the woods, an archetypal schizoid character mirrors our schizoid contemporary culture. We like to think of ourselves as the sons and daughters of pioneers, having just emerged from a clearing in the woods. But hey. Come on. After damming the rivers and scalping the woods comes the dawning realization that we can conquer and control the wild. We do so at our peril, destroying what we most love about the place. The nature-buster as literary hero gives way to characters who learn from—take their cues from—the natural world.

Northwest fiction came full circle in the last half of the twentieth century. While we once focused on how humans shape nature, we now celebrate how the land shapes us. Kesey got it both ways. He charted the course for the Norman Macleans and Molly Glosses and Craig Lesleys and David Duncans who splash in his wake and write so well about the continuing struggle for place.

Yet the seriousness of Kesey's writing is often eclipsed by his sensational capacity for real-life fun. Galling to me is Kesey's obituary, last Sunday, in *The New York Times*. Christopher Lehmann-Haupt's lengthy summary of Kesey and his work mentions *Sometimes a Great Notion* way late in the article and then only in passing, noting that some critics were annoyed by its wordiness. Along the way, Lehmann-Haupt condescends toward Tom Wolfe and the LSD-fueled movement that Kesey led, as if the whole deal were just a caper, as if no good has come from a time in America when nothing seemed impossible.

Tom Abbey, a wise friend in California, called me the other night to lament Kesey's passing and to fume about *The New York Times*. The establishment doesn't get it. "They're even taking the Sixties from us!"

The provinciality of New York publishers and critics is no surprise to those of us who toil at literature in the provinces, but Abbey has a larger point. America, not just American lit, is much the richer for those tumultuous and psychedelic years when Kesey and the Beat poets were straining at social bonds and ripping the mask off a settled and somnolent culture.

After Springfield High School and the University of Oregon, Kesey enrolled at the Stanford graduate writing program under Wallace Stegner and Malcolm Cowley, the legendary editor of William Faulkner. While there, Kesey signed up as a paid subject in drug experiments at the Veterans Hospital in Menlo Park. 1959, this was. Whoa, what's this lysergic acid diethylamide? LSD? Intrigued by the mind-bending possibilities, Kesey stayed close to the source by hiring on as a night attendant at the hospital's mental ward.

That ward became the setting for *One Flew Over the Cuckoo's Nest*. Kesey later claimed to have been stymied with the manuscript until he hit upon the brilliant and peyote-inspired notion to write the story from the point of view of Chief Bromden. Bromden, an Indian inmate who had been electro-shocked into silence, glimpses Randle McMurphy and Nurse Ratched between brief clearings of the hospital's "fog machine," and from there the darkly hilarious romp unfolds.

Right on the heels of *Cuckoo's Nest* came two years' work (just two years!) on *Sometimes a Great Notion*. A stranger all his life to moderation, Kesey was in a zone. He was a writer on fire. He had to have known how good it was, and couldn't stop. And because he couldn't stop, he busted the chains of literary convention every bit as wondrously as had James Joyce or Mark Twain before him. He gave us multiple points of view in the same paragraph. Why not? Here comes a generational time-shift, just when you think you knew where you are. What a trip. Wing it! Kesey blazed right through this book, and what we got in 1964 was the great Oregon novel.

And then . . .

And then came the elephant in the room that nobody talks much about. Kesey had accomplished all this before he was yet thirty years old. Following this frantic and inspired output came a string of forgettable books scattered over the next thirty-five years. His writing lost the old zip. For whatever reason, he never again collared the manic energy and wild brilliance that infused those first two books. To be sure, he directed that rascally energy in different directions, still jousting at convention and railing against the system. But when Kesey a couple of years ago took off in a replica of "Further"—the International Harvester school bus of Merry Prankster fame—to tour England, it was somehow sad, like Willie Mays, late in his career, stumbling about center field for the Mets.

Had he continued his writing in the same early vein, Kesey might have caught even New York's attention and become the Northwest's one-name rep in the pantheon of American lit, like Hawthorne for New England, like Faulkner for the South.

But if he had continued at the same early pace, he'd have died at thirty-six.

The title of his big book? It's from "Good Night Irene," by Huddie Ledbetter and John Lomax:

> *Sometimes I live in the country,*
> *Sometimes I live in the town;*

Sometimes I get a great notion
To jump into the river . . . an' drown.

Like I say, I get goose bumps. I can imagine Kesey's latter-day frustration at the idiots who wanted more. So, Michelangelo, when are you going to paint another ceiling? He'd done it. He'd nailed it. With *Sometimes a Great Notion*, Ken Kesey got it all.

Battle

One Saturday in Clatskanie, to stretch out, I began walking out of town along Highway 30. On the left, a crowd had gathered at the ballpark. The parking lot was full, and pickups straddled the highway shoulder. Kids were taking infield. I angled through the parking lot until a scratchy loudspeakered National Anthem brought me to a halt. Fans rose to face the American and Oregon flags in straightaway center. It was a nice little field, scaled to kids' dimensions and enclosed with a four-foot fence. Merchants' ads—Stimson Lumber, Hump's Restaurant, Hazen Hardware—filled plywood panels along the outfield fence.

The announcer, from a booth behind the backstop, read the starting lineups for Rainier—in Dodger blue and gray—and St. Helens, wearing aqua jerseys and black pants. Then she, the announcer, delivered a short speech about sportsmanship. St. Helens fans packed the wooden bleachers along the first base side, Rainier fans along third. Some sat in lawn chairs down both lines. I could have squeezed into the bleachers, but the smell of buttered popcorn drew me to the green snack booth. I nabbed a hot dog and joined a row of hefty men at the left field fence, looking in.

I hadn't meant to stay, but it was pretty good ball. The umpire—not in uniform—stood behind the pitcher and applied a sensibly generous strike zone. Pitchers threw "strikes." Batters were up there to hit, and the teams were well matched. Each squad had two or three players who knew baseball chatter and to whom this game was evidently the pinnacle of their lives so far. The Rainier shortstop charged ground balls with authority. The St. Helens centerfielder made an over-the-shoulder catch look routine.

Next to me stood a thickset blond guy working a toothpick hard. He had meaty forearms and wore red logger suspenders and might have been recently crawling under a truck.

We struck up a conversation.

"Whaddaya know?" he said.

"Not much."

After a while, when I asked, he said his kid was the Rainier third baseman.

I said no, I didn't have a kid here. I'd been out on the river and just stopped by. Turns out this was the final game of a tournament. Clatskanie, Scappoose, Astoria, and other river towns had been eliminated earlier. I had stumbled into the championship game, the 7 p.m. final, for all the marbles.

"Looks like rain," he said.

It did. A weather system had rolled in off the Pacific. Ominous gray clouds piled up like blimps against the foothills. But the first few innings went quickly, without walks. The Rainier shortstop threw out a runner from deep in the hole. A pudgy catcher's squeals of encouragement carried all the way to the outfield. I heard a raucous crow taunting the Rainier hitters—"caw! caw!"—after each swing-and-a-miss, but then it dawned on me that the right fielder was issuing a pitch-perfect mimic of avian scorn.

There were other nice touches. When the announcer misidentified a Rainier hitter, he stepped out of the batter's box, grinned up quizzically, and told her who he was.

"Sorry," she announced. "Eric Kristofersen. Number 8."

When a ball popped out of play on the first base side, it splashed down beyond yellow crime-scene tape at the high-water mark, into a blind slough. That happened often enough that a fresh white baseball was nearly always in play.

I grabbed another hot dog and returned to the fence.

After three innings, the scoreboard read Home 1, Visitors 1.

"Little League?" I asked the stout logger on my left.

"Nope. Just local."

Daniel Martinez, the Rainier second baseman and lead-off hitter, was not much taller than his bat. But his cap was squarely blocked and the bill curved just so. The sleeves of his dickey extended just beyond the jersey along his toothpick arms, and his pants cuffs dropped to his shoe tops, which is the style. Martinez had mastered the spit, the scratch of the butt, and the pawing at dirt as he set himself in the box and faced the pitcher with a malevolent glare and ripped the 0-1 pitch on a line to the third baseman's glove and ran it out anyway, as he'd been taught. I would have pegged him for the son of the coach if his coloring had been pastier.

If somewhere in his genes lurked a growth spurt, this kid would be a ballplayer. I caught myself thinking what it is to be a ballplayer, to pick up these skills that get passed on from human to human as surely as the coloring of a wood duck. I wondered. Maybe there is something adaptive about hitting a baseball, an act that maybe a long time ago was related to athleticism in the capture of food, rewarding the best eyesight, the most precise firing of synapses to trigger muscle spasms that results, today, in the ability to strike a sphere with a cylindrical club so that it flies away in a straight line. Hitting a baseball is a wondrous skill with no adaptive utility. Except. Except maybe a Daniel Martinez's mastery of it captures the attention of his coaches and me, and might give rise to admiration in his community that could boost whatever his social niche might otherwise have been. It might even be more likely that Daniel Martinez, like the wood duck, will be more sexually attractive, when it comes time for that, to the girl of his choice.

But Daniel Martinez, unlike the wood duck, *learned* what sets him apart. I'd wager that his dad played ball. It's in the family. We teach our kids.

~~~~

My own daughter, raised in France, missed out on baseball. By the time we got back to America and I set out to right this cultural wrong, Heidi threw, as they say, like a girl. The mistake was mine. I never taught little Heidi to throw a ball. And by age ten, she had no interest in throwing. But on a much later camping trip, up the Clackamas River, Howard Durand and I taught adult Heidi to throw an axe. She took to it. Within an hour she had the wind-up, the release, and the follow-through. She could whip that double-bladed axe over her shoulder, blades-over-handle, and stick it—thunk—into a tree. We had to knock it off before destroying the tree, but she learned to throw. Heidi may be the only fine artist in all of New York City who can bury an axe in a tree at twelve paces.

I won't guess what's adaptive about that, but it just goes to show you.

Where am I?

I am thinking nature and nurture. I am watching riverpeople pit their offspring against one another in battle.

~~~~

By the time the first Euro-Americans reached the lower Columbia, native people had evolved a wonderfully civilized way of pitting their warriors against one another in canoes. Village versus village, the Chinookans settled disputes—a contested fishing site here, a wrongful liaison there—with an athletic display that had all the trappings of naval warfare except the killing. A favored site for these mock battles was right out here upstream from Wallace Island, where the Columbia widens and there's a bleacher-like pitch to the beach.

Author Rick Rubin, in *Naked Against the Rain*, sifts through written accounts that have come down to us about native "combat." The first riverpeople could muster a force of three hundred warriors in forty canoes, each half the circumference of a western red cedar and up to thirty feet long. A canoe could hold a dozen men, sitting in pairs from front to back. Armed with bows, the warriors favored a two-part arrow with a main shaft of light cedar and a fore shaft of hard yew, tipped with a stone arrowhead. Brightly painted shields could stop an arrow. Warriors protected their chests and torsos with parallel wooden slats bound together. They had leather helmets. A defensive maneuver was to tip the canoe away from hostile forces. Attackers were shielded by the high gunnel, while others paddled on the low side.

Alexander Henry wrote about seeing a battle at Nayagogo ("Where There are Blows," now St. Helens) where the headman of the home forces "opened fire at long range without intending to kill anybody, as in that case they might rush in and fight at close quarters." You'd have more bluff and guile than bloodshed, more spectacle than loss of life. There was little risk of sacked villages or burned lodges. No. As in baseball, the action seldom progressed as far as hand-to-hand combat. It was a display of physical prowess that would have, if not for the rules of engagement, led to mayhem.

~~~~

A woman approached the ballpark fence with a Ziploc bag bulging with coins and one-dollar bills. She sold me a ticket to the "half-and-half." There will be a drawing, she explained. The winning ticket gets half the pot. The other half pays for baseballs lost to the slough.

~~~~

Contemporary riverpeople draw a field of play into a riverside clearing and follow the rules, fair or foul. Little ones learn codified competition and limited aggression. No one gets killed. Teamwork and fair play are one thing, but baseball is also an individual game, broken down to small units of pitcher against hitter. Quintessentially American, fundamentally capitalist, baseball makes a hitter stand in there against a scary opponent hurling heat, even if he's quaking in his cleats. Bluff and guile vie with speed and coordination and strength as twelve-year-old kids in the lee of 250-year-old trees go about the national pastime without even knowing how we shape and protect them.

Baseball shaped my own family. Born to a life in the woods, Dad and his five brothers grew up in a gyppo logging family where the old man moved from rivertown to rivertown, from White Salmon to St. Helens during the Depression, in search of the next working sawmill. When there was no work at all, Uncle Pat finagled a fifth year of high school to play baseball with my dad, his younger brother. The shortstop and second baseman, they parlayed baseball into college degrees at Oregon Normal School, in Monmouth. Summers they worked at the mill and starred for the St. Helens Papermakers, the local horsehide nine. Pat and Bob became teachers and coaches. Baseball got Dad out of the woods. Baseball got him not just educated but also interested in learning.

For me, too, baseball opened up a world I would not otherwise have known. My baseball skills caught the eye of Portland alumni recruiting for Yale. I would have gone to college somewhere. But Yale? Once there, baseball was the one thing I could do better than others. It nurtured the friendships and defined the limitations a young man comes to understand. Bluff and guile don't compensate for a lack of speed and size, but baseball helps explain why I am standing here at the outfield fence thinking about nature and nurture.

～～～

In the parking lot a small child stepped again and again with great purpose into a mud puddle. Near the snack booth, two boys improvised a see-saw with a plank over a fifty-gallon drum.

On the field, players busily acted out time-honored rituals and conventions. They practiced baseball chatter—"humm babe," "two down," "can of corn"—a language all its own.

Another foul ball sailed toward the slough. Little kids chased after it. The announcer—a young Nurse Ratched—barked, "KIDS!!! Don't go past the yellow tape!"

～～～

Beavers do that. Beavers guard their young.

At Hideaway Slough, a beaver cruises past *The Turtle* shortly before sun-up, and again after sundown. Every day, the same routine. One morning this beaver was accompanied on her (or his) rounds by a young one. First time out in the world? The kit spied the boat and came swimming straight toward me. Mom caught up with the curious little one and nipped at his side, heading him off from what could only, to her, be an encounter to be avoided. Mom, after all, was a beaver whose ancestors never got skinned before producing more beavers. Fear of hairless creatures is not wired in. It's taught. A beaver's survival strategy is to have only one or two kits, and *watch those kits*.

Beavers make their way in the world like we do, damming waterways, building shelter, and nurturing their young. It's an uncommon strategy among life forms. On the other end of the nature-to-nurture scale, we have Pacific salmon and mosquitoes and fir trees and yeast and such who are all nature, no nurture. They never know their parents.

What gets me is the variety—the range—of strategies for life on Earth. I looked at the big dad on my left, watching the ball game. If I'd told him I appreciate his work for the species, he'd have fled in alarm. But you know what I mean. There's a lot to be said for parents and grandparents.

~~~~~

Bottom of the seventh. Home 1, Visitors 1.

After a close play at the plate—"OUT!!"—yelps and groans arose from the St. Helens side, but there was no sustained agony over a play that could have ended the game. Nobody yelled at the umpire. Only once, all game, had a coach raised his voice in frustration at a ballplayer. What's going on here? These people seem to understand that it's just kids. It's just baseball.

~~~~~

The visitors, in Rubin's account of Indian battle, lodged with their enemy or camped down the beach. Warriors painted themselves black, red, and yellow and devoted the evening prior to battle to whooping and dancing, chanting and hurling insults from camp to camp. But the battle itself usually ended before anyone got hurt. In even the most grievous feuds, hostilities ceased as soon as a warrior of both parties had been killed. Always, at the conclusion, came the exchange of presents. If the naval battle hadn't ended in a victory, peace could be secured by marrying a woman to a man of the other village.

What we know about the first riverpeople makes them seem so sanely moderate, so reluctantly fierce. Native culture on the lower Columbia went into eclipse without a fight. East of the Cascades, in the dry country, whites mobilized a territorial militia to put down an Indian uprising in the wake of the Whitman Massacre, and the Cayuse waged bloody guerilla fights before succumbing to the Treaty of 1855. Chief Joseph the younger famously resisted as late as the 1870s. But here on the lower river—as in most of the wet country of the Pacific Northwest—the Indians were here and then they were gone.

Were they less resistant than dry-country natives to exotic diseases introduced by the newcomers? Or was there something in their culture that led to passivity? Maybe it had to do with their not needing a lot of territory to sustain themselves before the visitors took over. The Plains Indians had to band together into tribes and defend their territory. Here on the lower river, a living came to the people. They didn't have to roam far for their salmon and berries and roots and venison. Their social groups more closely resembled clans than tribes.

~~~~

Daniel Martinez had hit the ball hard but right at somebody three times. He was oh for three, with a walk. But that's baseball. That's life. As they played on, it began raining. Some fans opened umbrellas. Others went to the parking lot and came back wearing rain slickers. Still others sat or stood in the warm rain and, like me, got slowly soaked.

After two extra innings, the game was still undecided. One to one.

A chip truck on Highway 30 honked in support of who knows which team, or just at the wet shiny world of it. A surprise, when I looked up, was that the traffic had headlights on. Dusk had crept over the hill without my noticing it. But the game kept going. Out on the river, the beavers would be making their evening rounds. In Portland, the game would be called for lack of visibility. These boys played on.

In the top of the tenth, St. Helens scored two runs. The St. Helens fans whooped and pumped their umbrellas up and down. Now the game *couldn't* be called. Rainier had to bat in their half of the inning, or you'd have to declare it a tie.

Bottom of the tenth. The St. Helens pitcher's arm was shot. He'd gone all the way. Now he gave up two walks and an infield single. I could barely make out the ball, in the darkness, and I hoped these kids had better eyesight than mine. One of them did. Daniel Martinez cracked a single to center that took a dog-leg hop past the lunging outfielder. His three-run walk-off double won the game, 4 to 3.

There was pandemonium in the Rainier bleachers, but only comic resignation on the other side. "Those walks will kill you," said a mock-anguished St. Helens fan, as parents folded up their umbrellas and gathered their offspring and drove away, up the river.

One More Word Outta You and . . . You're Gone!

In the Portland Baseball Umpires Association we had a good young ump, Brad Lehrer. We older guys thought Brad could make it big. He could be a professional umpire. Brad had a barrel chest and a square jaw and a command voice. He never lost concentration like some of us during a game. He ironed his shirts and polished his shoes and barked his calls and stood his ground like a Douglas fir. Brad had played ball all his life and read the rulebook like some people memorize the Qur'an.

We encouraged him. "You should go to umpire school, Brad. You could make a living at this."

Tell you the truth, it's something I'd fantasized about, myself. Shoulda. Coulda. Why didn't I go to ump school instead of taking that master's degree? By now I could be out there working three hours a day for big bucks and per diem. I'd travel to storied ballparks. Rub mud into major league horsehide before the game. Make that big call at the plate and the replay on the big screen would show I was right.

If I'd only known there *was* an umpire school.

Well, there is. And Brad Lehrer took us up on it. In the off season he attended the Harry Wendelstedt School for Umpires, in Ormond Beach, Florida. Every ump in our PBUA, which officiates amateur baseball from junior high through college games in the Portland area and beyond, was pulling for our Brad.

When he got back, we were all over him. *How'd it go, Brad?*

"I didn't make it."

How can that be? What the hell are they looking for?

"I messed up the written tests."

No way. The rules?

"No, I aced the rules. And I did fine on mechanics. I did great. But they have this psychological test. An intelligence test. I scored too high on it."

I thought Brad was putting us on. But no. He explained that a prospective umpire can be too attentive to nuances. He can think too much. See it. Call it. They don't want deep reasoning, let alone second thoughts, at ump school. Brad was too smart to be a professional umpire.

That's my excuse, too, when I stink up a high-school game. But the Harry Wendelstedt School is onto something. A good umpire is a special kind of smart. He makes a snap decision and knows in his bones that what he saw and what he called was right. He doesn't weigh the options. No hesitation. No reconsideration. Forget that, even umping high-school ball. Especially in high-school ball. Fans and coaches are so close to the field they just talk to you. *You're missing a good game, Blue.* I had rabbit ears. It's called rabbit ears, but how can you not hear them? *That pitch wasn't low!* You think maybe they're right. A liberal education is of no use. A make-up call will be recognized for what it is.

Umping was harder than I'd thought it would be. I don't have a barrel chest. I don't have a command voice, or even a command personality. Don't tell anybody, but I practiced my strike call at home, in front of the mirror. It involves getting your chin right. I had to lower my voice an octave and boost the volume. You have to muster up the confidence—no, the arrogance—to take the field like you own it. I didn't have a lot of flint in me.

Is that Norman Bates?! Hey, Blue. I saw you in "Psycho."

And because I'd played a lot of ball, I had to unlearn some things. A hitter has to commit early on a pitch. He'll get fooled by a good pitcher. The umpire has time to sit on it for a beat. See it all the way into the catcher's glove before making the call. Same thing on the base paths. Let the dust clear. It's not what you *thought* should happen but what actually did.

I don't know. Am I boring you? But it became unreasonably important to me to be a good umpire. And it took a while.

I did have advantages. For one thing, I had no job. The PBUA Commissioner could put me on a game anywhere, any time, on a moment's notice. High-school games start at 3:30 or 4:00 on weekdays, and it's hard for the commissioner, Al Parent, to find enough capable sober men free at that time of day. When the rainouts and make-up games start piling up, Al has to cover a 2 p.m. doubleheader, say, or a 3:30 start at Hood River. Not even teachers can get there. I could get there. I often partnered with a waiter or a night watchman or a burglar out on parole, whoever Al could scrape up.

Another advantage was I know the rulebook. I always did, even when playing and coaching. The baseball rulebook—you should read it, really—is as good as Goren on bridge. PBUA umps could ask me about almost any situation. You might think all the umps know the rules. You'd think all umps can read. But I stood out. I was an odd duck, in this regard. My first year in the PBUA was not even complete when, at a meeting for nomination of officers, an ump stood up and said, "For Secretary? How about Cody. He can spell."

I liked these guys' company. After a ball game I'd go for a brew at The Ship and listen to baseball stories: Ring Lardnerish yarns, but true. The owner of The Ship was our PBUA Commissioner, Al Parent, and some of the best of the stories were told by Al or told about Al.

~~~~

Al Parent is the umpire, behind the plate at West Linn. This is a night game, an American Legion game, back when the lights at West Linn were like flashlights on telephone poles. Bruce Williams, who later signed with the Milwaulkee Brewers, is pitching blurry little pellets of white-hot hard stuff. Pro scouts are timing the kid's pitches with a radar gun. Ninety-plus. Al is a little guy, stocky, all torso, with stubby arms and legs, and he stands back there ankle deep in dust like a forward-leaning fire hydrant, peering past the catcher. Two outs, seventh inning. One out to go, and Al is thinking cold beer. Miller Time. Let's get this over with.

Here comes a pitch, pecker-high and rising over the inside corner. The ball deflects off the catcher's glove and smacks Al in the throat, between the mask and his collar bone. It lodges there (!) and drives him to the backstop.

Al lies in a heap, wondering if he will ever swallow again. He is making plans to get some air into him when the West Linn catcher—a red-headed bruiser, Al remembers him well—leans over him and extracts the ball. "Come on, Ump," the kid pleads. "Just one more out. We gotta finish this thing."

~~~~

Al Parent grew up in Portland's Multnomah district. A squat high-energy dirtball, he was dumb and eager enough to be the catcher. But he could hit with power and run fast, too, and when they saw him throwing the ball back to the pitcher harder than the pitcher had delivered it, Al became the pitcher. In defiance of the laws of physics, this stubby little guy could throw the ball *past* people. Al could hum it.

He worked at odd jobs to pay his own tuition at Columbia Prep, the Catholic high school that dominated city athletics in the late 1940s, early '50s.

Even while in high school he played semi-pro ball in Portland. Al graduated number thirty-one in his class of thirty-two at Columbia Prep and won the Outstanding Athlete Award, a Parker 51 fountain pen and pencil set. The Navy, next, was just another baseball league. Anti-submarine warfare meant pitching a one-hitter in Morocco or playing a midnight doubleheader in Iceland. After the service Al came back to Portland State, where he relied on his fastball more than a Parker 51 fountain pen.

Baseball can be a metaphor for life. To Al Parent, life is a metaphor for baseball.

"Baseball, Al Parent," he answers his phone at home, a big green ramshackle house off Barbur Boulevard that serves as the PBUA headquarters. The voice is gruff, gravelly, a what-the-hell-do-YOU-want kind of voice that scares mild coaches and rookie umps. On the phone Al sounds like a man six-foot-six, bearded, who lost a leg in a logging accident.

Al in his baseball war room works three phones at once when the fields outside are wet. His umps need to know which games are still on. A chaw of Red Man tobacco bulges from Al's lower lip. He lifts a Blitz Weinhard bottle from his cluttered desk to spit into it—yecch—a brown slurry of used juice. He checks the whiteboard above his desk for games completed, rained out, rescheduled. I'm here with Al, on stand-by, because my game has been cancelled. He might need me where a field is playable and they're short an umpire. Al knows I don't mind working a JV game alone if it comes to that. I need the money.

He's on the phone now with an athletic director. Al is pissed. "NOW you tell me," he says. He slams down that phone and makes another couple of calls. The trouble is, they've switched the Oregon City-Putnam game to Hood River. Fields are soaked on this side of the Cascades. Hood River will be dry, but Al can't get ahold of Masa Miyaki, the plate ump. "Getcher ass to Hood River," he says to me. "Plate. Game starts as soon as you get there."

〜〜〜

"Saturday doubleheader at Tillamook," says Al to me on the phone. "Rainier at Tillamook. Can you go?"

Can I go? Is he serious? Al knows I love to put Portland in the rearview mirror and haul up into the Coast Range and wind down the Wilson River

Highway and out onto the spongy green cowpasture flats of Tillamook. The Tillamook Cheesemakers have a field you've never seen the likes of. It's all grass, except for sliding pits of sand at second and third, and circles at the mound and plate. The ball comes from the pitcher's hand out of a backdrop of deep green firs. On a sunny day in May you get a salty sea breeze with a hint of sweet cow manure, and there is no bluer sky or greener turf at a baseball field anywhere in America than in Tillamook, Oregon.

Can I go? he asks. Does a bear shit in the woods?

Big jolly crowds pack the bleachers behind Tillamook High School, and pickups nose into the fence down the first base line. Dairy farmers sit in their trucks and listen to the radio as they watch the game through the windshield and honk for great plays. Yes, high-school baseball here is on the radio. The announcer sits in an elevated booth just behind the umpire, so close you can hear him comment on your work. *That pitch was outside, but Cody rang him up. That's all for the Cheesemakers in the bottom of the . . .*

Baseball fans everywhere think close calls go against them. But it's different here. These folks *know* life is unfair. People who can't accept bad breaks left Tillamook a long time ago. The downtown area is knee deep in Tillamook Bay every third or fourth year. Mud slides can close the Wilson River Highway for weeks at a time. Cows get stuck in the muck. A fishing boat capsizes at the bar. The most devastating forest fire in Oregon's written history was the Tillamook Burn. Tillamook's first white man lived in a tree. Really. Early settlers had to build a ship to deliver their butter to market. Life is hard in Tillamook. Dairy farmers and fisherfolk don't expect any breaks.

The Cheesemakers' coach, Randy Schild, is also a math teacher. He's a stickler for baseball mechanics and player behavior. He beefs. His ballplayers don't. Schild's wife keeps the official score in the dugout. His kid—the batboy, in uniform—brings the plate ump dry baseballs. It's a time warp. I was the batboy when my dad coached the big kids. In those days, bats broke. Louisville Sluggers were made of clear-grained Vermont ash. With tiny nails and adhesive tape, I fixed cracked bats and kept them. I could choke up on a Ted Williams 34 and hit rocks into the river until the barrel splintered. Boy. When I got old enough, Dad coached Babe Ruth ball. My sister Mary Jane kept score.

But anyway, the Tillamook trip is a good payday. In the 1980s you'd get $28 for a varsity game, maybe $45 for a doubleheader, I forget exactly. Plus mileage for the ump who drives. Because I had some seniority by that time, I'd pick up my partner and drive my Honda Civic to the coast. And in Tillamook, something always happens. Think you know baseball, do you? Think you've seen it all?

I was on the bases in the second half of a doubleheader when Ed Hessler—or was it his brother, Carl?—kicked the home team scorekeeper—the coach's wife—out of the game for calling him a walrus.

Or this. I was on the bases again. Rick Lattell, an excellent umpire, had the plate. I had *told* him—we drove there together—Rick, this is not the Metro League. You can loosen up your strike zone here. But in Tillamook he called strikes like you see on TV, knees to the belly button. This is my strike zone and I'm sticking with it. Coaches were O.K. with that. The radio announcer, right behind Rick, wasn't. I was at first and could hear this on a pickup radio. *Ball two, he says. Whoa. I don't know where* that *pitch was*. Rick got hot back there. You can't adjust an established strike zone without getting into even deeper weeds. With runners on base I had to move away from the pickup radio and didn't hear what finally set Rick off. But he tore off his mask and wheeled on the broadcast booth and threw the announcer (!) out of the game.

Somewhere else you'd get wonderment, at least, about where in the book does it say the umpire can boot the radio announcer. But here the fans so honkingly appreciated the scene that the decision stood. The game continued while another guy climbed up to the sound booth.

Can I go to Tillamook? You know me, Al. Who's my partner?

"Game time is two o'clock," he says. "Come to the house here at noon. I'll drive."

~~~

Baseball umpires are an aggrieved subspecies of *Homo sapiens*. It's only natural that when we gather among ourselves we remember the times we had to throw a coach out of the game. Nobody remembers his good games. And it's not always the umpire's fault when a game goes bad. All it takes is a questionable call early in the game—not a bad call, but maybe a close one dispatched with a hint of indecision—and an umpire's day is shot. Coaches and players then start looking for confirmation that this umpire is incompetent, a dimwit, a fool. Fans get on him. An ump hears the carping, and his effort to remain impartial gets mixed in with his need to show he is not intimidated. From there, things get worse.

Al remembers a game at Lakeridge High School, where Coach Royce McDaniel was a gifted umpire-baiter. Maybe Al did have a little trouble that day finding his rhythm on balls and strikes. In the second inning, McDaniel charged the plate and had it out with Al.

"Where the hell is your strike zone?" McDaniel screams, for all to hear.

"Wherever the hell I decide to put it!" says Al.

When McDaniel says the magic word, Al banishes him from the field, which is just and proper in baseball. McDaniel watches the rest of the game from the woods off third base. Al can see the heat rising off him out there like a potato baking. When the game is over, it's time for the umpires to get paid by the home team coach. That's how it was done in those days. The base umpire, Al's partner, says, "Don't worry about it, Al. You go to the car. I'll pick up both our checks."

"He won't give you my check," says Al.

"Sure he will," his partner says. "Don't worry about it."

Al goes to the car to peel off his shin guards and chest protector. He slips on a dry T-shirt, thinking cold beer. This Bud's for You. And here comes his partner, walking back from McDaniel, who is still in the woods, steaming.

"He wouldn't give me your check."

Al trudges through the parking lot toward the woods and McDaniel. Al knows what will happen. When he reaches for the check, McDaniel will drop it. He'll let it flutter to the ground. Al will have to stoop and pick it up. If McDaniel does this, Al's going to deck him. A left to the mid-section, a right cross to the beet-red face. Al doesn't care if he never works another game in his life. But maybe some self-preservation mechanism has clicked in McDaniel's cranium. Or maybe all he wanted in the first place was a quiet way to apologize face to face. After discussion about stupid comments ("What I said, or what you said?"), McDaniel hands Al the check. Then he extends to Al his hand, which Al grips with enormous, life-giving relief, as if it were a frosty mug of Coors.

~~~

But anyway. Here we go. It's the Saturday of the promised doubleheader at Tillamook. Al loves Tillamook baseball as much as I do. He's been there many times, over many years, but as commissioner now he can break away from the phones only on a Saturday. I get to Al's house at noon, the appointed time, and we toss our gear into his plum-and-silver Dodge van and head out the Sunset Highway toward the coast.

We're telling stories.

Al's telling me the time Lee Pelekoudas of the Seattle Mariners called him about an exhibition game with the Toronto Blue Jays scheduled for Portland in April. Could Al supply the umpires? Al worked this major-league exhibition game at first base, sorry only for the lack of high-profile names on these teams, big stars he could add to his snapshot collection. Al with Pete Rose. Al with Hammerin' Hank Aaron. "It was a piece of cake," Al says. "The ballplayers told us afterward it was the best umpire crew they'd seen all spring. They didn't know we just do amateur ball."

And I'm telling Al the time I blew—may have blown—a swipe tag by the first baseman that let the winning run score in an American Legion game at Pier Park. Brett Young and I had to sidle sideways, back-to-back, to our cars with beery fans screaming at us. That's a tough summer crowd at Pier Park.

"I know it," says Al. "Six o'clock games. Those dock thugs and steelworkers have time to hit the tavern before the ballpark. I've had umps' tires slashed at . . ."

Anyway, we're telling stories. Al misses the Highway 6 turnoff, and we are rising into the Coast Range on Highway 26. We're headed for Seaside, not Tillamook!

"No sweat," says Al. "I know a cutoff."

Al turns off at Elsie onto the twisting two-lane Necanicum River Highway. Log trucks can't take it fast, and we can't pass log trucks. At quarter to two we should be watching infield practice—Al says, "Put on your plate gear." I climb to the back of the van and strip down. Chest protector and shin guards. Cup. Steel-toed plate shoes. Run the belt through the ball bag and tuck in the shirt without standing up.

Back in the passenger's seat, it's two o-clock and we are not yet to Wheeler. "It'll be on the radio," says Al. I spin the dial and find the announcer speculating about where the umpires are. We hear that Coach Schild has gone into the school to call the PBUA Commissioner, in Portland.

Our Dodge van wheels to a gravel-scattering stop behind the stands, twenty minutes after game time. When we pile out, old timers recognize the stubby ump with the lizard grin. They know Al from years back, and here he is. They've lifted a cold one with Al at the Barn, after games, and relieved him a time or two of his game fee at the blackjack tables upstairs. Al strides out to the field to catcalls and applause. Not ironic applause, either. Big Al, the head honcho, the chief ump, has come back to Tillamook.

~~~~

After the games, Al says we ought to stop by the Barn. We're both hungry, and it wouldn't hurt to knock back a brew. And so here we are, and Al is telling a story to the locals. I've heard this one more than once but never tire of it. I can tell it myself.

Al Parent is the umpire, behind the plate at Hillsboro, and he is having one of those games that an umpire dreams about. The pitching is sharp, the fielding tight, the weather crisp. The strike zone is outlined in blue laser lights that only the umpire can see, and whatever he calls is *it*. Nobody says a word. He calls a third strike, and the batter just turns with his stick to the dugout as Al raises his mask to spit a brown stream of tobacco juice into the dirt. Baseball, by gawd. Batter up. There is the smell of the fresh-cut grass and the sharp crack of white leather, well hit, bounding toward the gap in left-center. This is Al's bell. This is Al's bell, ringing. Maybe somewhere there's a whiny child or a dented fender or a chipped tooth, but right here and now there's a baseball game, tied three to three and going into extra innings. Aloha at Hillsboro.

In the twelfth inning each team scores, and it's four to four. In the seventeenth, the score is five to five, and Aloha is out of pitchers. "They bring in what's-his-name," Al recalls, "you know, the kid who signed. Wally Backman, later with the Mets." Backman is a shortstop, not a pitcher, but he battles. The game is in its sixth hour. Al's shirt is dark with sweat. It's the longest game in Oregon high-school baseball history, as far as Al knows. He hopes it will never end.

In the bottom of the twentieth inning, Backman is still pitching. He runs out of gas. The bases are loaded, two outs. The batter takes a huge, air-clearing swipe and sends the ball bleeding along the ground just a few feet up the third-base line. Fair ball. Holy horse feathers, Al thinks, what a way to end a great game.

But Backman comes charging in. He scoops the ball, while losing his footing, toward the catcher and a force-out at home. The ball gets there in time. It's a great play, in a game filled with great plays. But Al sees, to his horror, that the catcher's heel has risen *off the plate*. The catcher was not touching the plate when he caught the ball.

In the dust and confusion at home plate, Al is the only one in the park who knows that this great play is no good. "SAFE," he says, extending his stubby arms in a gesture that breaks his big heart and brings the wrath of all Aloha down on his sweaty head. Six to five. The dream game is over.

"Oh," says Al, his eyes bright with the memory, "how I hated to make that call."

Steelhead: A Mystery

"In other words, even on the perfectly ordinary and clearly visible level, creation carries on with an intricacy unfathomable, and apparently uncalled for."

Annie Dillard
Pilgrim at Tinker Creek

Rain on *The Turtle*'s roof woke me up near daylight, but the songbirds were excited. And they were right. The weather soon cleared. I sat at the stern of the boat on morning watch. Hearing a good splash off the bow, I stood up to see a summer steelhead complete the last two of her three leaps. She was mint silver and over two feet long, maybe an eight-pound fish. Her leaps took her completely out of the water and parallel to the surface. A bullet-headed package of genes—and what a package!—came rocketing in from the sea.

Steelhead look and behave a lot like salmon. But unlike Pacific salmon, some adult steelhead survive the act of spawning and go out to the ocean again and back. Salmon don't usually pursue prey on their push to the spawning grounds, but maybe a steelhead does. Maybe some winged morsel, invisible to me, brought this one up and out of the water. Maybe some threat from below? Maybe she's trying to shake off sea lice. I don't know.

〰️

In a drift boat on the Clackamas, Dad at the oars kept the boat balanced while I switched from side to side to face the water-borne fury of a steelhead on the line. We followed the fish through a riffle and then for dives and leaps from a deepwater pool, where the fish exhausted itself and me. "Keep the tip up!" he said, meaning the pole tip. When boat and fish came together, he pulled the oars in and grabbed the net. My pole sprang straight, relieved of its counterweight, as he lifted the steelhead into the boat. Along with the triumph of landing a nice one came the marvel of fishness here in the boat. I held a live steelhead in my hands.

A fish doesn't have eyelids. A fish can't close its eyes as it goes flopping about in the net, jaws gaping, gills fanning at the suffocating air. A sharp blow to head with a sawed-off Louisville Slugger—the fish priest——put this steelhead out of its surprise. Sleek as a letter opener and armored with overlapping scales, it had a coat of mucous slime, as if greased. Even dead, it could squirt from my grip if I didn't hook my fingers into the gill slot to steady it. With needle-nosed pliers, I wangled the hook from its jaw.

Fish bleed. Don't tell me fish feel no pain. But it's wrong to feel sorry for a fish, and I didn't. This steelhead would be dinner—two dinners, and a packet of smoked snacks—for us predators.

~~~~

But here on the Columbia, in from the sea, had come a survivor. There wasn't a mark on her. She was in the fourth or fifth year of her life, having left the estuary for the ocean two or three years ago as a five-inch smolt. Now she will seek colder and swifter water to reach the upstream place of her hatching.

Where could she go from here?

Dams on the Columbia will not block her upstream migration. Fish ladders zigzag in a watery stairway up and around each massive block of concrete. Dams take their toll on young ones migrating out, but to an adult salmon or steelhead they are a less imposing barrier than was, in the old days, Celilo Falls. For all I know, this steelhead could be headed for the Eagle Creek hatchery, off the Clackamas River, downstream from all the dams. But she could—some do—reach the headwaters of Canada's Okanogan River, passing four federal dams and five public utility district dams. If she's headed for the Middle Fork of the Salmon River, in Idaho, she'll swim another seven hundred miles, or as far as from here to San Francisco.

The homing instinct in steelhead and salmon is still a mystery. In the ocean, they may take directional clues from the angle of sunlight penetrating water. The earth's magnetic fields might have something to do with it. "Smell" is a likely key. Returning from the sea, a salmon or steelhead may read in reverse a chemical map of where she has been. Fish biologists can implant a computer chip—the size of a grain of rice—in a young fish to monitor electronically *where* it goes. But it's a mystery how they do it.

Their itinerary is not inborn. It's not imprinted on the genes. Hatchery broodstock from the Wind River, in Washington, when raised in acclimation pens on Oregon's Umatilla River, will return to the Umatilla. They ignore the river their parents returned to.

～～～

Like all species in the animal kingdom, *Homo sapiens* strike a balance between how many offspring to have and how much biological energy goes into nurturing those little ones. Whales, beavers, and deer are much like humans on the scale of where to invest that energy. They, like we, give birth to few young but spend a lot of time incubating and nurturing them.

Salmon are different. Salmon are really different. Salmon, like steelhead, are all nature, no nurture. A spring Chinook hen will spawn thousands of eggs. She bets her entire genetic future on the push to reach home. Once she does, there will be no sitting on the nest. No leading by example. She'll die before the eggs hatch.

By the time she reaches the shallow, swift-flowing, gravel-bed spawning grounds, a salmon is depleted of all the flesh and oils that powered her there. She's a leprous package of scales and bones and eggs. The males, too, are gaunt and reddish-brown with sunken eyes. The upper jaw grows to curve like a hook over the lower. These fish lose not only their interest in feeding but also their capacity for it. Throats narrow. Stomachs shrink. The female uses her head and tail, wriggling, to hollow out an elongated cavity in the gravel streambed. She makes a pebbly depression in the shape of her own body.

A male begins to circle the female, his orbit around her ever closer. The two come together, parallel to each other, with the male slightly upstream. When she releases the eggs, the female floats off the nest, or redd. The male releases his milt in a pale watery cloud that floats down across the redd to fertilize the eggs. The female then moves upstream and swishes her tail in the gravel to send a fine cover of pebbles and small stones down over the redd.

Again, there could have been no instruction, no learning from example, how to do this. Soon after spawning, both adults belly up and die. The rotting carcasses add nutrients to the streamside ecology as food for scavenging crawdads and eagles.

～～～

I first saw spawners by accident. Trout fishing on Wade Creek, in Estacada, Gary Barden and I came across these huge beat-up Chinook idling below the mill pond at Park Lumber. I'd never seen so many big fish in so little water. Unable to pass the spillway on Wade Creek, they fell back into the pool downstream. The salmon were so thick in there you could walk right in and grab one. And I did. I waded in and scooped a big one into the streamside bushes. I should have known she was a spawner, but I was too young and excited to think it through.

When Dad saw the spawner I brought home, he was furious. "Knothead" is about the worst word you could hear from Bob Cody. The way he said it. "You knothead." He would keep the eggs, of course, for bait, and he stood over me as I slit this spawner's belly. Those bright red-orange eggs. My toes curl even as I write this recalling the smell of those wasted eggs, the slime on my jeans and hands. The whole history and future of that package of fishness had been snuffed out, and it was my fault.

~~~

I've known Karl Becker since we met in college, he from Massachusetts. We fell into a rooming group that stuck together, and later in life we kept in touch. Karl, more directed than I, headed from college to law school and on into mergers and acquisitions. When I saw him a few years ago he had alit via golden parachute on Hilton Head Island, South Carolina. Donna and I visited the Beckers at their amazing-to-us homestead, a perfectly manicured and beautifully landscaped haven on a woody barrier island of the eastern seaboard. Everything but the humidity was under control. Deer looked as if they would obey the deer-crossing road signs. On Hilton Head Island, bad animal behavior is not tolerated.

"What is it about the salmon?" Karl wanted to know.

He reads *The New York Times*. The National Marine Fisheries Service had declared twelve species of Columbia Basin and Puget Sound salmon and steelhead to be protected under the Endangered Species Act. WILD SALMON CALLED THREATENED; VAST CHANGE LOOMS IN NORTHWEST. For the first time, Portlanders faced the economic consequences of halting the decline of a native species. Taxes would go up to acquire riverside greenspaces and remaining floodplains. Building restrictions would ratchet tighter around city and suburban streams. Northwest people would have to pay more for our "cheap and abundant" hydropower. More water would be devoted to fish migration, less to generating electricity. To Karl it made little sense. A quirky provincial folk were supposed to change an economic way of life in order to rescue some token fish?

"What's the big deal about salmon?" he asked.

I remember his bafflement because I'm afraid I did little to allay it. He'd caught me off guard. A good friend asks you, *What's the big deal about reading books? Why do you like walking the beach?* Try to explain something you've taken for granted and assumed was self-obvious. Where do you start?

I don't remember how I answered, only that I fell short. Maybe I trotted out the usual stuff. The wild salmon is our indicator species—our canary in the coal mine—for clean rivers and healthy habitat. Our proximity to active nature is what sets us apart. We have to back off, while we still can back off, to keep a magnificent natural creature from going the way of the Plains buffalo, the California grizzly. In saving the salmon, we are saving what we like best about this place for our children, our grandchildren. If we can't save our favorite symbol of wildness, we will soon be indistinguishable from other American places. Portland will be Omaha, just a lot of people on the banks of a big river.

I believe those things. Karl was skeptical. He didn't *say* this is sentimental attachment to thin stuff, but he gave me a look. Only a host's politeness probably kept him from lawyerly cross-examination.

I didn't, but I would today, take the argument a step further. The world is watching, or it should be. Portland and its rivers are a test case. The planet is under huge pressure from human population growth and increasing consumption of natural resources. If *we*—in the biggest urban area of the greenest state of the richest nation on earth—can't sustain a balance with nature, where can it be done? This is a test of human evolution, with consequences for humanity's future. These fish have been here a lot longer than we have. They deserve to stay. From the beginning, the riverpeople here looked to the salmon not just for sustenance and trade but also to nourish the human spirit. Salmon were a people, a great race who returned from the ocean each year to affirm the mysteries of creation and life. Religious ritual grew up around the life cycle of salmon, and the celebration each spring of the first fish to appear in the river. If we allow our rivers to be poisoned for our economic comfort, we become deeply, unspeakably, poorer.

~~~~

Fish story, O.K.? The big one that got away. Witnesses are dead, so you'll have to take my word for it.

Salmon fishing with Dad and Frank Marshall, on Frank's boat, I put out my orange treble-hook plug deeper than the others as we trolled the Church Hole, across the Columbia from Astoria, near the Megler Ferry. I was young, so this was probably in the early 1950s. I hooked a fish bigger than any of us had ever seen. That fish was on for a good half hour before I even winched it the first time to the surface. Instead of leaping and splashing like the silvers we'd been catching, this one—a fall Chinook—came up to roll, and to roll again. I saw all of him before he sounded to the depths. I almost had him up to the boat when the drag on the reel screamed again and the fish surged *under* the boat. As I swung the pole around, the line got fouled on the propeller blade. The line snapped.

It was the first time in my life I'd said *fuck* in adult company, and Dad and Frank launched into derivations of *fuck* I had never heard before or even imagined.

~~~~

Columbia River salmon are smaller than they used to be. In the 1950s, the winner of the Ilwaco Salmon Derby each year had caught a fall Chinook upwards of fifty-five pounds. Five decades later, a fish in the mid-forty-pound range often takes the prize. It's not a controlled experiment, but it's a large sample—hundreds of fishermen each year for decades paying a little for a shot at the annual jackpot.

We can't study adult salmon under laboratory conditions, but smaller creatures with rapid rates of reproduction are well watched and documented. Among the books I have on the boat is Jonathan Weiner's *The Beak of the Finch*. It's about how evolution of species happened not just over unfathomable periods of time past. It's happening now, and we can watch. And we can make it happen.

Weiner cites an experiment with water fleas in lab tanks, sieved every four days with fine-mesh nets. In one tank scientists threw back the little fleas and killed the big ones. In another tank, the opposite. Because water fleas reproduce so rapidly, it doesn't take long to see a dramatic evolutionary response. Where lab workers culled the small water fleas, fleas began growing faster and delaying the age of first reproduction. Fast growers faced better odds. The survivors were those whose genes delayed the sex act until they were older, bigger, and safer in that environment. Big water fleas ruled.

The opposite happened in the other tank. The water fleas that stayed little the longest passed on their genes for smallness. Over time, small water fleas ruled. The changes were predictable and rapid. They took about fifty flea generations.

So why not in Pacific salmon? It's no stretch of Darwinian thinking to imagine the evolutionary squeeze we are causing. It's been about one hundred and fifty years, or thirty salmon generations, since people with nets began to swarm the river. A fishing net is an efficient accelerator of natural selection. Commercial and Indian fishermen in the river—as well as trawlers at sea—use nets. They snag the big ones. Smaller salmon are more likely to wriggle through. Big ones are less likely to spawn copies of themselves. After straining successive runs of salmon, it's survival of the smallest.

We've cut salmon habitat, too. Grand Coulee Dam, completed in 1942 without fish ladders, blocked forever the biggest of Columbia River salmon from their spawning grounds. June hogs, they were called, for the timing of their run and their oily bulk that powered them a thousand miles inland and half a mile high, well into Canada. Those runs, along with all the upper Snake River runs blocked by Hells Canyon Dam, are extinct.

Other dams, with fish ladders on the lower river, eliminate a bigger fish's advantage by making upriver migration *easier*. Before dams, only the strongest and best leapers made it past the cataracts at Celilo Falls. The Dalles Dam, in 1957, flooded the falls. Now an adult salmon must navigate only a watery staircase—the fish ladder—of no more than two-foot risers to pass the dam. Smaller and weaker may not be fitter, but just as good. A salmon can be, but does not have to be, muscled with unusual heft to pass on its genes. Smaller salmon do just fine.

It's not finished. No evolutionary story ever is. Organisms adapt to selection pressure.

Hatchery managers have incentive to produce more fish, not necessarily bigger and stronger fish. Hatchery salmon have the benefit of a coddled and predator-protected beginning. A much larger percentage of them survive their first year. But when released into the wild, they are less wary to the ways of the world. Visit a fish hatchery at feeding time. A hatchery worker walks along the edge of a narrow concrete rearing pool sowing handfuls of feed-pellets onto the water surface. Fish see the feeder coming. Fish surge like iron fillings to a magnet toward the human's shadow. The pellets hit the surface to a churning frenzy of fingerling salmon. Imagine those fish, conditioned to such a life, released into the wild. They surge in a Pavlovian rush toward a shadow at streamside. But the shadow is thrown by a heron—not a feeder but an eater.

That's conditioning, not instinct. Nurture, not nature. But there is a genetic disadvantage to hatchery fish too. Although they are wired with the same ropy loops of DNA as their wild cousins, there is less genetic diversity within each run of salmon. Hatchery fish are from relatively few mixes of milt and eggs. When they compete with wild ones for food and habitat, a fish run becomes more homogeneous, more susceptible to parasites and disease. It's as if the Portland school system were gradually flooded with brothers and sisters and first cousins. If one kid has a weak heart, many others are apt to. If one fish hosts a deforming parasite we're more apt to see an epidemic of crooked fish.

Hatchery managers are getting smarter. They move roots and boulders into the formerly featureless rearing pools. They time-release nourishment in places more nearly analogous to where and how fish would naturally find it. They move young fish sooner from the elementary hatchery pools to a middle school enclosed by nets in real-life water. Fish sniff out these acclimation pens and consider them "home." When it works—as it has on the Umatilla River and elsewhere—these salmon will return not to the hatchery but to a natural spawning grounds. They will complete a life cycle as their genetic hard-wiring intended.

Fish learn, in effect, to go wild.

~~~~~

A Chinook salmon hen lays about five thousand eggs in her redd. No more than 10 percent of the eggs lain in late fall will survive the winter and hatch in the spring. Most of the others never got fertilized by so hit-or-miss a sexual act as spawning. Some are buried too deep in the gravel to benefit from the aerating effect of nearby bubbling rapids. A landslide or bad logging upstream can spread suffocating silt over the fertilized eggs. Cutthroat and rainbow trout feast on salmon eggs when they can reach them.

But emerging from each viable embryo in the spring is a tiny elongated transparency with an orange food pouch, a yolk sac, attached to its underside. For the next six weeks or so these small fry draw nourishment only from the yolk sac, gradually absorbing it into the body. Now it looks more like a fish, the size and shape of a fir needle. A salmon at this stage will flit away when a human appears at streamside. As a kid I could squat motionless in shallow water with the patience of a heron until a swarm of fry came close. I'd lunge and maybe get one in a jar to look at. But usually not.

Salmon fry stay in freshwater streams for one or two years, doubling body weight every three months until they're about the size of your finger. Fingerlings have faint dark vertical bands along their silver sides that help hide them from adult trout and winged fishers in the mottled sun-lit woods. When it's time to move out, they ride a spring freshet downstream, tail-first, into larger bodies of water. As they migrate, their markings change. Side-stripes fade into camouflage appropriate to open river. Dark backs make them less obvious to airborne predators. Silver undersides draw less attention from predators eyeing skyward from down deep. They're called smolts at this stage. Their metabolism, too, changes as they migrate down the river. Gills begin to morph to filter oxygen from the richer chemical mix of seawater at the estuary.

The trip to the sea was always hazardous. Dams make it worse. In the spring and early summer, high water flows over a dam's spillway. Some smolts flow with it, dropping as much as eighty feet in a crash of foaming river. The impact can crush a young fish. Seagulls dive and squawk at the base of a dam's spillway in May and June to collect fish that rise to the surface, dead or stunned.

Some smolts get drawn into the penstock that feeds water to the spinning turbines. Turbines don't puree them, but the hellacious ride bruises or batters a fish on that route. Again, smolts emerge stunned, if not killed.

A third and less deadly route of fish-passage bypasses the spillway and penstocks. Elaborate screens deflect smolts into a watery chute that delivers them speedily to an outlet a mile or so below the dam. Even there, you'll see seagulls and herons congregate for easy pickings.

The river itself is a vastly altered habitat. Dams create reservoirs. Instead of a wild springtime rush of water to the sea, the Columbia falls to sea level in tame stages. A smolt's physical and metabolic changes from freshwater to saltwater are hard-wired to occur in three or four weeks. Now the trip to the sea can take three months. A slower river means a warmer river, more direct exposure to sun and different predators. Walleye and bass—introduced as sport fish in the reservoirs—are smolt-killers. Squawfish, too, take their share of out-migrating smolts.

Shores, too, are unnatural. Gone are riverside oxbows and backwaters where a migrating smolt could formerly find food and cover. Through the Columbia River Gorge, shoreline is mile after mile of railroad or highway bed, lifeless as quarried rock.

Some smolts ride in barges past the dams. The U.S. Army Corps of Engineers, at upstream dams, siphons millions of them into barges and chauffeurs them in a swimming pool through the locks of eight federal dams. The smolts debark one hundred and forty miles and a couple of days later below Bonneville Dam. From there they have unimpeded passage to the estuary. Arguments rage about whether or not barging works. Critics point out that the only way to measure success is not how many smolts reach the sea but how many adult fish manage to get back. Fish need to stay in the river in order to trace their way back. The Corps answers that it cycles river water through these barges as they move downstream. Many barged fish do find their way back upstream. If we hadn't been barging for forty years, there might be fewer upriver salmon left to save.

Until recently, the idea of removing dams was unthinkable. Dams were essential to a region that draws nearly half of its commercial and residential electric power from the river. Now some smaller dams are coming out. Portland General Electric blasted a dam out of the Sandy River, and Pacific Power & Light will do the same on the White Salmon. Power companies decided that fixing those dams to provide fish passage would cost more than the dam generates in electricity. Take it out. Those were economic, not environmental, decisions. But they help.

Free-flowing rivers are better for healthy salmon runs. If we put salmon recovery as the region's first priority, we'd remove or breach four federal dams on the mainstream Snake River that have nothing to do with flood control. They supply little irrigation and generate a relatively low proportion of the region's hydropower. Remove just one of those dams, though, and the river shipping route between east-of-the Cascades wheat ranchers and western markets would be interrupted. An Oregon governor has called for Snake River dam removal, but the four dams in question are in Washington, on the way to Idaho. Political and economic arguments have prevailed, so far, against breaching or removing a major Columbia or Snake River dam.

~~~

For all I know, this steelhead rocketing through Hideaway Slough could be headed for Eagle Creek or Clear Creak, tributaries of the lower Clackamas, where she won't encounter any dams at all. Whatever her route, she's already a hero. Luck plays a role in her magnificent journey. She's one of the handful— from thousands—of brothers and sisters to have made it up from the redd, out from freshwater to the sea, three years out there, and back into the Columbia past a gantlet of harbor seals, sea lions, and sport fishermen at the mouth of the river. It's not just luck. Only those with genes for sharp eyesight, fast reflexes, and wary behavior would have survived that kind of selection pressure.

Coming in from the sea, she is. What a heart-stopper she is.

If Salmon Were Truth

*The Indians will be allowed to take fish . . . at all the usual fishing
places and this promise will be kept by the Americans as long as the sun
shines, as long as the mountains stand, and as long as the rivers run.*

Governor Isaac Stevens
Walla Walla Treaty Grounds, 1855

One of the great real-estate deals in American history was consummated in
1855, when Isaac Stevens—the first governor of the Washington Territory
and superintendent of U.S. Indian Affairs—took title to millions of acres of
prime forest and potential farmland in what are now Oregon, Washington,
and Idaho. In return, he assured the native people they would be allowed to
hunt, to gather roots and berries, and to harvest salmon at all their usual places
in the vast Columbia River drainage system.

What separates this deal from other great ones—the Louisiana Purchase for
three cents an acre, Alaska for $7.2 million—is the manner of compensation.
The French and the Russians solved short-term cash problems, and few of their
citizens were displaced. The Pacific Northwest natives got reservation land and
a promise in perpetuity: a solemn pledge, or a pile of dusty old-fashioned
words.

Not even Stevens—a champion of Manifest Destiny—could have anticipated
the effects of industrial and commercial development, dams, clearcut logging
and off-shore harvests on what was thought to be an inexhaustible supply of
Columbia River salmon.

Now, well into perpetuity, the battle over who gets what proportion of
the fish has developed into a legal and cultural conflict that pits commercial
interests against the Indian fishermen.

～～～

David SoHappy, the Indian fisherman, says the clock by his bed showed 5:53
that morning when the feds moved in—June 17, 1982. "I heard the rap on the

door," he says, "and the cops kicked the door in. They didn't have to do that. Before I could get my clothes on, three of these fish narcs got in. They stuck a big pistol in my face and held it there."

Two other agents went to the next room with his wife, Myra. "They watched her get dressed. They herded up grandchildren," SoHappy says. "One boy had the stitches ripped out of his hand when they jerked him out of bed. They locked those kids in a trailer without food or bathroom until after 10 o'clock." SoHappy says the agents sacked his shack and confiscated fish, gaffs, cleavers, phone numbers, papers . . .

"We counted thirty-six cops," he says, recalling the raid on Cooks Landing, a bleak huddle of Indian dwellings and fish-drying sheds on the rocky mid-Columbia River shore. SoHappy says the sting operation included three airplanes, two boats on the river, and more cop cars than Indians living there.

Arrests came later, when seventy-five Indians—not all of them Cooks Landing people—were rounded up. The trials were moved from federal court in Tacoma to Los Angeles, where most of the charges didn't stick. But David SoHappy was found guilty. His wide-eyed grandchildren watched him carted off in leg irons toward Terminal Island, where heavy steel doors clanked shut on the lean old man with long gray braids and a wrinkled-leather face.

His cell mate asked the time-honored question of all newcomers. "Hey, man, what are you in for?"

"Fishing," said David SoHappy.

~~~

"No, no, no . . . It wasn't like that at all," says Wayne Lewis, Chief of Law Enforcement for the Northwest Region, National Marine Fisheries Service. Lewis planned the bust, coordinating state and local law-enforcement agencies. He was on the site that morning, riding with the Skamania County Sheriff.

"SoHappy says 5:53 because he knows our warrants were not good until 6:00. Nobody pulled a gun. Of course we were armed. Some of our people have been led around at gunpoint by Indians. We went in with twenty-six men – two per vehicle. We wanted a vehicle at every structure on the landing. We were dealing with women and children, too. The last thing I wanted was somebody roughed up.

"We were limited, preparing," Lewis explains. "With agents coming from all over the U.S., one from the Virgin Islands, we had only three days to rehearse. We built a model of Cooks Landing, for practice, at an abandoned fish hatchery. I played the part of David SoHappy at one point and they put those handcuffs on me. That was painful. So I made sure we got them loose enough."

According to Lewis, his task force used one little seaplane, that's all. The only boat involved was when the plane spotted an illegal net on the Oregon side of the river. Oregon police came out to get it.

"One of the SoHappy boys shoved an agent. He was arrested on the spot. But otherwise everything was smooth. Peaceful," Lewis says. "One woman took a stroll with her baby carriage through the landing. Another was watering flowers, so I turned off the water, just to avoid confusion. We were ready to leave, but a train came between the river and the highway. It blocked our exit. We were lined up there and this woman opened the back door of her car, which we were confiscating. She threw her baby into the back seat!

" 'Take the car. Take HIM,' she screamed," says Lewis, shaking his head. He was dealing here with unreasonable people, people who will do anything to make the law look bad.

~~~~

Stop! Take it easy.

If Truth here were a spring Chinook, it long ago would have been canned by one guy, smoked by another, and fileted by a third. When they gather around and cry, *Look here at my spring Chinook . . . This is the truth . . .*

Well, maybe so. I see what you have there, but . . .

~~~~

"Fishing," says Jack Schwartz, counsel for the Indian defense, "is all these people know. The salmon has been their livelihood, their sustenance, their theology, their *currency*, for generation after generation. Telling David SoHappy he can't fish is like telling you and me we can't breathe."

Schwartz, thirty-two, is a tall, slim, intensely engaging New Yorker with rimless glasses and hair too long for a lawyer. His low-rent Portland home is his office. People who need legal help and a place to spend the night can use the upstairs bedrooms.

"It's in the treaty," he says. "You can look it up. Private ownership of the land was unfamiliar to the Indians, but they said, OK, you white folks can own the land. Just don't mess with our fishing and hunting places. Clams, roots, and berries. Deer. Fish. Give us equal access and you guys can come ahead. Northwest history has been a process of chipping away at the Indians' treaty rights to make way for U.S. commerce," says Schwartz, who can talk up a coastal storm. "A landmark 1969 federal court decision gave the Indians access to half the predicted Columbia River salmon runs each year. Not that they're going to *catch* half the fish. But half the run should be left to migrate past traditional Indian fishing grounds like Cooks Landing and Celilo.

"That looked good to the treaty Indians at the time," Shwartz says. "But it doesn't take a genius to figure out that half of zero will be zero. The boardrooms and legal chambers of America need someone to *blame* for dwindling fish runs. Lewis's Fisheries Service is under the U.S. Department of Commerce. So. Who do you think Commerce is going to blame? Indians! Each cog in the criminal justice machine, through bias, ignorance, and a lack of guts, has chewed into one of the last indigenous American communities in the lower forty-eight. These river people live free of corporate paychecks and government jobs. They've been catching and trading fish since the first wagon trains came over the hill and began recording time for them.

"If the government—with electronic surveillance and aerial photography—can eliminate the last of these river people, there won't *be* a legal question about those treaties. They're not going after *white* poachers," Schwartz says. "Vindictive and selective prosecution, this is called. Ethnocide."

〜〜〜

Wayne Lewis, the fisheries lawman, has flown from his Seattle base to Portland, where the state police whisk him across the river to Vancouver and into a closed-door meeting of federal, state, and Indian law-enforcement agencies. Afterward, Lewis accepts a ride with me back to the airport and blanches at the mention of Jack Schwartz. Lewis, a native (as we say) Oregonian—Portland State, Lewis & Clark Law, Oregon State Police—wants one thing understood from the start:

"This is *not* an Indian vs. non-Indian problem," he says. "Anybody who presents it that way is just trying to polarize the issue. The Supreme Court settled this treaty business years ago. We're talking here about criminals, pure and simple."

Lewis, forty-seven, with neat thinning hair and glasses, could be one of the "you're-in-good-hands" people on television. Sincere, trustworthy. He explains that what the press has called SAMSCAM began a few years ago when patrolling agencies documented isolated cases of disappearing fish. Lewis called the law-enforcement heads together. "Nobody said, 'Let's get the Indians.' But we'd investigated the lower river, too, and where was the trouble most concentrated? Above Bonneville, where Indians fish."

At a table in the airport lobby, Lewis sheds his gray herringbone jacket and continues. "We set up an undercover fish-buying operation. April 1981 to May of 1982. We had scales and ice trailers at an isolated farmhouse—a beautiful old place—up in the hills behind Cooks Landing. Advanced Marketing Research, it was called. As a result of our agents' contacts with Indian fishermen, we can document fifty-three tons of illegally sold fish. Mostly salmon. Some steelhead, some sturgeon. $150,000 worth. We took the fish to Seattle and sold them to help pay for the operation."

Wait a minute. $150,000 divided by seventy-five crooks? That's just $2,000 apiece, spread over thirteen months.

"Well, yeah," Lewis says. "That wasn't really enough. But consider our dilemma. Here we were, charged with protecting the resource. If we kept the operation going we would have been a party to destroying it. So we moved in. This never would have been necessary," he says, "except for a total lack of enforcement by the tribal police. The tribes issue permits for subsistence and ceremonial fishing. Nobody argues the Indians' right to that. But they weren't checking. And we couldn't get Skamania County to move against poachers."

Lewis stretches. He rubs his tired eyes and checks his watch. "You'd think the tribal police would have come down hard on the renegades," he says. "It's taken the Indians years to gain what they've got through the court system."

〜〜〜

Oh yeah? Well look at this. Jack Schwartz knows a dirty fight when he's in one. He leaps from the dining-room chair and pounces on a cardboard file box. He pulls out a press release issued by Lewis's Fisheries Service before the Indian trials began. The release led to extensive pretrial publicity in local papers all over the Northwest. Lewis is quoted: *We are dealing with professional, well-organized business people who quite frequently handle thousands of dollars a day in illegal fish. The market for these fish is worldwide.*

"He's talking about the Mafia, right?" Schwartz says. "Swiss bank accounts?"

Lewis is quoted again in these half-page articles: *Biologists estimate forty thousand adult fall Chinook are lost each year between Bonneville and McNary dams.*

Schwartz goes bonkers, digging in his files for a follow-up article. Yes, here it is. "Now *after* the bust," he says, showing an article from *The Oregonian*, April 23, 1983, "the same agency comes out with its biologists' new theory. Those forty thousand missing fish might have adapted their run and begun to spawn *below* McNary Dam."

Schwartz waves his arms in frustration. "There *weren't* any forty thousand missing fish."

〰〰

Oh yeah? Well, look at this. Wayne Lewis is in a dirty fight. He digs in his traveling case and comes up with a memo from one of his undercover agents. The agent swears he overheard Schwartz—off-stage at a trial—say he hasn't read the material evidence against the Indians. And he doesn't intend to.

"Schwartz," says Lewis, "wants to draw out these legal proceedings until they become so expensive, so bothersome, that the states will dismiss the cases. That's what kind of attitude you're dealing with here," says Lewis, his jaw muscles tight.

〰〰

Hold it! Calm down, you guys.

If Truth were a spring Chinook salmon, it would be a sacred emissary to one guy, recreation for another, livelihood for a third, and cat food or fertilizer to another. When they gather around and start slinging the evidence . . . *Look here at my spring Chinook . . . This is the truth . . .*

Well, maybe so (flinch). I see what you mean (duck!!). But . . .

〰〰

Eight miles downstream from Hood River, across the Columbia, sits Cooks Landing, Washington, population three this January 1984. Pipes are frozen. The east wind howls over low shacks, campers, and boats scattered like driftwood on a sharp rock promontory. It might be a clever visual trick that the SoHappy dwelling even stands in the teeth of this gale. But inside, the place is warmed by a potbellied wood stove and by the effervescent—*What? Me worry?*—cordiality of Myra SoHappy. No wonder she was acquitted in Los Angeles "of drying fish," she says with grandma-giggle.

SoHappy himself, fifty-nine going on seventy-four, is free pending appeal of his five-year sentence. He sits nearby in blue-striped slacks and sneakers, with gray braids and a face weathered by time and the river. "Poaching, they got me for." He flashes a gap-toothed grin at the absurdity of it. "For it to be poaching," he says, "the fish have to belong to somebody. If the King of England owns the land and a man sneaks in and kills an animal, that's poaching. That's where the word comes from."

SoHappy tells more of the law he learned from his grandmother, then forgot until he found Felix Cohen's *Handbook of Indian Law*. "My grandmother was right all the time. There is no law that can keep me off the river."

SoHappy, with four sons, three daughters, and a total of nineteen dependents, grew up at Celilo Falls, a fisherman since age five. Some of the fish he catches these days are for ceremonies marking funerals and births and the creation of the Earth. Some are to eat. Others are to sell, so he can run his battered boats and van and . . . well, make a living. This is what he does. It's what he teaches his sons to do. He has never been on welfare, he says, never taken food stamps from what he considers a foreign nation. His boys have a token twenty-foot hoop net in the river right now, out of season, although few fish are running. "I have a right to fish in all the usual places, just like it says in the treaty. If I didn't fish," he says, "I'd be abandoning my rights."

SoHappy's law books are well worn. He is a true believer, as well, in the old ways. "A long time ago people were more advanced than we are now," he says. "The dead would lie in state for five days, and then come alive. They'd tell us, 'Here's what I've seen. Here's what's going to happen.' Now they get cut up and embalmed. We've lost touch. Here on Earth everything seems so complicated. It's not. Until the Indians get things the way it should be," he says, "your government will spend billions of dollars on weather-related things. Like ice storms. Winds. Mount St. Helens. When the ocean fish don't come back? This is nature's way of making people pay."

~~~~

Defense Counsel Schwartz has to drive to a 9 a.m. court case in Hood River, and he's not sure this ten-year-old ruby-rust Subaru—given to him by a client who could not pay—will start. Another client who tuned up the car to pass DEQ inspection has not come back and fixed it to run. But finally Schwartz gets it going and tunes his non-stop talkathon to geopolitics and autobiography.

Before passing Multnomah Falls on his drive up the river, Schwartz gives an account of his years on five different college campuses, climaxed by a Kent State-related takeover of the New York State Capitol at Albany and trumped-up charges against him, including murder. By Cascade Locks, Schwartz graduates with honors from Albany State, finishes law school at American University, and hooks up with the great William Kunstler for the Sioux Indian uprisings and trials at Wounded Knee. These days he is *the* expert, from San Diego to British Columbia, on Indian defense law. Few other lawyers will work on the Indians' side. There's no money in it.

At Hood River Schwartz unfolds his long frame from the car and sniffs the air around the putty-colored courthouse. Walking up to it, he passes the windows of a day-care center, where kids sport bright paper headbands and feathers. "Indians," Schwartz smiles. "Watch out."

On trial today is Bruce Jim, thirty-eight, David SoHappy's nephew and one of the SAMSCAM seventy-five. Jim was charged in federal court and in Washington State with salmon dealing. Here in Oregon, he's on trial for selling a deer to fisheries undercover agents for $100. Jim will be found guilty.

An air of country vaudeville infuses these proceedings. Four dozen Hood River county citizens are here for jury selection. As a juror's name is pulled out of the box, the owner of that name groans. Others, not chosen, laugh. Bruce Jim sits stoically in a red plaid shirt, his back to the prospective jurors, listening. Two young Indian men, to be called later by Schwartz as witnesses, pick up the mood. One belches. The other cracks his knuckles.

Called to the witness stand, undercover agents Richard Severtson and Penelope Fields—like anchorpersons for the evening news—are smooth, polished, persuasive. Bruce Jim and his two young witnesses, when called, are hesitant, scared, underdressed, and unpersuasive. The two sides' versions of the facts, as the trial stretches on into early evening, are significantly different.

At a break in the trial, Schwartz says, "This is what it always comes down to. Who's lying? The white cops or the Indians?"

When the jury goes into seclusion, Bruce Jim sits in the hallway on a metal folding chair, waiting for the verdict. Agents Fields and Severtson walk by, stiff with the strain of what has been a long day. Severtson is a former Green Beret and Oregon police officer who had befriended and arrested Bruce Jim under the alias of Mr. King. The Indians had called him King Tut, for his golden pockets. Severtson stops now in front of Bruce Jim's chair and points down at him, as if to scold a naughty child.

"I've lost all respect for you," he says to Bruce Jim. "You perjured yourself today."

Bruce Jim is stunned. He knows he cannot rise and punch this smug business-suited cop down the stairs of a white man's courthouse. He sits there and takes it. "You lied, too," he replies.

"Not under oath in this hallowed court," Severtson says, as if reciting lines from a civics text. Agent Fields listens to this. She says nothing. Her face is puffy with anger, or maybe with alarm that her partner has overstepped his professional bounds. "I'm speaking man to man," Severtson continues. He thumps his thick righteous chest. "From the heart. I never thought you would lie."

~~~~~

Time out! Break. Everybody take a deep breath.

Now if Truth were a spring Chinook . . . whoever saw it for himself, not secondhand, would see it battered and beaten and struggling upriver to spawn in changed and tainted waters . . . *Truth, you old spring Chinook. I knew you when you were bright and silver. How did you get so ugly?*

~~~~~

The day after the Bruce Jim trial, Jim Walker—the mayor of Hood River—drives through town at the wheel of a big maroon cruiser and says, "Hey, there's no wipe-'em-out mentality here. We were doing fine until the federal government moved in. If the Indians stepped out of line, the tribe would send in its own cops. They'd thump a few heads and take care of it."

The mayor is also President of Hood River Bottling Company. He has a bushy mustache and a maverick grin. "I don't know anybody who resents an Indian man a subsistence living off the fish," he says. "They've always sold some. Now if they waste the fish—put a net out, leave, forget to pick it up—that's another matter. People get steamed. But I'll tell you what. This isn't Portland. There aren't many hunters or fishermen around here who never bagged a deer out of season or doubled their limit on steelhead. I've done it myself."

Walker is appalled at the public expense of these Indian trials. "People I've talked to," he says, "just think it's a big joke."

He guides his car onto the gravel parking lot at the Hen Hut, a sportsman's coffee shop. Strong-willed citizens—wearing everything from business suits to orange ball caps—are gathered around Formica table tops with thick coffee mugs. Over the course of two or three hours, with the cast of participants moving in and out, this forum offers nothing like consensus, but some points give rise to affirmative grunts and nods.

These men agree that most Indian people follow reasonable tribal fishing laws. Sure, there's resentment toward Indian fishermen who don't follow the rules. But non-Indians cheat, too. And there is tremendous pressure on the river itself. You see slimy growth at the edges. You smell funny odors. Indian fishermen are the least of the problems, but they contribute to the collective strangle. Before, it didn't matter. The forum swings naturally toward the future of salmon. Stopping *all* in-river fishing might not save wild fish. Dams, industry, pesticides, and off-shore harvests are much bigger threats to salmon than are in-river fishermen. Years from now this forum might convene beside a big dead river and think back on this year, 1984, when the mighty Columbia lay low with a heart condition and a hangnail. The government went after the hangnail—its Indian fishermen—with a sledgehammer.

While David SoHappy guards his ancient tradition and his defiant little net, while Wayne Lewis flies off for a summit meeting, and while Jack Schwartz polishes his lonely outrage for yet another in a series of Indian trials that will last well into the summer, a deep sadness settle over the riverside forum. "All we're doing," says Tom Gibbon—the guy in the orange ball cap, formerly with the sheriff's office—"is fighting over who gets the last fish."

~~~

Oh Chinook, my old friend truth . . . You spawn new hope even with death. Always did. This can't be true? Can it?

Emotionally Disturbed

Kids on my school bus keep an eye out for the great blue heron. This heron is something to see, all right. We're driving north on 33rd Avenue, just after bridging a couple of spooky sloughs. On the left is a DEQ station and then a plush golf course. On the right, Portland International Airport. "Hooo, big bird!" they'll say. It *is* a big one, regal, standing tall in short grass just thirty yards off the road. The first two mornings we saw the heron at the same spot, manifesting the same attitude.

"That bird alive?"

"That some fake bird."

The next morning, the heron was not there. *See?* I told them. It was a live bird. But do they believe their bus driver?

"Somebody took it down."

I was momentarily puzzled. The wipers shuddered across my windshield. Somebody took it down?

But as the school days rolled on, we saw that heron in different positions. We saw other herons. Once, with big air-thrashing flaps, our heron took flight. Boy. You'd think Portland kids who've never seen a great blue heron must be little kids, but these are teenagers. On this route I carry delinquent juveniles to a reform school. They've been expelled from their neighborhood schools for disruptive or dangerous behavior, so I drive them to and from a set of dreary medium-security classrooms and a small gym out on Marine Drive. It's their last chance to attend school while living at home. Next stop, for them, might be MacLaren Youth Correctional Facility. They don't know rivers or animals. Their dads never took them fishing, I thought, until I came to understand they don't have dads.

I tell them. *When the heron stands facing the water, or in it, he's fishing. When the heron is up on the bank like that, he's hunting. For field mice? I don't know. You'd think the heron is just chillin', but that's how a heron makes a living. He waits, patient as a branch.*

Ours is a short bus, with just half a dozen kids and me on it. If two or three are listening I might drive around the block a time or two to finish a story before delivering them to school. This is only slightly bad bus driver behavior. Buses will be late due to traffic or due to a 10-55, the radio code for students at each others' throats. So what's a little late to finish a story?

One day I approached the school with them too soon. School staff won't open the doors to this bunch until precisely 8:40, so I re-routed onto Bridgeton Road, along the Columbia River dike.

DROP THE HEADPHONES, PEOPLE. We're taking the scenic route.

These metal garage-looking structures on the water are where the rich people keep their yachts. Over there, that's Tomahawk Island. Those are some really important yachts with more living space than my house. These others with tall poles on them are sailboats. You can hoist a sail up that pole when the wind is right and go somewhere on your boat without a motor. There's a floating restaurant, the Island Cafe. And these here are houseboats. People live here.

"Nice places."

I stopped the bus so those on the left could unbuckle their seatbelts and re-buckle on the right side for a better look at the houseboats. This neighborhood is not exotic to me, but to them we were in Dubai, or Lake Oswego.

"What if the water come up?"

These houses float. The sidewalks, too, float on top of the water. When the river rises, they go up. Those rust-colored poles keep the house in place, while the docks go up or down. A few years ago, when the rivers got really high, a string of houseboats like this broke away. The whole neighborhood went floating down the Willamette River on the current. I saw this on Channel 2. It was pretty exciting.

"What happened?"

That's what happened. They floated away. I don't remember what happened. Maybe nobody knows. The river leaves town, you know? It goes out to the ocean. Those houseboat people could be still floating around out there, eating their dogs, their cell phones out of range.

They were all quiet. I saw their wide eyes in my overhead mirror. Uh-oh. Broken kids can't tell when I'm putting them on. I pulled up to the school, but I didn't open the bus door. *No, wait. I remember. What happened was tugboats came to the rescue. They lashed that string of houseboats to the bank. When the water went down to normal, they tugged the houses back up the river where they belonged.*

"Aw, man."

"Aw, man," was right. By telling them what really happened, I'd ruined a believable-to-them story. These kids know in their bones that they have come unmoored from the world. No help is on the way.

I chose this route because the hours are good and because Ivory Broom moved to Hawaii a couple of years ago and because boredom can be a problem with slow or obedient children. Not here. My passengers are old enough to have stories of their own, and they will occasionally spill them. Sad stories. No. They have the *beginnings* of life stories that I'd like to turn around and play backwards. Dad comes home, Mom kicks her meth habit, and the cops turn out to be good guys after all.

A pale teenager with zits and a bad haircut trudges to my bus from a shabby house with its screen door off the hinges, a window Saran-wrapped, and a broken television set in the yard. He's not expecting a rescue. This neighborhood is known to us bus drivers as Felony Flats. He slumps in his seat reeking of cigarettes and resentment. He's been sentenced to this demeaning short bus that teenagers city-wide call a "retard bus." Emphasis on the first syllable. REtard bus. It kills him to be seen getting on or off it.

None of them would be on this bus if they didn't have a tortured relationship with school. And most of them have a fractured home life. They live with a grandparent or an aunt or a step-someone. Of the four boys and two girls on my route right now, only two have the same surname as an adult of the house.

~~~

On a dry run to drop a time card for a new student, I come to a large well-tended old house set back from Woodstock Boulevard behind two tall firs and a neat lawn. A foster home. Two cheerful teenagers rush to answer my knock. No, Teresa's not here. Yes, she lives here. They call for Tom, a bright young dad-like guy. Tom and I are on the veranda with paperwork. I expect to pick up Teresa at 7:58 each morning and bring her back by 3:40, starting Thursday.

But here comes Teresa now, from the sidewalk and up the front steps. She sizes up me—a stranger with picture ID on a lanyard—and I see pure terror in her lovely dark eyes. Teresa clings to Tom's elbow, pleading, and says to him, "Are they going to take me away?"

Imagine. It's not Mom and Dad and the kids, but Teresa has found a home here. She has an adult elbow to cling to, yet her world is so fragile.

~~~

You'd like to step in. Do something about this. Anybody would. But I am fifty years older than they are. I don't like their music and I don't know an X-Station from a Play Box. It's hard to understand their language. They don't get mine. It's not just the words but how an elder tries to use words to bridge a yawning socio-cultural chasm to reach a youngster he'd like to help. They don't dislike me. We are curiosities to one another, failing to connect.

"I don't need to read."

Yes you do. Everybody needs to read.

"I'm going to be a welder. My uncle's a welder and he makes $32 an hour."

Welders need to read the instructions. Work orders. The sports section.

"My uncle can't read."

~~~

Or you'd like to shake them. Anybody would. Take this knucklehead with swagger and shades who imagines himself the bull seal of the bus. Dejarvis (I'll call him) began rapping aloud one morning to vivid lyrics on his CD player about killing cops and fucking people. "Run, Nigger, run. POW. POW."

Others, laughingly, picked it up in chorus. They paid no mind to my reasoned pleas. *Give me a break. This is inappropriate language.* Weak stuff like that.

At school I secured the bus and went chest to chest with Dejarvis to block his exit. We exchanged ill-chosen words and then stood there surprised, eyeing each other unbudgingly across the void.

Bus driving is not like teaching, not like coaching. They don't know the bus driver's name and would not recognize him on the street unless they came up behind his bald spot or saw his face in some overhead mirror. They hate school. You can't think of a story to tell them. Nothing is funny. They withdraw behind their shades and into their headphones. One week's worth of mornings you idle the bus outside the sorry house of a kid you've come to like, and he doesn't come out. After another week you write it up and the school won't—or can't, by rule—tell you what happened to that kid. By December you have seven passengers on the bus, but only two of them are kids you started the school year with. The others just disappeared as migrating birds flying north, you fear, for winter.

If I had a genie lamp I'd get them out on the river.

~~~

By rule now on the bus they drop their headphones when we approach our brief Wild Kingdom on 33rd Avenue. There might be a heron sighting. We have spied and identified buffleheads and golfers and scaups. We saw mallards, of course. One morning a pair of F-15 fighter jets went roaring above the road from the Oregon Air National Guard base. Another morning, due to fog, the approach to a PDX runway was strobing white and blue and red lights like a five-precinct police action. Talk about excitement, until I told them why.

We saw a beaver or a nutria. From a passing bus you can't tell the difference, but it's something to talk about. Which of them, beaver or nutria, would be more likely to swim about like that in broad daylight? Which of them got here before humans?

Some stories don't go far.

The coyote sighting, though, had legs. Ramon saw the coyote slurking guiltily off in the direction of PDX and mistook it for a dog, which sparked talk of wild versus tame. They get that. They understand lawlessness. This coyote was a pretty good story, wild in the city, scrapping a living between a plush golf course and the airport. You have to admire that. And I have coyote stories, from Indian lore, that kept us going for several trips although we never again saw the coyote. The Coyote of creation myth is a rich character, all the richer to these kids because he's an outcast, a shrewd horny outlaw with powers.

~~~

"O.K., Robin," says Sylvie "Last night? Guess what."

You apologized to your aunt.

"No."

What?

"Her stepson came over."

Is that good or bad?

"Good! We got a decent meal. We had steak on a stick. Squares of meat. We had that and corn and mashed potatoes!"

~~~~

They're kids. They're unfinished human beings. You never know. It turns out Dejarvis can be civil and funny when he wants to be. He's a smart guy, older than the others, and on the bus we talk basketball. He plays. I doubt if he truly believes that his bus driver has played and coached and refereed hoops. But we unwrap some language we both understand. The school has a team, he tells me. Yes, there are twelve of these alternative schools in the metro area. League play will begin in January.

Well, shoot. I wonder. Maybe I'll get on the court with these jokers.

At home, in the basement, I rummage up my old black-and-white striped shirt. The patch on the shirt: OSAA Basketball Official, 1993-94. Good gawd. Was it fourteen years ago I last wore this? The shirt is a tight fit.

~~~~

Come January and basketball practice, Dejarvis didn't come to the bus for five days in a row. Hoping he was just sick, I asked at school. *What's up with Dejarvis?* The principal told me Dejarvis got sliced up in the melee at Lloyd Center that I'd read about in the paper. "He'll be back when he gets out of the hospital."

I didn't know Dejarvis was a gang member.

"You didn't?!" said the principal.

~~~~

They come and they go. Why should I care? I drive them to school on a gray wooly morning, windshield wipers batting at a persistent mist. They wear their despair like two-G gravity blankets, and there's a vacancy in my chest where concern should be. Just get them to school.

OK, this is not a sob story. It's about *What can we do?* It's about the desperation of unloved kids. It's about the unspeakable bottomless aloneness of kids who have no support at home. Their need for recognition will drive them to disruptive and dangerous acts. I don't kid myself that Portland Public Schools can rescue all of these characters from the scrap heap of teenage angst, but that's what this "school"—the Pioneer Program at Columbia School—is for. It's a salvage operation. Every once in a while it works. Help is there, if the kids will put in the work. Teachers and staff are as gung-ho and brave as NCOs in Baqouba or Kabul, and more forbearing. Students get close attention and door-to-door transportation and breakfast. This is a year-around school. It's expensive, but the school will rescue some kids.

A tall disengaged beaten-down girl who avoided eye contact on my bus hooked up with a teacher who encouraged her ability to draw. She got the idea she should work at it. She did. And then, boy, could she *draw*. After months of smart work and good behavior, she earned her way back to Madison High School. On her last day with us she passed out Snickers bars to everyone on the bus.

~~~~

Or this. A foul-mouthed and sharp-tempered boy swallowed hook line and sinker the school's three-step program from Safety to Respect to Responsibility. He got the idea. It was up to him. He loosened up and began to get along. He felt free to needle me—*me*—about anger management. "Robin, I know a good case worker for you."

~~~~

You win some and you lose some. I lost Dejarvis. Basketball season had begun by the time he came back from the hospital. Dejarvis joined the team and showed some skills, but he was out of shape. He played puffingly for a couple of games, lost interest, and quit coming to school.

Dejarvis is gone, but I referee basketball.

At a dimly lit poorly ventilated crackerbox gym—come look—athletically gifted and under-loved street kids are hooping it up. And up. Some of them play above the rim. Some have stars in their eyes imagining NBA careers, and all of them run as if their shorts were on fire. Scores won't be reported in *The Oregonian*. There are no cheerleaders, but the girls come, yes they do. These girls rhythmically stomp and they musically chant and they groan in unison and they scream in delight.

It's hot in here. It's break-your-ankles *fast* in here. I whistle a foul and have to pause three or four beats for breath to say the call.

Now a guard makes a clean steal and breaks away. It's just him and the rim down court. The boy has springs. He'll try to flush this one. He'll put some mustard on it and have maybe a 60 percent chance of scoring. Dribble one, dribble two . . . he's there. A gasp from the crowd sucks air from the court for this rim-rattling slam as—instead—he goes up with the ball and with the tenderest touch lets the ball kiss off the backboard and fall gently into the net.

With a sheep-eating grin, he turns back up court and glances winkingly at the coach who had been urging him all game to *play under control.*

You never know.

~~~

Basketball is a virtual world for some kids. Others, on my bus, escape through hand-held gaming devices to a parallel universe they call Anime (pronounced Annie Mae). Anime has blood and meanness, but it also fosters virtual alliances and tribal loyalty. A kid from a broken family can create a new family whole.

After school one day a burly buzz-cut boy who is given to tears anyway tromped onto my bus sobbing, choking. He slammed his backpack to the floor and head-butted the window while taking his seat.

What's the trouble, Jake?

"Devin said my wife is ugly. I'm going to kill him."

In Anime, you see, Jake has a wife and three children. This emotionally slippery boy administers virtual care and assigns chores. In Anime, he is tough but fair. Others on my bus know that Jake's blustered desire to kill Devin for insulting his wife was an overreaction but not trivial. Jake is a family man.

~~~

Or this. A fifteen-year-old scatterbrained high-volume girl is always talking about her baby. She has no baby. But she tells me something new each day about her baby.

The baby has a birthday coming up.

The baby needs a check-up.

The baby died!

I am not her case worker. I am not even supposed to know, from her case worker, that Sylvie has had several "babies" who died. After dropping her at home I have to park the bus and collect myself. It's bad form for a driver to return to the bus yard with tears in his eyes.

~~~

But basketball. Do come look. In this tiny grade-school gym, players go straight up for a lay-in to avoid collision with a wall at one end and a stage at the other. Suspended from the ceiling are square wooden backboards. We play twenty-minute halves with running time except for the last two minutes of each half. No bleachers. A single row of chairs fills up early, and then it's standing room only with deafening—but seldom rude—fans. Fans of rival gangs evidently have settled on a détente. Good humor and civil behavior rule. Ballplayers, too, are surprisingly compliant.

Maybe that's not so surprising. They don't have dads, remember. A man in a striped shirt gets their respect. I've taken more grief from over-indulged high-school players and their parents than from these unloved boys of the street. It helps that my referee partner—the large easy-smiling Greg Taylor, who played junior college ball in Alabama and two years at Montana State—knows what we're doing. And Portland police are at the door.

Wondrous athletic ability and wildly chaotic basketball are on display here. A popular offense is to fire up a three-point shot and crash the boards. But they've been coached. They do play defense. They work on the high pick-and-roll, and I've seen a sweet bounce pass to a backdoor cutter that any high-school coach in America would die for.

One slender point guard dominated a game while taking no more than three shots, just with slashing drives and deft passes. On a break he tossed the ball hard off the backboard for a trailing teammate to jam it. This boy has a withered right arm like a thalidomide baby. He gets fouled a lot and makes nine out of ten one-armed free throws. He understands the overarching beauty of basketball played well, and it just breaks your heart to see a kid so athletic and smart and to know he's in trouble.

That boy's team won the league championship. At the end of the game, we had a good ten minutes of unrestrained joy before coaches could corral the players for a trophy presentation. Kids did cartwheels and back flips. They hung off the rims. They bounced off the walls. Really. Two of these bad boys—too heavy for standing back flips—went running at the wall *and up it* to launch their 360s.

~~~

OK, you're right. I am emotionally disturbed. I have witnessed the abandoned young of the species at the acme, the very pinnacle, of their lives so far. I want them to know more of this teamwork business, of getting along. But when you throw a shipwrecked kid a life rope there has to be something more to haul him in to. Family. School. Church. A job, maybe? I don't know. Basketball is not it, not in the long run.

On the morning after that final game's pure loopy joy, I learned about a robbery in the art room, where the winning team had dressed. One of the boys claimed to have lost $300 and had kicked out a window at the school.

Wait. What!? This kid had three hundred dollars in his wallet? What's that all about?

The ups and the downs of caring for these people are so extreme they will turn you inside out. The up-side news that same morning—from Dennis Christensen, Dejarvis's coach—was that our boy Dejarvis had applied for and landed a job (!) with Federal Express.

Let's hold out hope for Dejarvis. You never know.

The Swimmers and the Walk-Uprights

Up the Columbia River from Portland, past Bonneville Dam and through the wind-swept gorge . . . past The Dalles Dam and the drowned site of Celilo Falls . . . beyond John Day Dam and way out east here, two hundred and fifty miles from the ocean, an "extinct" salmon run is coming back. Spring Chinook salmon are reclaiming the Umatilla River. To native Oregon waters comes a fish long gone—erased, wiped out—for seventy years. For the span of a human lifetime, nobody saw a Chinook in the Umatilla because the river, at critical times of year, had no water in it. The Umatilla was so thoroughly tapped for irrigation that you could hop from one bank to the other without wetting your feet.

But this is April 1997. The water is back. Spring Chinook are back. Come look . . .

The Umatilla River, snowwater cold, surges brown over the spillway at Three Mile Dam, where Umatilla Indians are dedicating new fish-sorting machinery. The parking lot is packed on this hot Saturday morning. As word spreads—spring Chinook!—pickups and vans line both sides of the road for a quarter mile downstream. A ukulele band strums toe-tapping tunes, and red balloons fly against a sky as blue as paint.

At the fish-sorting station, a rectangular strainer rises through a section of fish ladder as the water drains out. Fish come thrashing into air, gleaming silver on a steel mesh. Mostly these are steelhead, the females red around the gills. Also with each lift come squawfish and suckers. But now a Chinook rises in the lift. She's bigger than steelhead, a thick twenty-pounder, with black speckles on bright scales. Kids go "Ooooh," and a farm wife "Oh, my!"

The Indian fish-handler just nods. This is special. This is homecoming.

There are speeches. Tribal elders, government dignitaries, and water board big shots congratulate each other. Kids begin squirming until Louie Dick, a Umatilla elder in long braids, blue shirt, jeans, and cowboy boots, rises to sing thanks to the Maker. Dick stares to the big sky. He sings in a language unfamiliar to most people here, but even the kids are rapt. When he finishes, you can hear nothing but water rushing over Three Mile Dam. In the air rises an unspoken question—*What does your ancient song mean?*

Louie Dick lets the question hang there for a while before answering. "The sun is watching," he says. "The earth is listening. The salmon is keeping its promise."

~~~

How can this be? A salmon success story? Nearly everything I read is about the decline of things—virgin forests, clean rivers, ocean-going salmon—that define the Pacific Northwest. Article after documentary says our legendary salmon are on the brink of extinction, our rivers fouled, our tribes and white fishers forced to abandon a traditional way of life. Coastal silvers, or coho, are on the verge of collapse. Wild Chinook are an endangered species on the Snake River.

Are the Umatillas, with their revived spring Chinook run, only a small blip in a steady decline? Or are the Umatillas onto something?

"Historically," says Donald Sampson, a Umatilla chief, "our promise is to take care of this land. It's a two-way promise. The salmon are keeping their promise. We are keeping the promise."

Sampson is chairman—nobody says chief anymore—of the Confederated Tribes of the Umatilla Indian Reservation's Board of Trustees. A solid cornerstone of a man, only thirty-six, Sampson has hereditary fishing rights, twenty-five years of braids to his waist, and a degree in fish biology.

"By treaty, we can fish in all our usual places," he says. "The elders woke up and said, 'Where's our water? Where's our fish?' "

The Umatillas chose to negotiate, not to litigate. Tribes worked with irrigators and the federal agencies on a huge plumbing project that piped water overland, from the Columbia River, to fill Umatilla reservoirs. That left enough water in the Umatilla for ocean-going and ocean-returning fish. When the Umatilla Basin Project—financed mainly by Northwest electricity users and engineered by the Bureau of Reclamation—began showing results, tribal biologists moved stocks of young spring Chinook from a hatchery on the Wind River, in Washington, to acclimation pens on upstream tributaries of the Umatilla. They began releasing thousands of young Chinook to the world.

In the spring of 1988, thirteen adult spring Chinook, five years old, homed in to the Umatilla River. They returned not to the Wind River hatchery but to waters they had grown accustomed to when they were little.

Thirteen is not many. From this fish-sorting station, a returning fish still has to fight upstream and find a mate and a place to re-start the cycle. Life is hard up there.

The next spring, 164 came home. That's still not enough fish—or for enough consecutive years—to be called a salmon run.

Then came a series of low-water years. Returns were up and down. But in 1996, the Umatillas greeted a run of more than two thousand spring Chinook. In 1997, again, twenty-two hundred came home.

From here at the fish-sorting station, adult fish will continue up the Umatilla River. They can branch off separately to Butter Creek, Mission Creek, Squaw Creek, Meecham Creek. Later in the season, some will be held here at Three Mile Dam to ripen for brood stock. Their offspring, planted out in the streams, will spawn naturally, not at hatcheries.

~~~

"These salmon," says Anton Minthorn, a Umatilla elder, "were part of our everyday life since time began. They were food, but they were not just food." Minthorn regards the return of the salmon with an awe that others might reserve for the Second Coming. He is good with words, but now he struggles over the English equivalent to a native word, pronounced *ke-NOY-et.*

"It means something like new beginning," he says. "But not exactly."

Renewing?

"Not the right word."

Restoring?

"Not quite right." Minthorn gropes for the right word. The native word is evidently not just about salmon. It's about what the salmon mean.

~~~

When we say Chinook, we're talking about seasonal runs called king salmon, elsewhere, or *tyee,* for "chief." Blocked from their far-inland spawning sites by ladder-less dams—Grand Coulee on the Columbia, Hells Canyon on the Snake—many stocks of Columbia River Chinook are long gone. Crowded by logging, grazing, mining, and road building in the tributaries that remain accessible, native Chinook today are far outnumbered by their hatchery-bred surrogates.

The parallels to Native American culture, though not perfect, are inescapable.

When we say confederated tribes, or Umatillas, we're talking about descendants of the Umatilla, Cayuse, and Walla Walla bands. Crowded by homesteaders and miners, they signed a treaty in 1855 with the United States of America. In exchange for assurances that they would forever have access to their usual places for hunting, fishing, and gathering roots and berries, the Umatillas gave up vast expanses of land east of the Cascades. Their reservation, too, got squeezed and sold off in parcels until the land—west of the Blue Mountains, south of the Columbia—became more populated by whites than by Indians, better known for watermelons and wheat ranches than for fish.

Native salmon lost habitat and lost numbers when hatchery fish spread exotic diseases.

Native people lost habitat and lost numbers when Euro-Americans introduced exotic diseases.

A fish culture that once dominated the watershed hangs on tenuous threads from a few relatively undisturbed spawning grounds.

A human culture that once dominated the Umatilla River hung for decades by a thread from a single village called Mission, administered by the Bureau of Indian Affairs.

Fish reared at hatcheries . . .

A people shunted to reservations . . .

But wait. Native-to-native similarities have swerved here into parallels between native culture and *hatchery* fish. The prevailing biology these days says hatcheries are part of the problem. Hatchery salmon compete with native salmon for food and habitat. Hatchery runs lack the hereditary tools, the genetic diversity, to revive salmon runs. Don't they?

~~~

Back to Donald Sampson. Sampson got his degree in fish biology at the University of Idaho in 1984. Having grown up in a fishing family, he brought to the classroom a river-wise practicality, an instinctive skepticism that often isolated him from professors and fellow students. Sampson recalls refusing to get in the boat when a lost-in-theory professor wanted to launch a class onto the wind-raked Snake River. "He could have drowned the whole lot of us." These days Sampson is especially wary of the academics who worship at the altar of genetic purity.

Of the Chinook I saw yesterday, he says, "Give them a chance, and they find their way. They find places to spawn. Their offspring will come back naturally."

Hatcheries, in Sampson's view, got a bum rap because fish science was applied only to support commercial and sport harvests. To supply meat, without regard for self-sustaining runs. "That's why some people want to get rid of all hatcheries," he says. "But with good science, hatcheries can be a tool for building a run. We repair habitat. We enforce fishery laws. Once they get going, the fish take care of themselves."

Even hatchery fish?

"Salmon have it in them. Give them room, they'll *become* wild. The salmon are reclaiming the river."

Reclaiming. Maybe this is the word, if we have one, that Anton Minthorn had groped for. The difference between reclaiming and restoring is rooted in a way of thinking about the world. It has more to do with the salmon themselves than what humans do for them. Spring Chinook are reclaiming waters that were once indisputably theirs.

Umatilla Indians, too, are reclaiming their cultural heritage. Cultural revival here has little to do with genetic memory and everything to do with reversing social ruin.

"We got domesticated," Sampson says. "We intermarried and lost touch with our traditional ways. We lost our language. They cut our hair, and we lost our place. The BIA made decisions for us. We got disconnected from the salmon, and the salmon lost their river. We lost any reason to tell our children, 'This is my place. This is my scaffold. This is my drying shed.' "

Tapped for tribal leadership four years ago, Sampson was thrust into the world of commerce. He led the drive, which others had begun, for economic self-sufficiency.

"The BIA did everything for us at Mission," he says. "Our challenge is to cut the cycle of dependency."

Tribal economic development today springs from the new Wildhorse Resort and Casino, where eighteen-wheelers and Winnebagos pull off I-84, east of Pendleton. Truckers and tourists inside feed video poker machines to pay for the Indians' new golf course and interpretive center. Sampson doesn't care what you think about gaming. Wildhorse Resort and Casino makes his people independent of the BIA. The Umatillas can to make their own financial decisions.

The Umatillas' deeper and still ongoing challenge is to rekindle the connection between a people and the land.

"In the late 1970s there was a resurgence of the Washat religion," Sampson says. "The Seven Drums religion. The teachings came to us from Priest Rapids, through Smohalla and that line. We had always practiced gratitude, following the seasons. That religion fell out of use. We started bringing it back. We're flourishing," he says. "Come to our longhouse Sunday. It's the ceremony of the foods. Roots and berries. Venison. Salmon."

~~~~

I want to be open minded, but I am leery of Indian ceremony. Hopis in costumes thump the earth for Japanese tourists. Glassy-eyed innocents in the men's movement drum in the woods. I hear the Atlanta Braves chant and see the tomahawk chop. The whole idea makes me queasy, and I wonder . . . How genuine can Indian ceremony be in the 1990s? But here. Come look . . .

At 10 a.m. Sunday the drumming reverberates across the parking lot from the longhouse at Mission. The longhouse is twice the length of a basketball court, and wider. Inside, bleachers run six rows deep on both sides. At the west end, eight men stand in a row. Each man beats an elkskin drum and sings in a language that Indian people here tell me is "Indian." A leader in white buckskin sings verse to the drummers' chorus. He rings a gold bell at appropriate intervals to signal thematic turns, from high praise to wrenching agony.

Women elders file from their front-row bleacher seats to the floor. Each woman wears a brightly colored dress, moccasins, and a lone feather in her hair. The women shuffle to the drumbeats around an earthen rectangle, an opening in the concrete floor. As younger women join in, the line of dancers grows. Children, too—boys and girls, all spiffed up—take their places in the snaking line. The dancers hop and slide and shuffle. Some two hundred people are in the longhouse, and half of them are dancing. Even the littlest kids know the steps. Several of them mouth the words, unintelligible to me. Men on the sidelines, as well as the drummers, wear brilliant ribboned shirts. Everybody, whether dancing or observing, mimes the act of beating a drum.

At noon, the dancing and drumming stops. Men roll out folding tables for the Feast of the Roots, as it is called. It celebrates not just roots but all traditional foods. The ceremony unfolds over the next three hours. Because the crowd inside the longhouse has swollen, it's a sit-down dinner for four hundred. Before the meal itself, tiny portions—smaller than bite size—of huckleberries, five different kinds of tubers and roots, salmon, elk, and deer must be served and sampled and blessed in the native tongue.

I eye my neighbors at the table to know what to taste, when to stand, and when to mime drumming. I am reminded of having visited a Catholic service, not knowing what to do when, and of the comfort we take in ritual when we know it.

~~~

When the ceremony is over, I approach the white-clad bell ringer and ask if he will translate for me some words. About the salmon, in particular?

He looks at me pitifully, disdainfully. He could never begin to explain. I couldn't possibly—just look at me—understand. He turns away.

Donald Sampson, again, throws me a life jacket. "Come sweat with us," he says. "Tonight."

~~~

It's Sunday evening on McKay Creek, a tiny tributary of the Umatilla. Sampson, carrying the youngest of his four children in a backpack, tends the barbecue grill in his back yard. Family members arrive by van, and on foot across fields, to gather around picnic tables. Donald's father, Carl, gives thanks before dinner. They are a fisher family. Carl fished Celilo Falls as a kid. Donald's wife, Ellie, a Shoshone-Bannock, helped defend a traditional fishing hole against Idaho Fish and Game men in riot gear when she was only twelve. For Donald, the first Umatilla chief not to have known Celilo Falls first hand, fishing is the way to bring his children into the larger fold.

"We have to educate the children," he says. "The white culture is so pervasive. The children go to the schools. They play Nintendo. If we don't practice our spiritual philosophy, the children get lost."

He tells of Ashley, eleven, catching her first fish and yelling in glee at a scaffold near Cascade Locks.

Johnny, eight, was just watching on the Glass River when a salmon jumped onto the rocks. "It leaped right out of the water! At his feet. This was a special moment," says Sampson. "The story is told. We think he's going to be a special fisherman. It's in his blood."

After dinner, a nephew shovels hot rocks from an outdoor fire pit into an igloo-shaped structure of thick blankets over bent poles. The sweat lodge occupies one end of a plywood lean-to, with benches for undressing. Men first. Father, son, and grandson. Cousin, nephew, and me. Carl Sampson talks about connections, about a strand of religious practice—the sweat—that reaches as far back as he can imagine.

"We lost the language," he says of earlier generations, "but we never lost the sweat lodge."

Donald Sampson stands and walks to a concrete utility sink. With a pail he dips cold water and douses himself. He walks to the sweat lodge and—from a squat—backs into it. Cousin Mike, next, repeats this sequence. So do I. Soon the sweat lodge is filled to capacity with three adults, one teenager, and two small boys, all seated on warm earth. When the door—a blanket flap—closes, the sweat lodge is as dark as the inside of my eyelids. Someone splashes medicine water onto the hot rocks. With the hiss of steam comes a smell like damp wool and the history of the world. Sampson gives thanks to Our Grandfather, in the native tongue and then in English. Others, in turn, give thanks. After twenty minutes or so comes a round of appeal, addressing specific and current troubles. Someone is sick. Another needs strength to face down alcohol.

Steam and heat inside the lodge are intense, and intensifying. Sampson says anyone who wants to can leave. One of the small boys lifts the flap and the two of them scoot out. When the lodge is pitch dark again, the words coming from Sampson are all in Indian, evidently thankful. Others around the circle speak in English. Prominent in everyone's mention is the return of spring Chinook to the Umatilla River.

~~~

It's a small watershed, the Umatilla, compared to the Columbia River Basin as a whole. Hatchery fish can reclaim the Umatilla watershed without crowding out a native run. Whether or how to use hatchery science to supplement existing runs elsewhere is the grinding big question.

Can lessons learned on the Umatilla be applied basin-wide?

Sampson thinks they can. Experience here can be applied selectively, case by case, watershed by watershed. That's why he resigned his tribal chairmanship here in December, in order to devote himself to the larger complexities of Columbia River salmon recovery. Governor John Kitzhaber leans on Sampson for advice. Bruce Babbitt, the U.S. Secretary of the Interior, calls on Sampson when he visits the Northwest.

And what about the Umatilla people reclaiming their nature-based culture?

Sampson's talk of a people disconnected from place strikes a large chord. His words rise and spread to cover any culture that gets sapped of vitality by artificial rearing in unnatural settings. We Euro-Americans like to wrap ourselves in Northwest closeness-to-nature myths. But we still measure our well-being in terms of economic growth. Nature is close but *out there*. Nature is to get away to, when we find time. In that, we might be as estranged from the rhythms of rivers and woods as are any other settled and urbanized Americans.

Maybe the white-clad bell ringer was right. People like me could never understand. My ties to the land are relatively distant and theoretical.

Maybe the white-clad bell ringer is wrong. We do have, here in the Northwest, a broad tradition of non-native folk who take their bearings from the natural world. Parents who teach their children the rituals of rivering are passing on spiritual lessons. Taking cues from the wild, we defeat our sense of isolation in the world. More and more we recognize—in our literature, in our public discourse—that clean waters and healthy salmon run to the core of what it means to live here.

"I'm half Scot-Irish," says Sampson. "Did you know the Scots were tribal? Hunters and fishers. The Northwest is multicultural. Nothing in our blood prevents good science from serving kindred species. That's what salmon recovery is all about," he says. "Two nations—the swimmers and the walk-uprights—can reclaim their ties to nature."

Got a Call

Got a call from St. Helens Marina: "Your boat is taking on water."

Sunday, August 30, 2009. I drove there right away. It was bad. At St. Helens that evening I found *The Turtle* sagging at the stern. Bob the marina guy had roped a sling between two dock cleats to steady the keel. Floorboards were under water. The boat had come unhinged where the stern connects to the starboard side. The transom was rotten, and that would be all she wrote.

"How long have you had this boat?" Bob said, as if to say *I'm sorry. We've enjoyed having a wooden boat at the marina.*

Fifteen summers.

Bob helped me lift the motor from the transom. The gas cans and marine battery and a half-gallon of Atlantic Green yacht enamel—anything that could be a hazard—I lugged to the car. "I could break it down with a backhoe tomorrow," Bob said. "Rent a drop box, and haul it to the dump."

I'd known this day was coming. *The Turtle* is made of plywood. Plywood and water don't keep long-term relationships. The boat never left the river except for biennial bottom-scraping and paint jobs. I'd replaced a mushy floorboard toward the stern and rebuilt a loose mooring tooth. Cousin Kit had glue-glassed that wobbly intersection at the right rear corner. Daughter Heidi and I had replaced a dry-rotten vertical section of the bow.

She wouldn't last forever, but still . . . Break her down with a backhoe? Haul her to the dump?

I could have taken heroic measures to keep *The Turtle* afloat. An outfit in Woodland, Washington, accessible by boat, would foam-coat the keel for less than a thousand dollars. I could keep my boat on the water as a plasticized memorial to itself. But I didn't want *The Turtle* to linger. You know? She'd had a good life. We have physician-assisted suicide in Oregon. Sam McKinney chose that way out. That was the best way, for Sam. Two years ago friends of his gathered with our McKinney-made vessels at the confluence of Willamette and Columbia Rivers to tell stories and release ashes to the current.

In the morning at the marina Bob decided we didn't need to whack *The Turtle* with his backhoe. The dump—Columbia County Transfer Station—

would dispose of the boat whole. Find a flatbed wrecker, he said, and I could take *The Turtle* straight to the dump.

I called Grumpy's Towing, in Scappoose. Grumpy wanted nothing to do with a wooden boat. "If it doesn't come apart at loading, it'll break up on the highway." But Len, of Len's Towing in Deer Island, had a flatbed and said he'd give it a go. He had a Longview job that morning but would be here at noon.

I finished emptying the boat of its life jackets, anchors, cooking and cleaning gear. Bob's son, Brad, towed me in *The Turtle* over to the ramp. At noon I was ready. At 12:30, still no truck. I phoned, and a woman said state police had called Len and made him clear a wrecked car from the highway. But he'd be here.

~~~~

It was hot. By 1:15 I was re-thinking. Second-guessing. The whole deal took on the shape of a terrible mistake. What a heartless quitter I was. *The Turtle* looked serviceable and lovelorn, almost spiteful, there by the ramp. I could have . . . I should have . . . I walked into the river to cool off.

Len, a good old boy with his wife on the passenger side, drove up in a big white shiny wrecker. He turned it around and backed—*breep, breep, breep*—down the ramp to put his rear wheels at the water line. He stepped to the side of his truck and dropped the flatbed to the water at about a thirty-degree angle. I fixed the wrecker's hooks to *The Turtle* and swam behind the boat to keep it perpendicular, in current, to the truck bed. Len winched it up. Not bad. The boat went onto the bed only slightly askew, dripping two streams of water from the rear scuppers.

In my car I followed the wrecker through town to the dump. *The Turtle* looked waaaaaay bigger and more awkward out of the water and up on the truck. The woman at weigh-in directed us to the lane for Bay 4, and this boat on a wrecker stopped a lot of guys. One of them—shirtless, goateed, and buzz-cut—saw *The Turtle* and wanted it. "Free boat," I said. "Just pay Len, here, to take it somewhere." To be blameless, I pointed out to him the soft spots. Just paint, is what holds it together. This boat was sinking at the marina. Still he was interested. "Don't dump it," he said, and he stepped away. He opened his phone.

Bay 4 was about to open up for us when he snapped his phone shut and said, "My wife will divorce me if I come home with a boat. Any boat."

Breep, breep, breep, breep . . . Len backed into Bay 4.

A tall sandy-haired guy in Bay 3, shoveling junk from his pickup, looked up. "Omygawd," he said. "What is this? Wait." He jumped off his truck and came over to *The Turtle*. He walked around the boat. He touched it. I thought he might start jumping up and down. I began to explain how un-seaworthy *The Turtle* is. She's soft all over. But he cut me off. "No!" he said. "This is a playhouse for my daughter! I'm seeing a fort for my son!"

"Please take this boat," I said. "Where do you want to put it?"

I followed the wrecker and the guy's pickup out of town. Past Deer Island but short of Goble we turned up a long winding gravel driveway to a sensational clearing with a big new house and a horse pasture overlooking the Columbia River. The dad must have called ahead. Mom and those gaping kids, their eyes like out on sticks, were waiting in the front yard. The girl was ten or so, the boy maybe eight. Right up their driveway came this marvelous green *structure*. Inside, still, were cushions and curtains and an inch or two of water. I gave the kids two bright orange life jackets and an oar in case they ever wanted to pretend it was a boat.

Who would have thought of this?

Don't look at me.

It's a true story. *The Turtle* found its own way up off the river.

Note

Many of these pieces first appeared in *Northwest Magazine* (Jack Hart, editor) of *The Sunday Oregonian*. They are abbreviated and author-edited here for clarity, but not up-dated. In chronological order of publication, they are:

"Cutting It Close" (10/16/1983)
"Surf Savvy" (3/25/1984)
"If Salmon Were Truth" (4/28/1984)
"One More Word . . ." (9/2/1984)
"Driving Tunnel" (2/19/1985)
"Let 'er Buck" (4/27/1986)
"Birdman in the City" (2/1/1987)
"Deaf Basketball" (11/16/1988)

Others are adapted from articles that first appeared in *Portland Magazine* (Brian Doyle, editor) of the University of Portland:
"The Swimmers and the Walk-Uprights" (Spring 1998)
"Miss Ivory Broom" (Spring 2003)
"Battle" (Winter 2005)
"Emotionally Disturbed" (Autumn 2008)

"Killed in the Woods" is reconstructed from articles in *Willamette Week* (1982), in the *Clackamas County News* (1993), and in *Left Bank*, the literary quarterly.

"The Clackamas River" first appeared in *Ultimate Northwest* magazine, July/August 2008.

"Further and Beyond" appeared in *The Sunday Oregonian* (11/18/2001).